Motorcycling Stories

Adventure Touring
from the Northwest Territories
to the Yucatan Peninsula

by
Piet W. Boonstra

CONTENTS

I dedicate this book to the memory of my beloved wife Lillian, who was the kindest, gentlest, most generous person I have ever known. She was creative, optimistic, hardworking, caring, and compassionate. She appreciated beauty and loved nature, wild flowers, adventure, music, going to the movies, and walking in the autumn leaves; and yes, she loved to ride on the back of my motorcycle.

INTRODUCTION

I attended college for a while after World War II, but I got sidetracked when I took my first motorcycle ride, which was a lap around a quiet park in Michigan with a friend's Harley Flathead in 1946. A year later I bought my own new 1947 Harley 74 OHV, the "knucklehead." When I arrived at Jack Tracey's in Yonkers to pick it up, I had to make a U-turn from where it was parked -- something I had never practiced. This one involved crossing two sets of streetcar tracks and some rough bricks. I started out by giving it far too much throttle and kicking in the clutch, causing the powerful machine to lurch forward and roar across Broadway. I had almost regained control and completed my turn when the crash bar hooked the front bumper of a new Nash parked on the other side. The bike jammed itself between the Nash and a '37 Packard coupe, throwing me over the handlebars. I landed on the roof of the Packard and continued to roll across the hood and into the gutter. My dealer came running across Broadway yelling, "I thought you could ride that thing." With great embarrassment I said, "So did I." After visiting the local Nash dealer with the car's owner, and after Tracey replaced a few bent and broken parts on my new Harley, I was off again. There was still a good-sized dent on the roof of the Packard but I never did find the owner to make the proper reparations.

From the start I was interested in riding motorcycles on the dirt. I tried it a few times with the big Harley, but it was far too big for riding in the woods. In 1956 I bought a little Harley Hummer and got involved with enduros. I rode enduros for more than 30 years, wearing out at least 15 motorcycles before I began to look around for other forms of riding. This book begins in 1977, 30 years almost to the day from when I flew over the handlebars of my new "knucklehead" in Yonkers.

Piet Boonstra
Buchanan, NY, January 2002

ACKNOWLEDGEMENTS

I wish to thank my many friends who encouraged me to compile some of my motorcycle touring adventures into book form. I thank Jake Herzog for helping me to come up with the proper title. For basic printing and publishing direction and for my cover design, I am very grateful to Sandra Hardy. Last but far from least, none of these adventures could have been possible without Lilli's tolerance with my wanderlust.

ALASKA ONE - MY ROOKIE TOUR

I recall sitting on a new Suzuki GS750 in Don Pink's showroom in White Plains during the spring of 1977. It was on a Thursday evening before one of our weekly Crotona club meetings. I was daydreaming and wondering if someday I might break down and buy a road machine and do some touring. Motorcycling for me had consisted mainly of riding enduro competition for more than 30 years, and since my enduro riding was becoming much less frequent, I was considering taking up another form of riding to fill the void. During the meeting that evening my mind wandered a lot, and by the time it was over I had put together a plan to ride to California and visit with my youngest daughter Donna in the Air Force there. Before leaving Pink's that evening I owned the machine. A few weeks later before taking delivery, my original plan developed into something much larger: I figured since I was going to be on the west coast anyway, it would afford an excellent opportunity for me to launch my long-dreamed-of trip to Alaska. For an extra challenge I included the Arctic Circle and even Prudhoe Bay into my plans.

I took delivery on the bike in April after having a few extras installed like safety guards to protect the engine cases in case I dropped it somewhere in the wilderness, a chain oiler with a manually-operated lever on the handlebars, a beefed-up rear luggage carrier, a Dunlop K81 front tire to perform on the dirt, an extra tooth on the countershaft sprocket for gas mileage, and finally a Windjammer III fairing and a touring saddle for my comfort. With all of these modifications I felt like I was setting up an enduro bike for a national championship event. While breaking the Suzuki in over the next few weeks, I proceeded to accumulate other necessities for the trip, including a tent and sleeping bag, although I had never slept on the ground or in a bag. I had never been away from my family for that long either, which was my major concern, but with Lilli's encouragement I continued to prepare for the trip. Following is a daily journal of that first major tour:

Day 1 - I left on Saturday morning, May 28th, with Knoxville, Tennessee as my first day's objective. "Don't worry about the kids," Lilli said as we made our good-byes. She was smiling but I was worried a lot about how she felt about the whole thing. I was worried about how my three sons, ages 12, 18, and 20 would react to my being gone for a month. All the way into New York City I kept wondering if I had forgotten something and if I was doing the right thing by heading out alone like that and leaving the total responsibility of the boys and our home with Lilli. As I merged onto the Cross Bronx Expressway and headed the machine west across the George Washington Bridge, I peered far out into the western sky. Chills of anticipation ran up my spine as I realized I was actually on my way and there was no turning back at that point.

After weaving carefully through the last of some slow-moving traffic around Easton and Allentown the metropolitan congestion soon became a fading memory. The few high clouds that drifted over the Pennsylvania countryside gave way to clear blue, as the beautiful Shenandoah Valley lay open and free of congestion ahead. It got hot in Virginia as the temperature climbed to above 90 degrees. I realized early that I had brought nothing to wear in the broiling sun. The sun was far too strong for me to ride with only a T-shirt, and the best thing I had to protect my skin was a green sweatshirt. It lived up to its name because the sweat poured off of me every time I stopped for gas or refreshments. A long-sleeve white cotton jersey would have served much better.

It clouded up around Bristol and I considered looking for a place to stop for the night, but since I didn't care too much for aborting my plan so soon I pressed on. About 60 miles short of Knoxville the sky darkened, thunder and lightning threatened, and suddenly the skies opened up. I sat out most of that late afternoon downpour beneath an overpass with two local riders on their way to a Saturday night stock car race. As soon as the heaviest rain passed, I put on my rain suit and left, only to stop again under another bridge ten miles farther down the road when the next torrential downpour hit.

I found a medium-priced motel a few miles west of Knoxville where I checked in at 9:45 PM. I covered 785 miles on my first day and I ate my first evening meal at a nearby KFC. When I returned to the motel I found that a water leak in the heater had soaked most of the carpet. The guy in the office expressed regrets but he said I had the last room in the place and there was no one available to fix it. The entire carpet was soaked by morning.

Day 2 - The day began in a thick fog, which soon gave way to mostly cloudy skies as the Suzuki climbed easily into the Cumberland Mountains. My back was a little sore between my shoulder blades, but otherwise I felt pretty good as I took in the sights. I could see remains of strip-mining operations from the interstate. It looked as though attempts had been made to grade the mined areas and to plant trees, but it will take years for the scars to disappear and natural beauty to return to the landscape.

As I descended into Nashville I sailed through two police radar checks. I was well over the speed limit but I was apparently within their tolerance because I didn't get stopped. By ten o'clock the fog cleared and the sun beamed down more of its unyielding heat. After crossing the Mississippi River near Memphis the land leveled and the weather got very hot and humid. All afternoon the temperature hovered between 95 and 100 degrees. It was very hot riding as the light-colored pavement reflected the heat and the darker pavement absorbed and radiated the heat. Sometimes it seemed like more heat was coming up from the road than down from the sun. I had planned to stop every 150 miles for gas and refreshments, but I was dehydrating so fast I had to stop halfway between gas stops for cool drinks. I also needed the occasional breaks from the sun.

Local community groups set up refreshment stands at a few of the rest areas for Memorial Day weekend travelers, where they served lemonade, cookies, and coffee, and they collected donations in a cookie jar. These extra stops helped considerably to ward off a serious case of dehydration. During one stop I met a rider and his wife from Washington, DC who were headed for California on a BMW 900 to visit their son at college. At another stop in Arkansas I chatted with a charming old lady who stayed in her car while her husband used the facilities. I mentioned that the heat was almost unbearable to me. She smiled and said, "You haven't seen anything yet."

Everything on the bike was running incredibly hot, especially the engine and tires. When I realized that the chain was also hot to the touch I soaked it with oil from a liquid-soap bottle filled with 20W50 oil that I was carrying. I had originally intended to use that extra oil on the chain when I got to the dirt roads. I put the bike on its center stand and ran a thin stream of oil along each set of O-rings and on the rollers. I repeated this operation at every gas stop for the remainder of the trip. My

9

aftermarket chain oiler just wasn't doing the job. My speed was too fast for any oil to reach the chain and all it did was spread oil over everything back there. The manual oiling seemed to do the trick because I rode more than 4,000 miles before making the first minor chain adjustment in California.

I detoured for about 20 miles along old US Route 70 in Arkansas where I saw many poor, dilapidated shacks like those I had seen in the movie "Sounder." What an awful way for people to have to live! I guess I didn't realize that so many people in this country still live that way. The detour also made me realize there was a great deal of interesting scenery that I was missing by riding on the interstate highways. It seemed that the most interesting part of the trip was the people I saw and sometimes met along the way. I was convinced I would return someday on a back-road tour of the USA.

On long stretches of highway in eastern Oklahoma I learned that early evening was the most peaceful part of the day and the best time for traveling, even though it meant riding directly into the setting sun. Most other travelers and truck drivers already quit for the day and the local commuter rush subsides. I enjoyed the solitude and cooler temperatures of the early evening and I usually covered another few-hundred miles before darkness settled in. I finally stopped in Oklahoma City after clocking 880 miles on the longest single day of my tour. I located a room at a Motel 6 and ate my evening meal at a McDonald's just before it closed at eleven. I managed to do my first oil change in a nearby vacant lot in the dark.

Day 3 - Early the next morning I rolled out of Oklahoma City under the clearest, bluest sky I think I had ever seen. It was a beautiful day, I felt great, and the bike was running smoothly on a fresh change of oil and a full tank of gas. I settled back, took deep breaths of the fresh air, and watched countless miles of lush farmland go by. I saw lots of corn, wheat, and other crops growing, and I saw large herds of cattle grazing in the fields.

Ten miles out of Oklahoma City a sparkling new eighteen-wheel rig out of Tulsa zoomed by looking like he really had places to go. The name "Bounty Hunter" on his rear bumper somehow seemed appropriate. Smoky must have been on holiday that day! When he was about a quarter-mile ahead of me where I wouldn't be buffeted by his draft I tagged along. I followed him until my main tank ran out after only 116 miles. I had been getting 37 to 39 miles to the gallon during the previous two days of heat and normal highway speeds, but now with strong head winds, higher altitudes, and higher speeds, up to 80 and 85 MPH, my gas mileage dropped to around 28 MPG.

After gassing up I continued to push hard along Interstate 40 through Oklahoma and the Texas panhandle, tailgating cars and trucks with CB antennas whenever I thought they knew what they were doing. I went through a few towns east of Amarillo where the interstate was still under construction and local traffic moved slowly through the towns. West of Amarillo the land was dry and barren, the road was flat for miles, and the weather was hot and dry. I stopped at a rest area in New Mexico for water. I drank some and splashed a lot over myself like a camel driver at an oasis. I was still wearing the green sweatshirt that wasn't helping my dehydration much. I wondered how long I could take this level of heat and exposure to the sun. I stopped that afternoon in Tucumcari for lunch and I sat for a long while in the shade, just resting and watching the people. I was in Navajo country and most of the people I saw were Navajo Indians. Of those driving, four out of five were in pickup trucks. I never saw so many pickup trucks in one town.

The farther I got into my trip the quieter I rode, especially in the afternoon after an apparent overdose of heat. In the mornings I would usually ride along singing to myself, but I would stop singing in the afternoon when I got really tired. Then I would usually get deeply engrossed in thought as I became completely preoccupied with my surroundings. Sometimes I would slip into a kind of trance. It crossed my mind that the heat was getting to me. The temperature in Santa Rosa was more than 105 when I began to feel emotional about some of the things I had been seeing and imagining. I thought about the hardships the Navajo apparently endure, living as they do out there on the desert with no apparent means of escape from the heat. I wondered what they saw in the area and what keeps them there. Then I began thinking about the early settlers and the hardships they must have faced as they trudged across the barren desert in the blistering heat in their broken-down covered wagons. I could actually visualize men and women getting down to push as the wagons became mired in the deep sand. Tears soon filled my eyes and began to run down my face. The heat, my exhaustion, and constant pain were all taking their toll.

I had a bad case of sunburn on my face and the backs of my hands and I had pain in my back, my butt, my neck, and my shoulders. Many of the enduros I rode through the years weren't nearly as tough as this.

Around 6 PM as I approached the Continental Divide near Gallup I was passed by what appeared at first glance to be the same eighteen-wheel rig from Tulsa that I had followed early that morning. Sure enough I spotted the sign "Bounty Hunter" when he zoomed by. He gave two short blasts of his air horn and threw puffs of diesel smoke out of both high stacks and then he really took off. I had only 30 miles of gas left in the tank but I followed him to the crest of the divide, where luckily I located a gas station just about to close for the day. The new wave of excitement helped to break my emotional trance that day.

Later that afternoon I had my first riding scare of the trip. The extremely high temperatures all day had softened the road tar in Holbrook, Arizona to a consistency where my front tire began to pick up wet tar and sling it up under the fender. The road surface actually got slippery and I almost lost control of the bike a few times right in town. The sticky tire would pick up gravel and sand that gradually built up on the wheel like a snowball rolling downhill. It built up to where the front wheel began to scrape and bind against the inside of the fender. I managed to get through town without mishap, but the tar stayed under the fender for several days and the clearance was reduced to almost nothing. For days every time the tire picked up even the smallest stone it would rip loudly through the close clearance and the wheel would bind a little. That night I had tar on the engine, the windshield, the tank, my shoes, and even on my face.

As I approached Winslow, the setting sun was directly in front of me. That huge bright globe was like a searing ball of fire resting right on the road surface. My shadow must have been a mile long behind me. Fortunately the traffic was light because all I could see was that giant, fiery-red ball resting in the middle of the road. It practically blinded me and I realized I should have brought sunglasses on the trip.

By the time I packed it in that night I had put in another unforgettable 800-mile day for an average of 825 miles a day for the first three days of my trip. I was getting really tired and sore and I was developing numbness in the back of my right leg from poor circulation. For the rest of the trip I would try to stand up

12

on the foot pegs every 15 or 20 minutes to allow the blood to circulate. That night I drank more than a gallon of fluids and swallowed a teaspoon of salt at the restaurant. My body absorbed every ounce of the fluid, since I didn't pass any all night.

I ate a late steak dinner at Sambo's where I met a couple of riders from Illinois. One had a Kawasaki 900 and the other was riding a Honda 1000 Gold Wing pulling a trailer. They were returning home from visiting relatives in Los Angeles. They had stopped at Las Vegas the previous night but talked mostly about their experiences in a blinding sandstorm around the Four Corners area, and how well the Honda handled while pulling a 350-pound trailer. They asked me about road conditions between Winslow and Albuquerque because they planned to ride all night to avoid the heat. I told them about my experience with the tar in Holbrook, but that certainly wouldn't bother them at night.

Day 4 - While getting gas in the morning I learned about a shortcut to the Grand Canyon. My original plan was to go into Flagstaff for a 2,000-mile service check on the bike, but that changed after I found the shortcut that local people called Old 66. It was a gently winding road with trees, green grass, and very few houses or commercial establishments. As I leaned hard into the sweeping curves I wondered if Earl Robinson used that same route when he set his coast-to-coast speed record on a motorcycle 50 years earlier in 1927. It certainly would have been dirt then. I envisioned Robinson charging along on his old Harley JD with determination fixed in his eyes. His head was pointed into the wind and there was a half-mile trail of dust billowing out behind as he reached down to give the engine another shot of oil from the manual pump on the tank. I think his record coast-to-coast time was 77 hours. I had already been at it longer than that, mostly on superhighways, and the worst desert was yet to come for Robinson.

The eastern entrance to the south rim of the Grand Canyon was a barren road intersection near Cameron where Indian women sold beads under rustic wooden shelters. A faded sign at the intersection said that the canyon was still 54 miles away. I wasn't too enthused about having to ride the same 54 miles in and then back out again. I would rather have gone the long way around through Flagstaff, but then I wouldn't have gotten to ride Old 66. The entrance road had a few scenic viewpoints like the Little Colorado where I stopped along the canyon rim for photos. At the main lookout near Grand Canyon Village I stared in awe at one heck of a big hole in the ground. I concluded it was far too big for Evel Knievel to jump across like he once said he would. I met three riders from Amarillo and we spent a few minutes swapping stories before I excused myself and headed for Mesa Verde National Park in Colorado where I intended to pitch my tent for the first time.

I stopped for a quick lunch at a small snack shop in Tuba City in the midst of Indian country and shared a small table with a few of the local natives. No one said a word during lunch. I couldn't even tell if they spoke English, but I'm sure they did. I think they were mainly studying me as I was studying them. The temperature had already climbed to over 100 degrees. After lunch I made a brief visit to Navajo National Monument, a small park near there, before pressing on for Mesa Verde.

Entering Monument Valley, Utah was like stepping into a whole different world. It is basically a sandy, dry desert with huge buttes of all strange shapes and sizes standing tall and silent everywhere I looked. Very few travelers were on the road that afternoon and being alone in this strange world gave me an eerie feeling. It made me feel like I was very tiny and that I was wandering in what I imagined to be a huge cemetery. On the approach road to the Visitor's Center I saw a sign that read, "No motorcycles or dune buggies allowed in the park." I thought it couldn't possibly mean me. The entrance road was in terrible condition with deep sand and washouts. I learned while struggling through the sand that my Suzuki was definitely not a dirt bike. The steering flipped uncontrollably from "stop-to-stop" as I churned through the sand with great difficulty, using both feet as outriggers for support. I worried that if I ran into similar road surfaces for any distance on my trip I would be in serious trouble. Maybe the "No Motorcycles" sign was meant for me after all. The poor handling was due in large part to the weight distribution on the bike, which had a short wheelbase and I had piled far too much weight on the luggage carrier behind the rear axle.

From Butte, Utah I planned to follow an obscure secondary road that I had seen in my road atlas for about 12 miles into Montezuma Creek. There was a note in the atlas cautioning travelers not to enter the area without a guide, but I thought it would afford an excellent view of the barrens of Utah, and I have a fairly good sense of direction. I also figured it would give me practice riding on rough, sandy terrain. When I inquired about directions I was first told that there was no such road. I eventually found an older man at the local hardware store who knew about it but he said no one uses that road anymore and washouts often wipe out all traces of it. He didn't sound very encouraging. After following his directions to locate the start of the road it led me across some of the most barren landscape I had ever seen. There was lots of loose sand and rocks that caused serious handling problems, while the extreme heat added to my troubles. After about 12 miles, when I thought I should have been within sight of the town, I felt sure I had gotten lost; but I figured it was safer at that point to keep going because I didn't think I would ever find my way back to Butte. With the help of the sun and a few lucky guesses I finally felt my way into Montezuma Creek.

It was time to buckle down for Mesa Verde because it was getting very late. I saw four natives loading a pickup truck and I asked them which road leads to Cortez. Three of them said they didn't know and the fourth said he thought it was "over that way." He said, "If you see a Texaco station on your left it's the right road." I double-checked my bearings with the sun and figured the road he pointed out was probably my best bet. After 40 miles of totally deserted two-lane tar road I did see a Texaco station on the left. At that point it was almost seven o'clock and I was really wiped out from a long, tough day. My strength was totally drained and I still had almost two hours to ride to reach Mesa Verde. From sheer exhaustion I began to have hopeless thoughts of actually not making it.

Just as darkness was settling in on the world around me and I was feeling almost complete helplessness, I finally reached the park entrance. It was a sight to behold with a steep, winding road that ascended toward a tremendous mesa, which loomed in a very intimidating way over the entrance road like a giant sentry staring down at me. Looking up at this huge commanding form against the darkening sky was a breathtaking sight that made me feel very small, weak, and insignificant. My long silent trances, coupled with almost total exhaustion, brought tears to my eyes as the bike climbed slowly into the park.

15

There was barely enough daylight left to set up my tent, which was a new experience for me, having never done much tent camping. I ate a hamburger at the park snack shop and later I drank a quart of milk that I picked up at the park general store. I called home from a phone booth and tried to describe my experiences of the past four days, including the almost unbearable heat, my impressions of the magnificence of everything I had seen, and how insignificant it all made me feel. When my voice began to waver I cut the phone call a little short so Lilli wouldn't think I had lost it.

While sitting outside my tent reflecting on the first four incredible days of the trip, a local native stopped by and struck up a conversation. He said he was half Apache and half Navajo and he played a guitar in a four-man group. I suspected from the way he moved and the smell of his breath that he had been drinking quite a bit. He told me he once owned a big Harley and he would sure like to have another bike. He told me he smashed his around a tree. He kept asking how fast my Suzuki would go and every few minutes he would ask if I had anything to drink or smoke. I offered him my canteen of water but that wasn't quite what he had in mind. I don't think he had tailor-made cigarettes in mind either. He chattered on and on for about a half hour and then he suddenly turned and disappeared into the underbrush like in an old John Wayne movie.

My first night in the tent and sleeping bag was not a good experience at all, to say the least. I took a sleeping pill, which didn't help. Soon after I slipped into the bag I began to sweat. It was a very warm night. I peeled off all of my clothes and got out of the bag altogether, but that didn't help either. I wondered what I might do if someone like my newfound Apache friend began to walk off with my bike and I had to chase him naked through the park. I just couldn't relax and I tossed and turned until almost dawn.

Day 5 - The tent was wet with dew in the morning and the ground tarp was dripping with condensation. I never realized how long it took to dry everything. I decided it was probably best to camp only when it was not possible to find a room. My alternative would have been to roll up everything wet. After drying it all and loading the bike I toured the park and visited many Indian ruins along the cliffs and on the mesa tops. The park museum is one of the best Indian museums I had ever seen.

16

The Anasazi, meaning ancient ones, who lived there, vanished several hundred years ago. Ranchers rounding up stray cattle discovered the spectacular cliff dwellings early in the 20th century.

It was almost noon when I left Mesa Verde. I stopped for steak and eggs outside the park, which served as my breakfast and lunch. Later I located a Suzuki dealer in Durango for my overdue 2,000-mile service. I wanted to be sure everything was OK after the bike's exceptionally hot break-in period. I knew I would have to wait for the engine to cool for the mechanic to adjust the valves that had been clattering. They finally got to my bike after servicing a GT750 for a guy from Illinois.

Route 550 was the most scenic road I had traveled so far on the trip. It scales three 10,000-foot passes and skirts alongside breathtaking drops. The Rocky Mountains in the background were covered with snow. A few times I experienced the thrill of hitting an unexpected patch of sand on the outside of a curve. It was especially heart stopping when the bike was leaning hard and the shoulder of the road was a mere foot wide with no guardrail. The drop off the edge in some places was several hundred feet. I reached Silverton, elevation 9,318 feet, with only a few miles of reserve gas left in the tank.

On the way down the west side of the Rockies I stopped several times to view the sights and take photos. I saw gold mines on the western slopes, a large rainbow falls, and I visited a box canyon in Ouray. A good deal of snow still blanketed the mountaintops. Late that afternoon I descended into Grand Junction and back into the heat. I pointed the bike west into Utah directly into the setting sun not thinking about my gas. A short while later the main tank ran out on a desolate stretch of interstate. By the time I finally reached the first highway exit I was already 15 miles into my reserve. A guy at a construction office there told me that the nearest gas was 16 miles back via the old road or 42 miles ahead. I chose to go back and drove slowly to stretch my gas. I barely made it to the station as the engine began to sputter.

Later I located a motel in Green River and ate a home-style meal at a local restaurant while planning the following day. I had told Donna that I would be in Yuba City, California from Friday night until Monday. Since it was already Wednesday

17

there wasn't enough time for any meaningful side trips like Yellowstone, so I decided to continue in a direct line to Yuba City with a possible stop for the night in Reno or Lake Tahoe.

Day 6 - The day began with bright sunshine and clear blue skies. I was happy that it was a little cooler than the previous five days. I followed US Route 50 for a long time though very sparse cattle country. Occasionally the open range would appear lush with thick green grass, but mostly it was dry and desolate with sagebrush and tumbleweed. It was a long, tedious ride with great distances between gas stops. I rode one 82-mile stretch where there were no gas stations at all and not much of anything else.

Nevada was generally greener and the cattle were fatter than in Utah. I rolled through Reno a little ahead of schedule. The truck traffic there was heavy. I decided to press on for Yuba City and spend the extra time with Donna. I stopped for gas near Lake Tahoe and spoke with a young guy from Pennsylvania on a BMW 750. He was headed east after having toured much of California. He raved about the coastal highway north of San Francisco. At Donner Pass the temperature dropped and I had to dig for more clothes. I tried in vain to contact Donna a few more times and finally I called home to ask Lilli if she would keep trying so Donna would know that I was arriving a day early.

The strong smell of evergreens mixed with the delicious aroma of steaks cooking over open campfires filled the air as I rode leisurely through beautiful Tahoe National Forest and into Nevada City in the peaceful early evening. Donna was still out when I got to her home so I ate dinner in town and reminisced the day's events. I had covered 775 miles that day for a total of 4,200 miles in my first six days. By the time I finished dinner at a small restaurant, Donna had returned from food shopping.

Day 7 - I slept late Friday morning, washed the bike at a do-it-yourself car wash, and took it over to the local Suzuki dealer for service. It needed different shims in the exhaust valves again, new plugs, points, oil filter, and the first chain adjustment of the trip. I figured I had oiled the chain more than 30 times during the first six days. The only bike problem was with the very light front end, especially in sand, gravel, mud, or hot tar, or whenever I made tight maneuvers below 30 MPH. I was sure it had most to do with my having too much weight on the rear luggage carrier.

Day 8 - I didn't ride at all on Saturday. Donna and I went to a giant flea market in Sacramento with her car where she searched for something she never found. We wandered through acres and acres of junk in what seemed to be one of the world's largest flea markets. Later we visited an arts and crafts exhibit at the Air Force base where Donna won first prize for her macramé and second prize in a photo contest. We stopped at the Base Exchange where I picked up a few things. That evening we went into Sacramento with her date for a steak at the Victoria Station Restaurant, which was an interesting reproduction of an old English railway station. After dinner we visited Old Sacramento, a reconstruction of the city as it was in the 1850s.

Day 9 - On Sunday I took Donna on a bike ride through 1849 gold-rush country. We took several photos in Grass Valley, Auburn, and Sutter's Mill where gold was discovered. We generally followed California Route 49, which was named after the "forty-niners," and connects many of the historic points of interest. We stopped for lunch at a quaint roadside ice cream parlor near Coloma. The temperature rose to 105 and we both became exhausted from the heat. We returned by way of Sacramento where we stopped briefly for gas and some much-needed liquid refreshments.

On a two-lane highway leading back into Yuba City we came upon a serious two-car crash that happened only seconds before we got there. It was obvious that two people had been killed and three others were in grave condition. At least one of the others looked like he wouldn't make it due to massive injuries. I tried to comfort him but there wasn't much I could do. He was in shock and somewhat delirious. The other two survivors looked very critical and also appeared to be in shock. We stayed until the paramedics arrived. I learned later that the man died on the way to the hospital. It was the most horrendous sight either of us had ever seen and it left a very somber impression on both of us. I was sorry that we had to stop but we were first to arrive on the scene and we couldn't just pass by.

Day 10 - Monday morning I visited Beale Air Force base as Donna's guest. We chased U2 touch-and-go landings in a Chevy El Camino. One of the pilots drove and described the operation as we sped along. As the U2 aircraft entered final approach, nearing touchdown, the El Camino would pull out onto the runway practically alongside the descending aircraft.

Driving one-handed down the runway at 90 and 100 MPH, the driver would speak into the microphone he held in his other hand, "Three feet, two feet, two feet, one foot," etc., informing the pilot how far his wheels were from the ground, because landing visibility is very poor in the U2 aircraft. Donna introduced me to her Commanding Officer and several of the pilots in the ready room. She was assigned at Beale as a video photographer working with the landing support team to record all U2 landings for training purposes and as a permanent record.

I left the base around 11 AM and headed due north. I was tempted to use the scenic coastal highway but I used the interstate instead in the interest of time. I was anxious to get on with my Alaskan adventure. Temperatures in the valley were expected to reach 110 that day. The peach orchards and rice fields seemed to absorb water as fast as the farmers irrigated the fields. I wondered how they could spare so much water for farming after I had heard that water was so scarce in the area. I could see why the valley is famous for fruit and rice production: The soil is very rich, the temperature stays hot, the sun shines most of the time, and the fields are kept continually wet.

The huge peak of Mt. Shasta was clearly visible from the interstate. In spite of the extreme heat in the valley, the top of the mountain was covered with snow. This sharp contrast in temperatures caused a thick white cloud shaped like a huge halo to form around California's tallest mountain peak. Except for that single cloud the sky over the Cascade Range was deep blue and crystal clear. The sweeping mountain curves offered a very enjoyable ride with beautiful scenery in every direction.

Soon after entering Oregon I began to look for a place to camp. About 20 miles south of Eugene I found a peaceful county campground with only a few campers. There was a general store nearby, but I decided to try one of the freeze-dried dinners I had packed for emergencies. The first one I grabbed from my bag was macaroni and cheese, which turned out to be awful. The scrambled eggs I tried for breakfast was even worse. That freeze-dried stuff may be OK as an alternative to starvation, but I decided as long as I could find something else to eat on my trips I would keep it only for emergencies. I also experimented with my butane hiker's stove and found that to be very useful for heating my meals and making tea or coffee.

I met a guy named Jeff from Ontario, California at the campground who was riding a Kawasaki 900. He said he was a radio disk jockey and that he was headed for the Canadian Rockies where he planned to "rough it" for a few days. He was sleeping under the stars in a sleeping bag with no tent. I didn't care much for that idea, especially with bears and other night creatures crawling into your bag or chewing on your face. He asked if I minded his company the next day. I enjoyed meeting people along the way but I wasn't too enthusiastic about riding with someone I didn't know. To avoid appearing antisocial I said he was welcome, but I added, "- if we're ready to leave at the same time." I would make sure I was ready to go early.

Day 11 - I woke at 6:30, washed up, and prepared the dried eggs that I eventually threw out. I only partially dried my gear in the early morning sunshine and got ready to leave. Jeff got up at 8:30 and said he needed to take a shower to wash the bugs out of his hair. He said he would be ready to leave in about an hour or so. I shook his hand and left. Soon after crossing the Columbia River into Washington I stopped at a Sambo's for steak and eggs. I was getting really bored with the interstate highways and I was anxious to get on with my northern adventure. Soon after passing through Seattle I turned northeast on a two-lane blacktop and headed for the Canadian border at Sumas. It felt great to be on a two-lane road again. I almost charged too fast into the first couple of turns.

I remarked to the Canadian customs guy what beautiful weather they were having. He said I should come by more often because maybe I brought the good weather with me. He said it was the first time they had seen the sun for three weeks. I learned later that the rain returned there the very next day. When I heard that, I thought maybe the good weather was following me after all.

The customs guy asked about my plans, "Are you taking the Alaska Highway or going by ferry?" I said "Neither. I'm taking the Cassiar Highway. I plan to connect with the Alaska Highway near Watson Lake in the Yukon." He frowned and said, "The what?" He reached for a huge map of British Columbia that he spread out on a countertop. He said he never heard of a Cassiar Highway and there were only two ways to get to Alaska -- the Alaska Highway or the ferry. He said, "Show me where you're going." I pointed to a faint dotted line on his

21

map and said, "There it is." He shook his head and said, "That's not a road. A dotted line means it's a trail." I told him his map was out of date and that I had read about a road opening up through there eight months ago. He said, "You're looking at almost 500 miles of wilderness. Are you carrying a gun?" I said, "Of course not. What would I do with a gun?" He said they had a preacher come through there the previous week who was carrying three guns. I said jokingly that the preacher must have had some problem I don't think I have. He continued to shake his head and strongly advised that I check with the Mounties before ever venturing into that area alone. After making a few additional comments about the risks of traveling alone, he wished me a good day and said, "I hope you make it." He didn't sound very encouraging.

I had a peaceful evening ride along the north rim of Fraser River Canyon. The river far below looked ideal for white-water rafting. The temperature climbed to around 85 degrees and I stopped briefly to peel off a layer of clothes before pressing on for Cache Creek in treeless butte country. The landscape around Cache Creek is made up of light gray hills and buttes as far as I could see. These strange-looking outcroppings looked like piles of powdered volcanic ash or remains from mining operations. I reached Cache Creek a little before nine and priced a few motels before paying $17 for the least expensive. It was the highest price I paid for a motel so far on the trip. The farther north I got the higher the prices seemed to be getting on everything.

Day 12 - The day started out clear although it was only 62 degrees. I skipped breakfast to get on the road as soon as possible. It felt good to ride in the cool morning air after so many scorching days. My skin was still burned from the sun. Before I reached 100-Mile House the temperature dropped ten degrees in 75 miles and it began to cloud over. I was stiff from the cold by that time and my fingers were hurting. It looked and felt like snow. I stopped for breakfast at 100-Mile House and lingered over a third cup of coffee to give the pain in my fingers a chance to ease. The local hardware store opened at nine and I was their first customer. I bought a pair of lined mittens to solve at least one of my problems. I put on another layer of clothes plus my rain suit before proceeding north. It began to drizzle lightly as I left the restaurant.

I got the feeling I was leaving the populated world behind as I continued to ride farther north into the evergreen forests of central British Columbia. I rode in intermittent light rain all day, which wasn't bad in my rain suit but a few times the rain changed to sleet and hail while I was moving at a pretty good clip. The sunburn on my face was still tender and the windshield didn't offer enough protection from the hail, no matter how close I ducked behind it. The tiny ice pellets would whip around the sides of the windshield and sting my already sore face like bullets. I stopped to dig out a face shield but by the time I found it the hail stopped. I found that the face shield was scuffed up pretty bad from being packed away. At one point the road was covered with tiny hailstones, making it a little slippery in spots. Later in some road construction the loose dirt and gravel presented similar handling problems.

I got several interesting comments when I asked at gas stations about the Cassiar Highway. A trucker in Quesnel who was also a biker said he wouldn't travel that road with his Honda 750 for anything. He said it cuts almost 500 miles off the trip from Prince George to Watson Lake, but when he traveled it the previous September in his truck he spent the entire trip bouncing between the seat and roof of the cab. He said it was like torture and he felt it wasn't worth the time he saved. Most people I asked never heard of the Cassiar Highway. If they did, they didn't know anything about conditions.

My original plan called for stopping at Prince George to replace my rear tire. Before reaching the cutoff for town I examined the tire closely to try and determine how many miles it had left and I pondered my alternatives. There weren't many places along my route where I could buy a tire and I knew that the trip into Prince George would probably cost me several hours. When I reached the cutoff I just kept going rather than going into the city. The tire still had some tread left and I guessed it might reach Whitehorse where I hoped motorcycle tires were available. At that point I was mainly concerned about reaching New Hazelton before nightfall and I was already running late for that.

It was almost nine o'clock when I finally reached New Hazelton. All of the rooms at the motel as well as the hotel were sold out. The people at the hotel located a room for me at an old hotel in South Hazelton, a few miles off my course. I took a short walk after dinner and stared with some misgivings at the ominous snowcapped peaks that loomed over my morning route. For the first time on my trip I began to wonder if it wouldn't have been smarter to have a riding partner along like my long-time enduro teammate Bud Peck. It had rained most of the spring season and I was envisioning deep mud, snow, and impassable mountain passes. I couldn't get a forecast of the area or find anyone who knew what the weather might be like. I wondered what I would do if I dropped the bike and broke something on it, or if I got really stuck in the mud. I tried to think about pleasant things to keep from worrying about it.

One bit of encouragement came from a guy I met after dinner. He said he worked on road construction along the Cassiar and he claimed to have traveled the entire length seven times in the past five months in a pickup truck. He raved about it and expounded on the virtues of this "vital link to the Yukon." He also got wound up talking about the gas shortage and how Canadians were preparing for it by breeding more horses to take over the farming and transportation. He said that in a few years Canadians all over the country would be riding horses instead of driving cars. He was starting to get a little too theatrical and he was beginning to lose credibility with me. I wondered if he really traveled the length of the Cassiar seven times.

I called home to make sure everything was OK before entering this phase of my trip. I kept thinking that in the morning I would make my "initial assault" on the Cassiar and I wasn't sure what communications I would have with the outside world for the next few days. It probably wouldn't have taken much of a problem at home for me to turn around at that point, but everything was going along just fine. At least Lilli said everything was fine. I had trouble getting to sleep that night, which may have been because it was still light at 11 o'clock, or it may have been because my anxiety was running pretty high.

Day 13 - I woke up early on my thirteenth day and went about preparations as if I were getting ready for a long, tough enduro. I ate a hearty breakfast of bacon and eggs before riding the 27 miles into Kitwanga where I topped off the tank, rechecked the luggage tie-downs, and checked the air pressure in the tires. I inquired about the condition of the road at the gas station but no one seemed to know anything about it. The Alaska Highway connection was 482 miles of narrow dirt road away, for which I allowed two days. As I left Kitwanga on the 102-mile first leg of the trip to Stewart Junction I left the hard pavement behind and moved out with some reservation onto the narrow, twisting dirt road. I began cautiously but I gradually picked up speed as I gained confidence in the road surface and the handling of the bike on the fairly firm dirt.

What a spectacular ride it turned out to be and what a beautiful day! The Cassiar Highway that morning was a dirt rider's dream. The first hundred miles to Stewart Junction was the most enjoyable part of my trip by far. Spring rains had given the ground just the right amount of moisture to hold the dust down and make the tires stick. The forty miles of construction I went through was a blast! I had a great time dodging bulldozers, graders, and surprised construction workers. I rode as if I were in an enduro heading for a checkpoint, and trying to stay "within my minute." It reminded me of the Corduroy Enduro in Ontario, and I thought about Bud Peck again. He really would have enjoyed this part of the trip. I probably wore a broad grin from the time I left Kitwanga until I rolled across the long single-lane wooden bridge over the Nass River into Stewart Junction.

On one curve I suddenly faced the massive grill and heavy steel fenders of a logging truck that spanned the entire road from ditch to ditch. He came at me at about 40 miles per hour with no apparent intention of yielding even an inch of the narrow roadway to a motorcycle. I was coming at him at approximately the same speed. My reflexes helped me to veer into the right-hand ditch as I simultaneously locked both brakes. I managed to stay upright and came to a bumpy stop in the ditch. The truck was out of sight in a few seconds and I wondered if he ever knew what happened to me, or if he cared. I remembered seeing a sign several miles back about the logging company having control of a large tract of land in that area and it said that I was on their land. I climbed out of the ditch and continued on my way, keeping a sharp eye for another one.

There was a small service complex at the junction with a gas station, a restaurant, a general store, and a repair garage, all probably owned by the same person. I didn't notice any other buildings around the junction. I dodged a few deep mud puddles as I made my way to the gas island and parked between the puddles. As I started pumping my gas a guy came out of the garage wiping oil from his hands. He walked toward me with a big smile and said, "Where on earth did you come from?" I told him Kitwanga and he looked surprised. He said he didn't know the road was open because he hadn't seen anyone come up it for about a week. He asked if I was interested in something to eat. I told him thanks because I was having too much fun to eat. I asked if it was true that the next service was 161 miles. He laughed and said, "The next anything is 161 miles." As I pulled out a few minutes later I heard him say, "Don't go near the female moose with newborn." Apparently they can be more unpredictable than bears. I glanced back to see that he was still smiling.

In that next 161 miles I didn't see a house, a car, or even a sign that anyone had ever been there, except that someone must have built the narrow dirt road and the small single-lane wooden bridges across the many brooks and white-water streams. For several hours I enjoyed total solitude. I was able to maintain between 50 and 55 MPH most of the way. I stopped at some of the most beautiful spots, shut off the engine, put the bike on the center stand in the middle of the road, and I proceeded to oil the chain. There were no sounds at all. I would look around for several minutes admiring the incredible beauty and serenity of it all. The dark-blue lakes reflected a mirror image of the evergreen trees and snowcapped mountains in the background. The lakes were so clear I could see pebbles very clearly through several feet of water. I took many photos and regretted not having brought a better camera.

The road was generally wide enough to be considered two lanes. The surface was hard-packed dirt, with some loose gravel between the tire tracks. Whenever I switched from one track to another, I would hold the handlebars a little tighter because of this strip of loose gravel. Most of the way I could maintain my desired speed, except on the small single-lane bridges. I usually slowed down for the bridges because the foot-wide tire planks were often an inch or more higher than the road surface. Occasionally I risked coming onto a plank a little faster if it appeared level with the road; but once, just before reaching one of these planks, my front wheel struck a stone, which threw me a few inches off course. I almost missed the plank altogether and nearly sideswiped the side rail of the bridge. I was more careful approaching the bridges after that close call.

Iskut was the first small village I saw on the Cassiar. I continued on to the second of two gas stations, which I understood from my Milepost Travel Guide included a complete general store. Iskut is a small Indian village of the Tahltan tribe. Several children and teenagers gathered to admire the bike as I shopped in the clean, new co-op store where I bought canned foods for camping. The proprietor was a friendly little guy from Vancouver who looked like Colonel Sanders. The first thing he said when he came out to the pump was, "Hi, are you a cop?" I laughed and said that I wasn't but he didn't seem to believe me. He thought I was a New York cop who had come up there looking for someone. He said that most people who come through are either cops or fugitives. He told me there was a fugitive on the loose somewhere in the area at that time.

I bought canned steak cubes and canned spinach for my dinner and a can of baked beans and another of grapefruit sections for my breakfast. The "colonel" talked nonstop while I was in the store, which he said was operated for the benefit of the Indians. I assumed it was government-owned. He showed me some of the odd merchandise he said the former proprietor had stocked. In spite of the fact there was no electricity in homes for hundreds of miles, he carried several small electric appliances, even an electric charcoal starter for backyard barbecues. I laughed when he said he was running a special on the charcoal starter. He said, "If you think that's funny, what would you say if I told you I sold six of them since my sale started?" I think he was joking.

I left after spending a few minutes talking with an Indian teenager who seemed to have fallen in love with my Suzuki. They rarely saw a motorcycle in the village and mine may have been the first big one they ever saw. Several of the children waved as I left. I planned to look for a campsite about 50 miles north of there near Dease Lake. The colonel said that I should be able to find a good spot anywhere along there. When I got to that vicinity I noticed a few small provincial campsites, but each one had a lone camper already parked there. I continued on because I preferred to camp alone.

About forty miles north of Dease Lake near some road construction with freshly bulldozed dirt, I found a logging trail that I followed for about a half mile off the highway. I rode through a few deep puddles and around some fallen trees before the trail ended at a swift-running, 75-foot-wide glacier stream. I found a suitable area large enough to set up my camp amidst tall spruce and balsam trees in the shadow of a huge mountain. The water in the stream was so cold that it was painful to dip my fingers in it for even a few seconds. I heated and ate my evening meal near the edge while sitting on a big rock and watching the water rush by. Although it was an incredibly beautiful setting I felt very alone and uneasy for the first time. I felt somewhat helpless as I thought about the problems that could arise there. I would be unable to hear anything approaching from behind because of the sound of rushing water. I was mainly concerned about animals, but I remembered what the colonel had said about a fugitive on the loose, and I also thought also about what the customs guy said about carrying a gun. As I prepared and ate my meal I kept looking around behind me, thinking I heard something.

A huge dark cloud suddenly loomed over the mountain and it began to rain. I got up, grabbed a few things, and ducked into the tent to finish my dinner, where I brewed a cup of tea. When the rain stopped I washed the utensils in the icy stream and cleaned away any odors that might attract bears. The rushing water played tricks on my hearing. I thought I heard something behind me a few times and I would turn quickly, but it was always just my imagination. After crawling into the tent and slipping into my bag I unsheathed my hunting knife and placed it close by my side. Still feeling a bit uneasy I unsheathed my small hand ax and placed that by my other side. As I lay there feeling somewhat vulnerable, I imagined a bear coming through the side of the tent with a single powerful sweep of his claw. I thought about attaching the weapons to my hands with duct tape to get at them quicker, but I thought what might happen if I got a mosquito bite in my sleep. I felt better after communicating with the Almighty, and I was soon fast asleep.

Day 14 - It rained during the night, which soaked the tent floor and part of my sleeping bag. I realized I should have dug a small trench around the outside edge of the tent to deflect water. The weather had turned much colder and frozen water droplets hung from the bushes and tree branches all around the tent. I heated and ate my breakfast outside and tried in vain to dry some of my gear in the morning dampness. Shade from the tall mountains prevented sunlight from getting through, so

28

finally I rolled up everything very wet and headed out. I planned to find a room in Whitehorse that night where I could dry everything. The sun was on the highway and I was anxious to get on my way. I remembered it was my 52nd birthday.

I had to ride into the town of Cassiar to get gas, an 18-mile round-trip from my main travel route. I paid the highest price for gas so far on the trip there. The average price per gallon in the US at the time was around 89 cents. In most of northwestern Canada it was around $1.25. I paid $1.50 in Cassiar. After oiling the chain I headed out over several miles of scarcely maintained tar road for the Alaska Highway junction, still 88 miles farther north. I recalled the guy I met in South Hazelton telling me that British Columbia would probably pave the entire Cassiar before the Alaska Highway is paved. He said contracts for road maintenance on the Alaska Highway are politically motivated and current politics favor maintaining dirt roads rather than tar. There were 400 miles of dirt remaining on the Cassiar in 1977, while the Alaska Highway still had more than a thousand miles of dirt in British Columbia and the Yukon.

The road surface of the Alaska Highway was in the process of being redressed. Workmen would soften the dirt with a mixture of water and calcium chloride that they spread liberally from a tank truck. This operation was followed several minutes later by two or three huge road graders traveling at 25 to 30 MPH. The road between the tanker and the graders often got very slippery. If there were too much water on the surface, either from the tank truck or from a sudden rain shower, it would turn to a deep quagmire of mud. I barreled onto a wet, slippery surface doing about 65 MPH and really had my hands full. After the surface was leveled by the graders and packed down by truck and RV traffic, it looked and felt like concrete. Then I only had to watch for loose stones that would get uprooted by the graders. They would usually snap out from under the tires of fast moving vehicles and fly like missiles into your windshield or headlight. Whenever a vehicle approached from the opposite direction, I learned to duck my face to avoid getting one in the kisser. I had several hit the top of my helmet while ducking, which would sometimes hit so hard they would make my ears ring.

I met a few brief showers, but generally the good weather held for me. I noticed there was almost no traffic, which I thought was odd because of what I had heard about heavy truck

29

and RV traffic on the Alaska Highway. When I stopped at a rest area to oil the chain, a guy from a big Winnebago asked how I managed to get by the landslide. Of course my answer was "What landslide?" He said that the spring thaw and heavy rains had caused landslides east of Watson Lake, and that they blocked the highway. He had been there for two days waiting for the road to be reopened. I was glad I had come up the Cassiar and I told him about it but I also warned him about the many narrow bridges and the road construction on the south end.

The Mounties stopped me twice that afternoon. They warned me not to stop for anyone on foot. They said two guys had stolen a car in Alaska the previous day. They crashed the border and eluded the Mounties twice, once with a shoot-out. The Mounties found the car abandoned and out of gas and figured they were on foot and probably desperate. I learned several days later that they were caught the following morning in Watson Lake without a struggle.

When I stopped for gas at Jake's Corner, I saw a sign at the pump, "Do not operate pump yourself." Another sign said, "Free ice cream with fill-up." Jake didn't come out right away but I figured if I ignored the first sign and pumped my own gas he'd probably get mad and I wouldn't get the free ice cream. He looked annoyed when he finally did come out and he said gruffly, "Whadda you want?" He was a big, burly guy with long red hair and a big red handlebar mustache. When I said I wanted a fill-up he jerked the nozzle from the pump and jammed it hard into my already open tank with a single sweeping motion. He put only about three gallons in the tank, which didn't quite fill it. As he was hanging the nozzle back on the pump I asked if he would please top off my tank. He answered gruffly, "You're full" and he put his hand out for the money. He scowled when I handed him a credit card because he had to walk back to the office to get the imprint and it was uphill all the way, with some steps included. After signing the receipt I asked politely if I could have my free ice cream now. He stood for a few moments glaring at me but finally he walked back up into the office a second time for the tiny cone. He returned and handed it over very begrudgingly. I smiled and said, "Thank you."

It was sunny and warm when I reached a 30-mile stretch of new tar that took the Alaska Highway into Whitehorse, capital of the Yukon Territory. Whitehorse is a small, friendly, and fairly modern city with department stores, supermarkets, and other cosmopolitan conveniences. I found a nice room for only $16 at a very old and rustic-looking hotel. I had ridden only 400 miles but I was exhausted from struggling with loose gravel and slippery mud most of the day. I hung my camping gear around the room to dry and went out for something to eat at a nearby KFC. Later I checked the bike over and oiled the chain. I noticed the chain still didn't need a second adjustment in spite of all the mud and dirt roads. Oiling it about every 75 miles while on the dirt was paying off.

Day 15 - The sun was well up into the sky when I left the old hotel that morning, with just a few white fluffy clouds around. Occasionally dark clouds would appear, seemingly out of nowhere, and soon after that it would rain. I rode through several brief showers that morning. I noticed there were more weather changes in the far north than any place I had ever been. I wore my rain suit constantly because of the unexpected showers and cool winds. The rain suit also protected my clothes from dust after the roads dried up.

The Alaska Highway just west of Whitehorse was in fairly good shape. The dirt surface was very firm, smooth, and slightly damp, with very few loose stones. I could go almost any speed I chose. I stopped often to enjoy the scenery and I took several pictures around Lake Kluane. The deep blue of the lake, the largest body of water in the Yukon, contrasted with the snow-covered mountains and sparsely growing, deep-green spruce and balsam trees in the background, making it an excellent picture. Almost every place I stopped reminded me of a scene from a picture post card. I ate lunch at a relatively new restaurant overlooking the lake. About every hundred miles or less there were service complexes along the highway, with gas, food, and usually lodging. There was almost no traffic on the road, which I assumed was still due to the landslide.

Thirty miles from the Alaskan border it began to rain steady, although the road surface didn't seem to get very slippery. It consisted of what appeared to be crushed black cinders, with a rippling washboard surface. The faster I rode the smoother it felt, but the suspension really got a workout. I checked through the US border and moved out on some fairly good blacktop pavement toward Tok Junction where I turned southwest for Anchorage. My first impressions of Alaska were that it was a Godforsaken place, and I couldn't imagine why anyone would ever want to live in such a cold, wet wilderness. The steady drizzle afforded an even less favorable impression. A single beam of sunshine glistened on the peaks of the Wrangell Mountains far to the south across hundreds of square miles of dark, foreboding muskeg, pockmarked with puddles of water that probably spawned the billions of mosquitoes for which the area is infamous. I also saw a few glaciers in the distant mountain range.

I rode through some construction while approaching Glennallen, which was the realization of my worst nightmare. The roadbed had been dug out, leveled, and covered to a depth of about four to five inches with bank-run gravel. Obviously they intended to pave over it but they hadn't gotten that far. I used my feet as outriggers and rode about 15 miles through the heavy, loose gravel. I tried to maintain 30 MPH because going slower made it even worse, and going faster was far too hairy for my blood. I got so completely exhausted from struggling for control that I had to stop several times to rest.

In Glennallen I met more people who reminded me of the guy at Jake's Corner. Of those I met, none were very friendly. Most seemed angry about something. I thought it might have been because of the oil pipeline that runs through their back yard, which maybe they resented, but I assumed most people there were associated in some way with the pipeline. Maybe they were not there so much because of their love of Alaska, but more for making money off the pipeline; and maybe I looked like I had come to compete for their jobs. People seemed surprised when I told them I was on vacation.

Most of the prices around the pipeline were very high. I paid the highest price for gas on the entire trip in Glennallen -- $1.65 per gallon, which was double the price in the lower forty-eight states. The least expensive motel in the area was $25, plus a $5 key deposit. The room was very old, dirty, and in a sorry state of disrepair. The water was so hard I couldn't wash in it and the night clerk advised me not to drink it. I looked into the adjoining restaurant and decided against eating there because of its "greasy-spoon" appearance. I found a small food market nearby and bought some Dinty Moore stew, canned vegetables, and a quart of milk. I bought baked beans and canned peaches for breakfast. I heated my dinner in the room on my camp stove.

Day 16 - The day began with a dark, overcast sky and drizzling rain. It was the first and only time on the trip I started in the rain. I thought my luck for good weather had finally run out. I took extra time eating breakfast and getting dressed because I was in no hurry to start, although I certainly didn't care for the idea of spending a day in Glennallen. It was one of the worst towns I had ever been in. When I went to the office to pick up my key deposit, the desk clerk said he had no record of any key deposits. Sensing my extreme annoyance, which is an understatement, he finally came up with my five dollars.

About an hour after leaving, the rain tapered to intermittent light showers and the day brightened. I stopped for gas in Palmer and quickly changed the oil there, and made my second chain adjustment of the trip. The weather was sunny and warm when I ate lunch at a small roadside cafe just west of Palmer. The people were friendly and the food was good, which was a welcome change from the past few days. I rode into Anchorage on Sunday morning and threw in the towel for the day. I had to catch up on postcards, replenish my film supply, and tend to a few other chores like washing the bike at a do-it-yourself car wash. I talked with three guys on two Kawasaki 900s from Sacramento who had taken the ferry from Prince Rupert, BC to Haines, Alaska, bypassing the most scenic, mountainous sections of the Alaska Highway.

Day 17 - Monday morning I threw open the drapes to another beautiful day and headed for the Alyeska Pipeline Company to request permission to use the pipeline road to Prudhoe Bay. My timing was terrible because within a week they were supposed to start oil flowing, and they were having more than their share of startup problems. They were concerned about the possibility of having to rescue me from a breakdown or worse, hundreds of miles up the Haul Road. If the press ever got hold of a story like that, they wouldn't know how to explain it to President Carter. I realized I had done very little planning for Prudhoe Bay anyway, so dropping the idea wasn't a big deal.

I left Anchorage at 10:30 AM, heading for Denali Park and Fairbanks. One of the things I noticed along many Alaskan highways was that almost all of the road signs had bullet holes through them. Some were literally riddled with bullets, probably done from moving vehicles. Many things about Alaska reminded me of the old west. Another thing I noticed was that

Alaskan motorcyclists never wave, even when I waved to them with plenty of time to return it. Waves I got during the trip varied from clenched fist salutes and thumbs-up gestures to the old-fashioned open hand, which I got often in Canada. I think waves tell a lot about the rider's personality, as does the absence of a wave.

I stopped about 90 miles south of Denali Park at a scenic overlook where I could see the entire Alaskan Range and the 20,320-foot peak of Mount McKinley poking through the clouds. Soon afterward it got very overcast and started to rain, mixed with hail, and it got very cold. I stopped at an alpine-type restaurant near the park entrance to warm up with a hot bowl of soup. I decided against going into the park due to the poor weather. I already knew that I wouldn't be allowed to ride the motorcycle past the Visitor's Center anyway.

South of Nenana I encountered a very rough section of road for about 30 miles with huge potholes and a lot of heavy washboard. The bike's suspension bottomed hard several times and the front forks got a severe workout on the extremely rough surface. I was concerned about damaging the machine but I continued to move at highway speeds and then some, because the weather was looking progressively worse. After gassing up in Nenana I ran into a heavy downpour and rode the next 25 miles in torrents of rain with thunder and lightning. I don't recall ever riding in heavier rain. At one point I was going less than 20 MPH because I just couldn't see. So much water was getting into my mouth that I felt like I was drowning. By the time I reached Fairbanks I was completely soaked, even inside my rain suit. I noticed that prices in Fairbanks were even higher than Glennallen. It was too wet outdoors for camping, so I looked for a motel. I found a plain one like the one I had paid $22 for in Anchorage, but they wanted almost twice what I paid the previous night. I asked the guy where I might find something a little easier on the budget and he directed me to a place about a mile down the road called the Frontier Hotel.

I didn't see an entrance as I approached the large, log-cabin-style building, which was a combination hotel and saloon of rustic wood-frame design. There were no windows on the first floor and a narrow walkway or porch encircled most of the second floor. There was no pavement of any kind around the building and when I ventured around to the back, looking for the entrance door, I got stuck in the mud. Finding no door there I went back to the front of the building and parked. I entered through a small-unmarked door that was ajar and I stepped into a large kitchen, where I felt awkward. I asked how I might go about renting a room. An oriental cook pointed a big spoon toward a narrow, unlit hallway. He said the bartender rents the rooms. My footsteps sounded loud on the thin wooden floors as I made my way toward the bar. I had to duck through a few low doorways that reminded me of John Wayne entering a hostile bar in the old west.

It took a moment for my eyes to adjust to the darkness, where the only light was coming from the floor behind the bar. The bartender was a tall, attractive blonde of college age, in white "hot pants." She had really nice legs that were further complimented by the lighting. She greeted me with a big smile and, "What will it be?" It took a moment for my eyes to adjust to the light and for me to regain my composure from seeing this beautiful person. I said I was looking for a room. "Private or semiprivate" she asked, going on to explain that she was referring to the toilet facilities. I said semiprivate would be fine. As I handed her the $12 that she quoted, I wondered what a 12-dollar room would be like when the price of rooms in the area was running $50 and up. As she handed over the key she said, "See you later, OK?"

The directions to my room were to climb an outside staircase to the second floor porch surrounding the building, where a heavy wooden door opened into a large community sitting room. I saw several pieces of shabby, overstuffed furniture and a badly worn carpet that only partially covered a dirty, wooden floor. An old black-and-white TV was turned on but no one was there to watch it as a dim, jittery picture flopped over every few seconds. I passed through the community toilet to get to my room. The toilet was WWII-army-style with a long, rusty urinal against the wall. There were metal stalls without doors, where I noticed dirty toilet bowls in some and dripping showerheads in others. A vile odor of urine emanated from the wet floor.

My room was seven feet by seven feet, and the walls were only seven feet high. It was actually a tiny cubicle without a ceiling built from old crate wood, and situated against the outer wall where a small window overlooked the parking area. Many other cubicles in the center of the building had no outside view. The inside of the huge slant roof was visible from where I stood. The building was constructed like a giant log cabin. The door to my cubicle was an old cross buck type with a hook on the inside to lock it. There was a small metal chest of drawers with no mirror, and a steel army cot with a musty-smelling cotton mattress. My window had no blinds, just an old, torn curtain. I sat on the edge of the cot, looking around at the dirt, the close, unpainted cubicle walls, and the heavy logs supporting the roof, as I tried to get some consolation from the $12 price. I rationalized that it was probably better than sleeping out in the tent on a cold, rainy night. My room was directly above the bar where I could hear the jukebox blaring away, and occasionally I could hear loud voices and laughter.

I took a sleeping pill around nine o'clock and tried to get some sleep in spite of the noise and the daylight streaming through my window. The thin floors offered very little sound barrier from the noises below. Radios in the other cubicles and the community TV in the sitting room competed with the racket from the bar. A guy spent almost two hours on a telephone right outside my room making calls to friends in Kansas. I learned from eavesdropping on those conversations that most of the tenants were young guys who worked on the oil pipeline. They paid $40 a week for cubicles similar to mine that I suspected were mostly located in the center of the building.

The noise from the bar continued until closing time at 3 AM, after which the heavy outside door slammed loudly every time someone left. Several patrons continued their conversations in the parking lot. It never really got dark outside, just a little dim between 2 AM and 3 AM. It was still considerably lighter than on a bright moonlit night. I looked out shortly after three and saw people clearly as they stood talking near their vehicles.

Sunlight began to stream through my window at 3:45 AM, just as the voices finally began to quiet down. The leaky showers dripping on the metal floors in several of the shower stalls became an annoying encore to the earlier racket. I got up around 4:15 and twisted all of the shower valves tight and tried to get some sleep. By that time the effects of the sleeping pill were just about worn off, and I only drifted in and out of a half-sleep for about an hour. When a few early birds in adjoining cubicles got up for work at 5:30, I gave up trying. I got up, packed my things, and left.

Day 18 - I was on the road by 6 AM. Like with Glennallen I was anxious to put Fairbanks behind me. I did ride around a few of the streets in the city to take a quick look but I soon turned east and headed out of town. I noticed that Fairbanks is only a fraction of the size of Anchorage. The bike was running pretty good, but the fork seals were weeping a little oil from the beating they took on the washboard surface the previous day. The rear tire was beginning to show significant wear and I realized I should have gotten one in Anchorage. It was raining lightly at the spot where the oil pipeline crosses the Tanana River. At first glance the elevated pipe looked like a highway suspension bridge. A security guard watched closely as I stopped to snap a photo.

My map showed the Taylor Highway turning northeast toward Dawson City at a place called Tetlin Junction. While getting gas there I asked the attendant for directions to the road to Dawson. He said, "That's it, right there." The gas station was at the intersection. I asked about the condition of the road and he said, "I don't know. I've never been up it." I asked if many people use the road and he said that once in a while he sees someone go that way but he doesn't know how far they go. The kid wasn't much help.

After I started up the road I saw a vehicle about every 20 or 30 minutes. About 50 miles from the junction while I was down on one knee oiling the chain I heard a sound behind me. I turned and saw a huge black bear crossing the road less than 60 feet from me. I was riveted for a moment, after which I fumbled for my camera but the bear disappeared into the low underbrush before I could get it out. I ran after him hoping he would pause for a moment in a clearing, but he was gone.

The first 75 miles of the Taylor Highway went through a portion of historic 1898 gold-rush country. The next hundred miles consisted of scenic, hilly tundra. The temperature was a very comfortable 70 degrees and the sun was out. There were patches of snow on the north sides of many of the hills, but the rest of the tundra was clear of snow and beginning to come to life with many varieties of knee-high greenery sprouting buds. I noticed a few small communities along the route consisting of a half dozen rustic shacks probably occupied by trappers and die-hard gold miners, but I saw no one around. I inspected a large abandoned dredging machine in a riverbed where it was apparently used in bygone days.

I got gas at a place called Boundary near the Canadian border. There were a few rustic buildings, a landing strip for planes, a gas station, and a place to eat. I could see the tiny community for miles as I approached across the rolling hills. The gas pump was the manual type with a large measuring jar at the top. A gasoline storage tank stood above the ground next to the pump. The tank wasn't buried because of the permafrost in the ground. The friendly middle-aged woman who came out to literally pump my gas using a four-foot-long handle called the antique contraption "an oldie but a goodie." When I remarked about the size of her tiny town she said with a smile, "Oh, we're pretty big sometimes, when we git agoin'."

Seven miles east of Boundary I came upon two buildings standing alone on the open tundra. They looked at first glance like a nineteenth-century military outpost in the treeless hills of western Nebraska. The rustic-looking US customs and immigration building on the north side of the dusty gravel road faced a clean, white-shingled Canadian building on the south side. I stopped and talked with the Canadian customs guy for several minutes. He gave the impression he would talk for as long as I was willing to listen.

Farther out on the tundra from vantage points near the highest elevations, I could see for almost a hundred miles in every direction. I could see rain far to the southeast, clearing in the west, and sunshine far to the north. Almost all of the vegetation was less than four feet high for as far as I could see. The rolling hills and shoulder-high growth combined to create an illusion of miniature mountain ranges and a miniature forest. I felt like a giant in the land of Lilliput. The close appearance of the horizons all around me added to the illusion that the earth was actually very small and that I was standing on top of it as it hurtled through space. A steady breeze against my face gave the feeling that I was actually in motion, which added to this strange illusion. It was one of the most fascinating perspectives I had ever experienced. Many people know the road from the two customs houses to Dawson City as 60-Mile Pass, although it is more widely known as the Top-of-the-World Road. It became one of my all-time favorite most-memorable rides.

I came upon what appeared to be an overnight rest stop for travelers of another era. It was a small, one-room log cabin with a dirt floor and grass roof. A sign outside said it was once used as a stagecoach stop on a regular route between Dawson City and Fairbanks. I climbed an embankment not far from there to get a better photo and I stumbled upon a lone, secluded grave near one of the highest and most beautiful spots on the tundra. Carved on a handmade wooden cross that marked the grave was the epitaph, "The Mad Trapper - The end of his trap line - R.I.P." A very old weather-beaten hat hung from the top of the cross. I understood why someone might want to be buried there: It was not only a very beautiful spot, but the strange top-of-the-world setting gave the impression of actually being closer to God. I learned later that there was once an infamous fugitive named "The Mad Trapper" who became a notorious legend in the Yukon for killing people for the gold in their teeth. It is said that the Mounties finally caught up with him, shot him on the spot, and buried his body where he fell. The exact location of his grave has never been known because the Mounties never made a map. I may have accidentally stumbled upon that grave.

I crested the final hill 175 miles after leaving Tetlin Junction and I saw Dawson City spread out in the valley far below. Dawson is in the Yukon Territory, in the heart of Klondike-gold-rush country. It is situated on the northeast bank of the meandering Yukon River, near its confluence with the Klondike River. I could see this entire panorama from where I stood. After a long, steep decline, the dirt road ends abruptly at the water's edge directly across the river from Dawson City. A small government-owned ferry that plies continually across the river and back came and dropped its steel ramp onto the dirt road in front of me. It looked like a double-ended LST. After boarding, I sat on a box beside the bike and held it to make sure it didn't fall over during the crossing. The ferry churned diagonally upstream across the quarter-mile wide, swift-running river. No other vehicles had boarded with me so I made the 10-minute crossing on the free ferry with two Indian boys and their dog. A steel ramp was then dropped onto the dirt road on the north shore, from where I rode a short distance into town.

Dawson City looked a lot like a frontier town with dirt streets, wooden sidewalks, and old, unpainted buildings. The town is intentionally kept just as it was in gold-rush days.

Tourists from British Columbia and Alberta often come there on bus tours. From Dawson they sometimes continue over the Top-of-the-World Road into Alaska. I stayed at the Downtown Hotel, a western-style hotel-saloon, where the bartender rents the rooms. The saloon entrance had traditional swinging doors at the corner of the building accessible from a wooden sidewalk. The establishment bore no resemblance to the Frontier Hotel where I had stayed in Fairbanks. It was clean, cheerful and quiet, and the bartender wore an old-fashioned gingham dress. It reminded me of Miss Kitty's Long Branch Saloon in the old sitcom, "Gun Smoke."

A strong wind blew through town soon after I arrived, raising clouds of dust along the unpaved streets. The sudden wind warned of an impending storm that made everyone scurry for cover. After it passed I found a nice restaurant and enjoyed a steak in the company of two secretaries on an auto trip from Kamloops, BC. We shared a four-place table, since the restaurant was crowded and they invited me to join them. They also invited me to accompany them to the Gay-Nineties Revue at the local opera house, but I declined because I needed time to service the bike, study my maps, and look into a possible side trip that I hoped to take up the Dempster Highway to the Arctic Circle. That night I adjusted the spokes for the first time and the chain for the third time. About ten spokes on the rear wheel and four on the front were quite loose. The rear tire was totally bald and almost showing its casing. I noticed several deep rock cuts that did reach the casing. Whitehorse was now my only hope for a fresh tire since none were available in Dawson City.

Day 19 - The weather was perfect when I left Dawson at 9 AM. I definitely had to forgo earlier plans of a ride up the Dempster Highway due to the condition of the tire. I learned that the Dempster was completed to just beyond the Arctic Circle at Mile 245. Gas was available at two maintenance camps -- at Miles 129 and 231. My problem now was getting to Whitehorse, 355 miles of rough dirt road away. I spent a nerve-wracking day dodging millions of sharp stones on the Klondike Highway. I tried not to think about how much I might get torn up if the tire blew and I came into contact with some of the sharp stones in the road at that speed. I kept pushing between 60 and 65 MPH though, because I was worried that the cycle shop, if there was one, might close before I got there. That evening I found a sport shop and bought the only 400X18 motorcycle tire they had, which was a soft-composition Yokohama sport tire. I changed it that night outside my hotel.

Day 20 - I backtracked in the morning over the same Alaska Highway route of the previous week. Traffic was very heavy since the landslide had been cleared, including a long caravan of Airstreams headed for Alaska. Many rocks hurled by vehicles coming from the other direction hit me. One stone broke the headlight lens and several others struck my windshield and the top of my helmet. By the time I got to the Cassiar Highway junction I was really fed up with oncoming trucks, RVs and pickup campers, so I decided to return by way of the Cassiar Highway rather than continue on my planned mountainous route down the Alaska Highway.

It hadn't rained since I came through a week earlier so the places where calcium chloride was not used were very dusty. Traffic had also increased so I was pelted several times by flying stones there too, and the dust choked me. I stopped for gas and food provisions at the same co-op store in Iskut that I visited on my way up. Later I located a beautiful lake about 22 miles farther south where I pitched the tent under some tall trees close to the shoreline. The silence there offered a sharp contrast to the steady roar of the glacier stream where I camped a week earlier. I think it was quieter by the lake than any place I have ever been. I would listen for a long while and hear absolutely nothing, not even a loon on the lake. For the first time since I began sleeping in the tent I enjoyed a very restful night.

Day 21 - I got up early with sunlight streaming through the trees. The lake glistened like a mirror. I hated to leave but my gear dried quickly as I prepared and ate breakfast, and I was soon on my way. The dust problem became much worse than the previous day. Fast-moving vehicles left a half-mile-long trail of dust -- quite a change from the total solitude I experienced on my trip up just a week earlier. Often when I got behind someone the guy would speed up and try to keep me from passing, thereby throwing up even more dust. Whenever I moved left to pass, the bike would drift on the loose gravel of the shoulder, making passing very difficult and dangerous. My drive chain kept getting coated with dust so I oiled it every 30 or 40 miles. I stopped at Stewart Junction for an early lunch of ham and three eggs with toast and coffee, which cost about double what it would in the US, but it was welcome.

Passing vehicles on the final leg of the Cassiar became even more difficult, because the road was narrower and the dust trails were longer. I could seldom get within 200 feet of another vehicle. I managed to get by one on the shoulder when a gust of wind blew his dust to the right. I charged in and went left but I had only inches between the side of his pickup and the ditch. Luckily he didn't swerve to miss a stone or other road hazard. I got by a camper after he slowly crossed a single-lane wooden bridge and hadn't resumed his speed yet. I passed another camper in some soft dirt in a construction area. I finally got behind a massive logging truck and tried several times to get close enough to attempt a pass, but there was never enough room. I really didn't trust the guy either. I eventually followed him for 15 miles into Kitwanga. When I got there I was a mess.

I tried to get the bike up to highway speeds on the blacktop, but I couldn't get the engine RPM up because the air filter was totally clogged with dust. I stopped at the first gas station and cleaned it in a half bucket of gasoline. I also made another chain adjustment and changed the oil there. I found a nice motel in Smithers after having traveled only 300 very-difficult miles that day. I visited a Laundromat that evening to wash my clothes and I washed the calcium chloride off the bike at a car wash. Later, I soaked myself in the tub at the motel.

Day 22 - I left Smithers at 7:30 AM feeling refreshed and rested. I headed out on some good blacktop on a beautiful, sunny day. I stopped near Prince George for a quick snack before beginning the long, steady, and very beautiful climb along the Yellowhead Route into the Canadian Rockies. It runs along the Fraser River to Mt. Robson Park, where the narrow and sedate Fraser didn't look anything like the raging white-water river I had seen earlier on the trip much farther downstream. The view of Mt. Robson's 12,972-foot peak near the Continental Divide was spectacular. I rode into Jasper Village for provisions and noticed the town was filled with young people on vacation. Jasper gave the impression of a mythical Shangri-la nestled in the mountains. I called home and thought I sensed some anxiety in Lilli's voice. I thought possibly she was having difficulty with the boys, although she wouldn't say so. I figured it was about time I should hightail it for home. I planned to camp that night before turning east in the morning and stepping up my pace.

I was in total awe of the sensational panorama as I rode south along the Icefields Parkway in search of a campsite. The view in every direction was spectacular. The road follows a broad clearing in the Athabasca River valley as it winds through the giant snow-covered granite mountains that stand back from the highway on both sides. I would have liked to capture the whole thing on film but whenever I looked into the viewfinder I saw only a very small piece of the spectacular panorama. There were beautiful lakes, huge ice fields and majestic mountains in every direction. I thoroughly enjoyed my evening ride, during which I rarely saw another vehicle. I traveled 95 miles before locating a campsite vacancy. I was in Banff Park by then where the scenery was no less spectacular. The Icefields Parkway is near the top of my list of most memorable rides.

My campsite was in the Thompson Creek Campgrounds on Highway 11 just off the parkway. I pitched the tent on a thick bed of pine needles in a grove of huge evergreen trees. Solid-granite mountain peaks surrounded the site. The creek from which the camp got its name trickled peacefully by my tent. I shared the campground with many recreational vehicles of all shapes and sizes. My site in the tent section had a picnic table and a hibachi. I heated and ate my evening meal outside as twilight settled ever so peacefully over the Canadian Rockies. The weather was clear and mild and I slept soundly on the soft bed of pine needles. In the morning my gear wasn't even damp. The ground tarp, which was usually wet from condensation, was bone dry. I prepared a hot breakfast inside the tent and packed to leave. It was a pleasure to pack my camping gear without having to dry it first.

Day 23 - Soon after returning to the Icefields Parkway, the early morning sunshine gave way to a heavy cloud cover. It got so cold I had to dig into my bag for more clothes. I wasn't sure of the elevation but I assumed it was quite high. I was in Banff Park at the time. I followed the parkway for another hour before reaching Trans-Canada One, where I turned east and rode about 40 miles before finally getting clear of the mountain clouds. It was midmorning when I passed through Calgary and saw many people on horseback in fancy cowboy regalia. They appeared to be preparing for a parade that I thought might have been associated with the Calgary Stampede, an annual festival held there.

I ran into the first really strong head winds of the trip on the prairie east of Calgary. My gas mileage dropped sharply, and at one time I got less than 100 miles from gas in my main tank. I wasn't aware at that time that Saskatchewan gas was a different blend that adversely affected performance. I continued to maintain a heavy throttle most of the day, while worrying all the time about the long overdue service to the valves. The engine seemed to be losing power even when there was no wind. It was impossible to find service on Sunday so I decided to look for a bike shop in Regina where I planned to spend the night.

Much of Saskatchewan is flat as a tabletop. The monotony of prairie scenery is broken only occasionally by tall grain elevators in the small towns and by tiny oil-well pumps rocking in the open fields. I got to Regina early in the evening, after passing through towns with names like Medicine Hat, Swift Current, and Moose Jaw. The weather was clear although the head winds were strong and constant. I found a clean, comfortable motel in Regina for less than $12 and got directions to the local Suzuki shop from the desk clerk before turning in.

Day 24 - I found the shop easily but I got there far too early, even after having taken extra time for breakfast. I decided to look for a shop later that morning in Minot, ND. I entered North Dakota at Portal and was ordered by the US customs guy to empty all of my bags. I figured I must have fit some kind of profile -- maybe just being a biker. It was the first and only time my luggage has ever been thoroughly searched at any border. I was detained for almost a half hour, unpacking and repacking my duffel bag on a large outdoor table. He went through everything with a fine-tooth comb, looking into every film container and every vitamin pill bottle. The guy acted very official and unfriendly and he responded to my light chatter with terse answers if he responded at all. Finally after satisfying himself that my luggage was clean, he acted a little more amicable. Unfortunately he never heard of a Suzuki dealer in Minot or anywhere else nearby for that matter.

Unable to find a dealer in Minot I pressed on. I came close to getting a speeding ticket about 10 miles west of Grand Forks when I sailed through a radar check at almost 75 MPH on a scarcely traveled section of US 2. I was sure I had "bought the farm." I chopped the throttle and coasted by the patrol car. I was preparing to stop and take my lumps but he never made a motion toward me. When I mentioned my good fortune to a gas station attendant a few miles down the road he said, "Oh, he wouldn't bother you. He's laying for those big grain trucks. They sail through there at speeds you wouldn't believe." It was late afternoon when I got to Grand Forks. I stopped to check the yellow pages for a dealer but found none there either. I called the Harley dealer, the only bike dealer in the book, and he seemed to get great pleasure out of telling me that both the Suzuki and Kawasaki dealers in Grand Forks had gone "belly-up" a year ago. He thought the nearest "surviving" Suzuki dealer was in Duluth, 265 miles east of there. I bought a quart of milk at a grocery store and picked up some chicken at a KFC. I carried my supper to a picnic area a few miles out of town since the weather was perfect for it. I figured if I made Duluth that night I would have covered 725 miles that day.

I stopped in Bagley, MN to call home and give Lilli my estimated arrival time. A few miles from there to my surprise I spotted a dealer in Shevlin. The tiny shop was in the midst of farm country with cornfields all around it. The corn was so high it nearly obscured the small building. It was still open when I pulled in at 8 PM but he didn't have time to work then. We made an appointment for 9 AM and I returned to Bagley for a room. I wrote a few final post cards and went out to find a post office. I asked directions from a guy sitting on his front steps and he turned out to be another biker who invited me on a tour of his garage where he had three motorcycles of his own.

Day 25 - The dealer re-shimmed five of the valves. Two others were also slightly off but he didn't have the right shims in stock so he shimmed them to be slightly loose. Two of the intake valves had been too tight, which may have contributed to my loss of power. He also adjusted the points, changed the plugs and the oil, and he checked the compression, which was still OK. Time passed quickly as I talked with a few competition drag racers who dropped by. When the dealer returned from road-testing my bike he said the lack of power in the head winds was probably due to the "tall" sprocket I was using. Apparently the Suzuki was designed to perform much better at higher RPMs. I found the cost of bike service in Minnesota to be far less than most other places I had been. My gas mileage improved considerably after the tune-up.

It was mostly cloudy that afternoon with a weather front moving in from Wyoming. I hoped to stay ahead of it because according to reports on TV it was accompanied by strong winds and heavy rain. I stopped for lunch in Bemidji and had a late supper at a Burger King in Ashland, Wisconsin, overlooking Chequamegon Bay on Lake Superior. I finally called it a day in Ironwood, Michigan where I estimated I was still two long days from home. I found a really nice room for only seven dollars. The room was large and clean with a double bed and a single bed. There was a color TV, wall-to-wall carpeting, and the bathroom had a tub as well as a shower. It was hard to believe that people could make a profit from renting rooms like that for seven dollars a night. The beaches on the north shore of Lake Michigan were practically deserted in spite of it being summertime. I saw a few sunbathers, but very few were swimming because of the cool weather. The cool weather and lack of vacationers could certainly explain the low motel prices.

Day 26 - The weather got noticeably warmer after crossing the huge single-span bridge at Mackinaw. I rode through Jack Pine Enduro country that day and reminisced several enduros I rode there in the 60s. I made a short detour to look for the famous Rifle River crossing that was used in almost every Jack Pine run that I rode, but I couldn't locate it. I noticed big changes in Detroit from when I went to school after the war. I looked for a room around Detroit but didn't find anything until I got to Toledo, where I packed it in after 775 miles.

Day 27 - I loaded the bike for my final day and left around 9 AM. Truck traffic on the Ohio Turnpike was very heavy. Exhaust fumes and other smoke pollution from factories around Cleveland were a sharp contrast from the clean air I left far behind. I realized that my tour was coming quickly to an end. I enjoyed the ride through Pennsylvania where truck traffic was lighter and I thought the scenery was much nicer than along the Ohio Turnpike. Most of the farms were clean and well kept with fresh paint on most of the houses and barns.

I did a lot of thinking about the trip and wondered as I rode where I might go the next time. I reflected on what I should have taken on this trip and what I'll certainly take on the next one. A long-sleeve white shirt was at the top of my list of things to take, while dried food was at the top of the list of things to leave behind. I'll also remember to take gloves and mittens for every occasion. Different weight jackets would be helpful, whereas on this trip I carried extra layers of sweatshirts. A pair of leisure shoes would have been useful -- aside from providing comfort in the evenings I could ride with them in the extreme heat. Good sunglasses are a must for my next trip. Two pairs of jeans seemed about right this time, as I wore a pair and carried a pair, and I washed one of them whenever I found a Laundromat. I washed some of the smaller things that would dry overnight like socks, shorts and handkerchiefs in motel sinks.

The next time I plan to travel on many dirt roads I'll carry an extra tire, a tire repair kit, spare tubes, tire irons, and an air pump. I remembered to bring my owner's manual, a spoke wrench, extra oil, a siphon hose, the warranty card, and my special insurance card for Canada; and I also carried a 25' length of quarter-inch-nylon rope for emergency towing. Fortunately I didn't need that. For some of the places I could have broken down it might have been the only way to get out. I need to figure out a way to carry a face shield without scuffing it.

For camping I would have benefited from a lightweight blanket for when it got too hot for the bag. My tiny butane hiker's stove was very useful. I used three butane cartridges during my trip. I stopped to buy Brillo pads for cleaning my cooking pots and I bought a small bottle of detergent for my dishes, socks, etc. I'll also bring a water canteen the next time. I remembered to bring mosquito repellent and used that a lot.

Fifteen dollars a day was more than enough cash to carry on this trip. I used my credit cards for lodging and gas and I could have used it to eat in many places. My rule-of-thumb for cash was that I would bring only as much as I needed to buy food and I would use the credit cards for just about everything else. I spent a total of $150 for bike service, which included the tire. With the telephone bill that I paid later the trip cost a little more than $1200, or an average of about $45 per day. Only about twelve dollars of that was cash. Buying canned food for camping kept my eating expenses down. Eating in travel restaurants and fast-food places rather than camping probably would have cost at least five to ten dollars a day more.

As for the bike, it averaged about 36 MPG on the trip. My gas mileage varied from around 26 in the very strong head winds in Saskatchewan to more than 50 with a tailwind, and especially when I kept my speed under 50 MPH, which was mostly on the dirt. The bike required a little extra care to the valve shims and the points during the trip than a bike with hydraulic lifters and electronic ignition. I dressed the points myself but the valves required special tools. The bike's handling on unstable surfaces left a lot to be desired and the ride was stiffer than a bona fide touring bike. Pain just below the back of my neck between my shoulder blades bothered me quite a bit on the trip. I lost about 15 pounds during the four weeks I spent on the road, but I felt good. The numbness on the inside of my thighs that I apparently got from the seat on the third day took a few months to clear up.

The weather front that chased me most of the way across the country was still a day behind when I crossed the George Washington bridge into New York City. I had covered 12,741 miles on my 27-day trip, for an average of 472 miles a day, which included the day in California when I didn't ride at all and a few other days that I rode only part of the day. I estimate that I averaged roughly 500 miles a day on my full-travel days.

ALASKA TWO - THE TOUGH ONE

My second trip to Alaska, four years after the first, turned out to be a struggle for survival. It was a tough trip from beginning to end. Almost every day I rode in rain, sleet, snow, or hail, and sometimes all four on the same day, and sometimes all day. During the trip I became stranded for four days in a blizzard near the Arctic circle, 231 miles up a closed road almost a week before it was scheduled to open for the season. I almost died from hypothermia in my tent. On my return home I rode from Anchorage all the way into Eureka, Montana, a distance of more than 2,400 miles, on mostly wet, slippery dirt roads, in some of the worst weather imaginable without ever seeing a bed, a shower, or the inside of a building for four days. I have never felt so cold and miserable in my entire life, before or since. Following is a daily journal of that epic adventure:

Day 1 - I left home at noon on Memorial Day, May 25th, 1981 and headed due north, having chosen a completely different route across northern Canada for my second trip. The odometer reading of 52,000 miles on my well-worn 750 Suzuki included my first Alaska trip four years earlier and two additional trips to the west coast. It was 80 degrees and humid when I pulled into my first gas stop near Warrensburg in the Adirondacks. I realized early that, like with my first trip, I had loaded far too much gear onto the rear luggage carrier, except that this time there was even more. It made the front end of the bike far too light and the handling, that was already poor on loose terrain, became worse than ever. Although I fully expected the problem, I couldn't find a better way to pack all of my gear and still have room to move around on the seat. A tank bag and saddlebags would have offered much better weight distribution but a tank bag would have restricted my movements. My load this time consisted of a tent, a sleeping bag, a fairly large suitcase, many extra tools, and a spare tire. Most of the heaviest gear was loaded well forward on the rear seat, but a lot was piled back on the luggage carrier too, directly above and some behind the rear axle. The front end of the bike raised an inch off the ground as I left the first gas stop.

I met the first of several rain showers that afternoon between Tupper Lake and Plattsburg, some of which were downpours. As I approached Montreal clocking a steady 70

MPH almost every car on the road flew by me. I got lost three times in the urban sprawl before finally locating Route 117. I ate at a Mickey D's in the city before heading into the Laurentians, where it rained for about two hours. The Laurentians are not very tall mountains but it was a scenic ride that reminded me of the Catskills. I stopped for the day at a small motel near Labelle shortly after 9 PM, having clocked about 400 miles on my first half day. When I asked about the security of the bike the owner said I could use his garage for the night. He said the bike would probably not be safe out front. With the garage space included the room cost only $14.

Day 2 - I eased the bike out of the garage at 6:30 AM trying not to wake anyone. I stopped for breakfast a few miles up the road. The waitress spoke very little English. She blushed a lot, dropped a few things, and seemed very nervous about waiting on an old guy on a motorcycle who didn't speak her language. It rained lightly and was quite cool as I maneuvered through the sweeping turns and rolling hills north of Labelle. The flora consisted mainly of pine trees, hemlocks, and white birches. The area reminded me a little of New Hampshire with the same kinds of trees and two-lane macadam road. Most people I met spoke only French or struggled a lot with English.

Near Mont-Laurier I dug into my bag for extra clothes. I was wearing a Belstaff enduro jacket over a few layers of sweatshirts and other shirts. As the temperature dropped below 50 degrees it was already becoming clear to me that I hadn't packed enough warm clothes for the trip. Deep potholes in the first of several construction areas jarred my teeth, making me wonder about the strength of the rear luggage carrier. All of the above contributed to a wicked headache, for which I stopped and dug into the bag again, this time for Anacin.

I passed an accident where a lumber truck had overturned in a ditch. He must have had at least 28 wheels and all of them were pointed straight up. I noticed that most places in Quebec fly their separatist flag rather than the Canadian Maple Leaf. The flag is light blue with a white cross in the center and small figures in the corners that reminded me of Boy Scout emblems. I saw this flag in many places including in front of commercial establishments like restaurants. The sun popped out occasionally but it was mostly overcast and cold. The wind picked up near Val-d'or and it began to rain. I stopped for gas at a Shell station where the girl cashier didn't speak a word of English. Around 4 o'clock I stopped for the night near Iroquois Falls when I couldn't stand the cold any more. I was wet under my rain suit and my feet were wet inside my shoes. My toes hurt constantly from the cold. I kept thinking that my idea of taking the northern route during late May might not have been very smart. I was already cold to the bone and I had barely started.

Day 3 - I parked the bike directly outside my window and very close to the building, hoping to make it as secure as possible. I still lost my only pair of sunglasses that I left in a case taped to the handlebars. I was getting a really unfavorable impression of Quebec. The temperature was in the high twenties when I left at 6 AM. I had to scrape a thick layer of frost from the seat before riding about 70 miles in search of breakfast. From the time I entered Canada I kept looking for a bank to exchange currency. The premium on my US dollars should have been around 20 percent in my favor but when places took cash for gas or food they usually did it on an even money basis, thus charging me the extra 20 percent. This also seemed more so in Quebec, since I didn't have that problem on my first trip. I used my credit cards wherever I could, but most small restaurants along my route in Quebec wouldn't accept my card.

The sun was out by midmorning although the temperature was still only in the mid-to-low 40s with a biting wind coming off James Bay. I was already wearing just about everything I brought with me and I wasn't even close to the Northwest Territories where I figured it would certainly be much colder. I was also wearing my lightweight coverall that I carried mainly for the dusty roads. I slipped my rain suit booties over my gloves to avoid digging for mittens, which were packed deep inside one of the bags. I found a mailbox in Kapuskasing and dropped a card to Donna about my ETA in Anchorage. The cold eased a bit around Hearst, Ontario where I peeled off the duster and the balacava. Ontario is generally flat in that area with short cedars, poplars, and balsams. Most of the farms looked very poor and small, and not much was planted. Of course it was still early in the season.

Whenever I met large trucks coming in the opposite direction with both of us traveling at 70 MPH or better, I had to really hold on. Wind spilling from the truck's front end would sometimes throw me a foot or more off course. I stopped every

150 miles or so to oil the chain. Sometimes I would have to go ten to fifteen miles to find a place where I could put the bike onto the center stand. The shoulders of the road were too narrow and slanted and the main traffic lanes were too hazardous. I would usually look for a bridge with a level space between the travel lane and the outer railing, or a culvert that I could get down into and back out of without struggling too much. That's also how I parked for photos. I didn't take many photos that day.

My main tank ran out in only 129 miles, my worst gas mileage so far on the trip. I figured it was probably because of the strong head winds but I thought it also could have been from the condition of the plugs and points. The price of gas in the area was running 50 percent higher than in the US. At one station east of Longlac the pump stopped with the price between two numbers and the girl read it as $8.60 instead of $6.60. I had to argue with her before finally convincing her that she was reading it wrong. I located a bank in Longlac and exchanged some currency. I got 18.5 percent, which was a lot better than the even money I was being charged.

Western Ontario is like one huge forest. The flora consists mainly of small balsams, cedars, and poplars, the growth of which might be stunted from the cold. I stopped about 50 miles before Thunder Bay to dress the ignition points. It was a good move because a huge lump had built up on one point and there was a hole burned into the other, which may have contributed to my poor gas mileage. The sun was shining around Thunder Bay and the temperature was up to 60 degrees. The relative warmth felt good for a change.

I took a wrong turn leaving Thunder Bay and accidentally headed for International Falls, MN. I didn't realize it until I had gone through 30 miles of really rough road construction. The bike handled very poorly in the soft dirt and I struggled with it for the entire 30 miles. After checking my map I decided to continue on that route in spite of the fact that it would take me about 100 miles off course, which was better than going all the way back through the construction. There were many rock outcroppings on both sides of the two-lane road, some of which was light-colored and looked like granite, while the other was black and looked like lava. The road surface was very coarse and rough, which made the tires roar. I figured it was probably causing much extra wear on them. I stopped for the night in Emo, west of Fort Francis, after having traveled 750 miles that day.

Day 4 - It looked like it would be a nice day when I left the motel with the temperature in the low 50s. I hurt all over from my first three days of riding. It was becoming much more difficult for me to get out of bed in the morning and it reminded me of starting a second day at a Jack Pine Enduro. I was continually aware of pain somewhere in my body, especially between my shoulder blades and on my butt, but I hurt all over. The area just north of Emo looked like a vacation spot with many picturesque lakes. I saw a seaplane take off from one of them. In contrast I saw a few small Indian villages that looked very poor and run down. Route 71, which eventually led me back to my planned route, was a great bike road, with 70 MPH sweeping turns. I got back onto my route near Kenora, and a short time later I picked up Trans-Canada One in Manitoba.

The sun broke through around 9:30. I noticed while oiling the chain that the countershaft sprocket was badly worn. I figured I could probably get a replacement along my route during the next few days. Thirty miles before reaching Winnipeg I emerged from the forests onto the open prairie. I put on my full rain suit when it started to rain, but a few minutes later the sun came out so I took it off again. I stopped at a McDonald's for a midmorning snack although I also snacked on peanuts while I was moving. I would put both feet up on the highway pegs and hold the jar between my knees to remove the cap. I could then drink the peanuts from the jar as I rode along. I couldn't possibly take both hands off the handlebars at the same time because the front end of the bike would immediately start to wobble and shimmy no matter what speed I was traveling, which was due in large part to the poor weight distribution.

The farmlands west of Winnipeg appeared almost black, like pure loam, and I wondered what could have made the soil so dark. Near Portage la Prairie I turned northwest on Route 16, the Yellowhead Route. While oiling the chain a short time later I realized that the new Michelin rear tire that I had mounted for the trip already showed significant wear. The coarse Canadian road surfaces were taking their toll on the tread.

I was gradually climbing to higher altitudes as I rode through the gently rolling hills around Neepawa, Manitoba. I saw mostly wheat fields and cattle farms, where the farmhouses

53

were miles apart. About every ten miles or so I would pass through a tiny community consisting of a few grain elevators, a few houses, and a garage for repairing tractors. I crossed into Saskatchewan just ahead of a heavy rainsquall.

A short time later I met another extremely heavy squall with 50 MPH crosswinds, hail, and torrential downpours. The wind almost blew me off the machine and the hailstones stung my face like bullets. It only lasted about five minutes but there were constant crosswinds of 40 and 50 MPH on the open prairie. I occasionally had to find a sheltered spot to stop and rest from the constant struggle with the wind. A cluster of trees around a farmhouse would usually serve as the only haven from the unrelenting crosswinds. I could see squalls coming for miles across the prairie. Sometimes the brightest spot in the sky was straight ahead, so I traveled as fast as I could in pursuit of it. A hundred miles east of Saskatoon I met the heaviest and most prolonged downpour of the day accompanied by fierce thunder and lightning. A gas station attendant said these were their first good rains of the spring season. What a difference from my first trip when good weather seemed to follow me wherever I went. It didn't seem like a very good omen for a trip where I intended to use my tent a lot more. I checked into a motel in Saskatoon after clocking 730 miles.

Day 5 - I had a light breakfast in my room of oatmeal cookies, milk, and prunes. I oiled and greased the chain and dressed the points before leaving at 6:40. I spoke with a guy at the motel loading a Blazer who was headed for Fairbanks. He said, "I saw you out there yesterday. Boy, you must have gotten soaked!" I told him I had never ridden in rain that hard for that long in my entire life. Ten miles out of Saskatoon I saw a sign, "Slow down and save your windshield." The road was torn up and covered with heavy loose gravel. Later on a hard-surface road a guy riding a Yamaha 750 SECA came up alongside and said he had three hours to get to work and he was running late. He was traveling at a steady 80 MPH or better. I watched him as he gradually faded into the horizon. The terrain west of Saskatoon consists mainly of gently rolling farmland.

I stopped at a McDonald's in North Brattleford for a midmorning snack. It was overcast and I was cold, and I just couldn't pass up the warmth of a Mickey D's. It rained lightly a few times during the morning and I could see several showers in

54

the distance. My gas mileage had gotten so bad that I was constantly looking for a cycle shop to buy a new set of spark plugs. I could tell that my strength was also waning when it got increasingly more difficult to get the bike onto the center stand to oil the chain. Of course part that was due to tire wear. The more the tire wore the higher I had to lift it to get it on the stand. I usually looked for a sheltered area to oil the chain because the wind would blow the stream of oil away long before it reached the chain. I located a Suzuki dealer in Lloydminster, Alberta where I bought spark plugs and a countershaft sprocket. I installed the plugs there in the parking lot and stowed the sprocket for later. Two of the four replaced plugs had cracked porcelain. The bike ran much better with new plugs.

Six deer ran across the highway in front of me shortly after I entered Alberta. The speed limit through most of the towns was 35 or 40 MPH. Most of the smaller towns had two or three grain elevators, while the larger towns had as many as six or eight. I rarely saw a police car. Sometimes I would ride for hours without seeing a provincial cop like state troopers back home. Cattle farms became more prevalent in Alberta. I bought a deli sandwich and a soda and I found a small picnic area where I stopped to eat it. An elderly couple was also having lunch there. It was clear and 65 degrees, which was the nicest weather I had seen on the trip so far, although it was short-lived.

Sixty miles east of Edmonton I rode through a small, picturesque town called Vegreville where I saw several Ukrainian churches. I had seen similar churches in several towns along the open prairie. I also spotted a small cemetery in the median of a divided highway near Vegreville.

A guy drove up alongside at a light in Edmonton and pointed to the bike saying, "Hey, you're leaking something." The #1 carburetor float was stuck and gas was gushing from the overflow tube. The end of the tube was swollen, indicating that it had been leaking for some time. After rapping the bowl to get the float valve to fall back into place I pulled the overflow tube out so I could keep an eye on it. Gas in Edmonton was 25 cents a liter, less than half what I paid in Quebec.

Most of the approach to the Alaska Highway between Edmonton and Dawson Creek was paved, except for one rough, dusty stretch that was under construction. My gas mileage seemed to recover a little after gassing up in Edmonton. I saw many natural gas fields in Alberta and occasionally I saw oil pumps rocking in the fields. I stopped in Grande Prairie for dinner after getting lost twice from poor route marking in town. I ate at a KFC near a window with the sun streaming in, which made me sweat as I sat there in my full riding clothes. It was 7:40 and the sun was still pretty high, so I continued riding to near Dawson Creek where I found a campground. My face was getting badly burned from the weather and I was tired.

Day 6 - I didn't sleep well at all. It was my first night in the tent on this trip and I heard people talking, laughing, and singing until around 3 AM. The thin sides of the tent didn't block out any of the sounds. I got up at 5:30 and used a little short of two hours to roll up everything, tie it to the bike, make my breakfast, eat, and leave. During that time I talked with a guy who worked for one of the Canadian oil companies and he solved at least one of my problems. I learned that most regular gas in Saskatchewan is only about 81-octane, and it has very few cleansing additives. He said that it gums up most engines and generally makes a mess of carburetors. He was sure it was the cause of my poor gas mileage, my sticking float, and my cracked spark plugs. If I had known earlier I certainly would have looked for high-test gas while I was in Saskatchewan, although high-test gas is not available at most gas stations on the prairie.

The official Mile Zero of the Alaska Highway is in Dawson Creek. I saw a sign that said Whitehorse is 1473 kilometers, or 913 miles from there. At Mile 34 I rode over a long, narrow bridge with metal decking, where the poor-handling machine gave me white knuckles as I clung tight to the handle grips. That part of the Alaska Highway offered mostly long hills and wide curves. I stopped at Fort St. John for a ham and eggs breakfast where the temperature was in the mid 50s. I rode on gravel with a lot of soft spots after the blacktop ended. The bike handled very poorly on the gravel. Fresh puddles began to appear in the road around Pink Mountain and 20 miles farther on I ran into rain again. It got much rougher after that, especially in hilly terrain and on steep grades where washouts were common. Most of the highway was built on high ground and I could sometimes see the road on the next mountain, far across the valleys. I almost dropped the bike once when I stopped to take a picture. The panoramic views from a few of the high vantage points were so breathtaking it brought tears to my eyes. I could see snow on far-off mountaintops. A group from Ontario that I spoke with at one of the lookout points shared my feelings. One of the men mentioned that he remembers the road in much better condition when he came up 13 years earlier. There was probably much less traffic to chew it up then.

I saw about a dozen horses running loose that appeared to be wild, but they probably belonged to outfitters who rent them for mining and other backwoods expeditions. A few miles farther on I saw another group of horses and came into some sunshine. Around mile 230 I spotted a huge caribou and a third group of horses, some of which had brands. I would ride for a while on very rough macadam with huge potholes, but mostly it was dirt. Occasionally there would be a stretch of new blacktop, but tar road in good condition was scarce. The temperature was in the low sixties when I saw a guy on a bicycle near Mile 250. What a way to travel to Alaska! I occasionally saw signs of the original road, which consisted of wheel ruts through the woods. I also saw signs of a natural gas pipeline.

Near Fort Nelson I was riding across some tooth-jarring bumps when a stone from a truck coming the other way hit the top of my helmet so hard it made my ears ring and I felt a little dizzy. Fortunately I ducked my head whenever I met oncoming vehicles. One big rock hit my arm and gave me a Charlie-horse. An old guy in a pickup camper sucking on a cigar didn't see me coming from behind, and he almost ran me off the road as I was passing. He suddenly swerved to miss a pothole while I was directly alongside. There was one eight-mile stretch of road construction where deep gravel covered the road. I was literally showered with rocks from vehicles coming the other way. I dropped the bike at a photo-op when I misjudged the balance point while putting it on the side stand. That balance point changes as the tires wear. I fell downhill with the bike above me. I got out from under it but when I tried to pick it up I couldn't lift it with the entire load of luggage tied on. I quickly untied everything as the gas poured out of the carburetors and tank vent, and while I was struggling with the weight. Part of my problem was my waning strength. Lack of sleep at the noisy campsite the night before was a major contributor. I was becoming totally exhausted.

A short while later I stopped for another photo-op and I dug into my bag for a snack and a sip of water. I got to

Steamboat Mountain with only about six miles of gas left in my reserve tank. I learned that gas was very scarce along that section of the highway. The gas attendant asked what part of New York I was from. When I told him Buchanan he said that at age 18 and with only three days on the job with Con Edison, he did the calculations for inserting the uranium rods into the atomic reactor at Indian Point. He said that now he wants to be as far away from there as he can get. When I told him I was headed for the Dempster Highway he offered information about road conditions. Mainly he said I should probably carry two spare tires rather than just one and that I should certainly carry spare tubes and a well-stocked tire repair kit because of the large amount of sharp shale on the Dempster.

Summit Lake was completely covered with ice. I saw a motorcyclist in his full rain suit coming the other way and I spotted a mountain goat with young. At Muncho Lake the road runs along the edge of the water for about five miles. It is one of the most beautiful spots along the Alaska Highway.

By six o'clock truckers and RVs quit for the night and I rode the next few hours without seeing anyone. A big porcupine crossed the road in front of me and I saw two Dalls sheep licking at the puddles, probably for the salt in the calcium chloride that's spread on the road. I saw a second porcupine and I chased another group of horses down the road. I noticed that a few of the horses had tattoos behind their ears. I swerved to miss some loose gravel and ran smack into a pothole that made the suspension bottom out and the center stand slam against the road. The bike was taking a terrible beating.

It rained lightly as I crossed the Liard River. I was often down to 40 MPH and less because of huge breaks in the pavement, many of which were less than a hundred feet apart. I saw hundreds of square miles of forest devastated by fire. I stopped for a light supper of cheeseburger and coffee at a roadside snack shop. A short while later I located a small British Columbia campground near a fast-running glacier stream, a few miles from the Yukon border. I pulled in at 9:45 and was set up and settled in by 10:30. I chatted with one of the only other campers there, an Air Force guy who was headed for Fairbanks. I covered 600 miles that day, almost all of which was dirt or badly broken macadam. It was raining lightly when I crawled into the tent to heat my evening meal. I reflected on my long day and thought it was probably the toughest day I had ever spent on a road motorcycle. I was totally exhausted after having been up for 17 hours on about two hours sleep. I was at least 14 hours on the road.

Day 7 - That night was a psychological disaster and the first real low point of my trip. I worried a lot about the poor handling of the bike in the mud and loose gravel, and I was getting increasingly concerned about the rear tire that had worn much more than I had expected. Things I had been hearing about the Dempster Highway compounded my worries and my waning strength was continually pulling me down. I dreamed about the match between Sugar Ray Leonard and Roberto Duran, where Duran put up his hands and said "No mas!" (No more!) I felt weak and completely inadequate for the trip and I felt the same as Duran. I had concluded that I was riding the wrong motorcycle for a trip up the Dempster Highway, I hadn't packed enough warm clothing, and I was gradually convincing myself I would never make it to Inuvik. The roads were already bad and would only get much worse as I proceeded farther north. To add even more to my poor state of mind, there was about an inch of water inside the tent when I woke up. It had rained all night and a lot of the water had gotten between the ground tarp and the bottom of the tent. I was actually lying in a huge puddle of water in the morning. My clothes, my bedding, and most of my gear were soaked. I felt really down. I prepared breakfast in the tent before rolling up all of my wet gear. I decided while packing to abort my plan to Inuvik and head for Anchorage, which I figured I could make in two days. The sky was gray and overcast when I left the campsite, as was my state of mind. I had given up the main purpose for my trip and I felt cold, defeated, and very depressed.

Traffic was extremely light that morning. I stopped to oil the chain about 50 miles out. I hadn't seen another vehicle for at least 20 minutes. The sun was shining on the road by then and the sky in the direction I was headed was clear blue. The entire horizon glistened with beautiful snowcapped mountains. For the first time in two days I could get the bike up to 70 MPH on smooth dirt and it really felt good. The highway in the Yukon was actually in much better shape than in British Columbia. I ate a second breakfast of ham and eggs at a Chinese place in Watson Lake and I stopped at a small super market there for provisions for that night. I heard about a bridge being washed out on the Campbell Highway and thought if I had still intended to go north, I would have had to detour all the way to the Klondike Highway on the far side of Whitehorse.

My full stomach, the clear blue sky, and much better roads west of Watson Lake all encouraged me to reconsider my original plan. I did a lot of soul-searching as I rode along, and finally decided it would be better to try for it and fail than never to try at all. I had at least a glimmer of hope of making it. I mustered up a fresh surge of courage and decided to go for it. I felt an immediate rush of emotion for having made the decision.

My duffel bag suddenly came loose from the luggage carrier and I almost lost it. I noticed that the longest and most critical bungee cord was missing. I turned around and headed back with only slim hopes of finding it, but luck was with me, as I only had to go back a few hundred yards. I had a close call passing another pickup camper when he veered from a pothole without checking his rear view mirror while I was alongside. I crossed the infamous Teslin Lake Bridge with its deep, widely-spaced steel grating, and I really got white knuckles from the poor-handling machine. I wondered what it would be like with that bike in the rain with wet, muddy tires.

The beautiful scenery in the Yukon went on for hundreds of miles with snowcapped mountains, sparkling blue lakes, and white-water rivers and streams. The blue skies and fluffy-white clouds further enhanced my panoramic views. The views around Muncho Lake, Marsh Lake, and Teslin Lake are as nice as anywhere I have ever been. I believe the scenery in the Yukon and British Columbia is even nicer than in Alaska.

I rode into Whitehorse without realizing it was Sunday. I needed to exchange currency but I could only get gas and I came right back out to the highway. Just west of Whitehorse I turned onto the Klondike Highway and experienced another rush of emotion as I headed the bike north toward the Dempster Highway. The rear tire had less rubber on it than the used Continental spare I was carrying, but even that didn't bother me. I was determined to go north and nothing was stopping me now.

I rode up the Klondike Highway a short distance before spotting a campground at Fox Lake. It was barely four o'clock but I needed extra time to dry everything that had gotten soaked the night before. I pitched the wet tent and hung all of my wet things out to dry in the warm breeze. I was on the west side of a sloping hill near the edge of the lake, which afforded maximum sunshine. I managed to dry everything and stow it away by 7:30. I proceeded to prepare my evening meal of canned chicken and hard rolls with canned prunes for dessert. My campsite was in a beautiful setting with the lake and snowcapped mountains in the background. Teenagers strummed their guitars and sang folk songs until very late. No one seemed to know much about the condition of the Dempster Highway. One guy thought I should check to see if the ferries were running because it was still very early in the season. He thought he remembered hearing that the first ferry was near Mile 320 in the Northwest Territories. I turned in around 11 o'clock and tried to get some sleep.

Day 8 - I got very little sleep again. The road construction crews worked until 3 AM. It was twilight but there was apparently enough light for the earthmovers and graders to do their work. The only sleep I managed to get was between three and five when there was no roadwork going on. Around 5 AM a huge water truck began to wet down the dirt for the next day's work. I finally crawled out of the bag and heated some baked beans for breakfast. The temperature was just above freezing. Wearing just about everything I had, including my balacava, I packed up and headed north. The gravel road was in fairly good condition and the meager bike service I managed to accomplish helped the performance a lot. My small 1940-vintage Harley mittens worked well enough against the cold, but it was difficult to operate my mini tape recorder with them on.

There was plowed snow on both sides of the Klondike Highway. The road was relatively straight and level with huge granite mountains on both sides that rise abruptly less than a mile away from the road. There were a few patches of green on the mountainsides but otherwise they appeared to be solid stone. It wasn't long before I began to get very cold again, including my feet. The dirt highway was freshly treated with calcium chloride and there was very little loose gravel on the surface. I held my speed fairly constant above 70 MPH. Occasionally a slight washboard surface would cause the forks to work extra hard. One of the fork legs had already begun to leak oil from several days of strenuous workout.

I got emotional again that morning as I reflected on my decision to go north. I learned from earlier adventures like my

61

first Alaska tour that changes take place in my psyche after long periods of physical and mental stress. Not having enough sleep for several days compounds the condition. The changes seem to come from struggling alone in an almost totally exhausted state while being exposed to extreme elements of nature. I've heard that the phenomenon occurs with lifeboat survivors, explorers, and mountain climbers. I usually feel closer to God during these trials and I am constantly aware of His presence. What may start as a simple motorcycle trip becomes an epic struggle for survival, where I use every bit of strength I can muster just to survive. When things finally go well I feel it's because God has granted me some relief from the stress and the pain; and then I sometimes just break down and cry.

The Klondike Highway north of Carmacks was in excellent condition. There were almost no loose stones on the surface and no dust, and traffic was exceptionally light. I stopped for photos a few miles north of Carmacks and again north of Pelly Crossing, where I saw bear crap in the pull-off area. I passed a grading crew where the fast moving, liquid-calcium-chloride truck was followed a half mile behind by two huge graders moving at roughly the same speed. About fifty miles from Dawson City it got very overcast and started to rain. At the Dempster Highway intersection there was a barrier across the road and a sign that read, "Closed for the Season - Open June 5," -- and it was only June 1st. While getting gas there I asked the attendant about the condition of the road. He thought it was passable for at least 231 miles to the maintenance camp at Eagle Plains but beyond that he wasn't sure. He heard that the ferries across two of the rivers weren't running due to heavy ice floes and that two of the highest passes in the Richardson Range were still being cleared of ice and snow.

I rode into Dawson City to stock up on provisions for my three days on the Dempster Highway. I planned to reach Eagle Plains that night. I figured my second day would be the longest and probably the toughest, which would be a 460-mile round trip from Eagle Plains to Inuvik, provided of course I could make it through the passes and across the rivers. The third day would consist of returning from Eagle Plains to Dawson City and hopefully beyond. It took about an hour and a half to make the 60-mile round trip into Dawson. I stopped again at the gas station near the junction to top off my tank and fill the two

Prestone bottles I was carrying with spare gas. I had made makeshift saddlebags from an old pair of Carhartt pants sewed at the bottoms to carry the extra gas. I inserted a bottle into each leg and draped the pants over the rear seat under my other gear. It was 1:30 PM when I squeezed around the barrier and started up the deserted Dempster Highway.

The scenery was outstanding. The road-surface of the first 40 miles was in excellent condition, which reminded me of my 1977 trip up the Cassiar Highway shortly after it opened. It was drizzling and overcast as I climbed into the Ogilvie Mountains. At times I was down into second gear picking my way around and through minor washouts on the steep, twisty incline. The view from the summit was incredible. I almost lost control of the bike as I turned to look and became totally mesmerized by the breathtaking view, which was a fantastic panorama of heavily snow-clad mountains. Snow was also piled high along the edges of the road. The entire scene was like a winter wonderland. I felt like I was getting my own private showing of the top of the world where I was completely alone, although suddenly I looked up and saw a guy walking toward me. I could hardly believe my eyes. A young guy with a beard, wearing a parka, was leisurely walking down this deserted road. I wondered whether he was a hiker or if he lived up there. We exchanged smiles and waves and continued on our respective ways. About eight miles farther on I saw a small, well-kept log cabin with a sign, "Pete Jensen, Outfitters." Tools and other paraphernalia for panning gold were strewn around the yard and hanging from the sides of the building.

A wide, flat plateau began around Mile 60 where an ice-covered stream ran alongside the road. I was traveling only about 30 to 40 MPH because of the billions of loose stones, which presented more and more of a handling problem. First there was just a strip of half-inch gravel in berms in the center and on the edges. Farther north there were many more stones of all shapes and sizes spread across the entire road, many of which were sharp, crushed stones, and some were crushed shale. My wheels kept crunching and snapping stones up under the bike. Stones constantly smacked against the underside and skittered out in all directions. It was impossible to pick a clear path through the stones. I was in a constant struggle to maintain control, with white knuckles and sometimes cramps in my hands from holding the grips so tight. I was getting totally exhausted.

I saw a small settlement that might have been an Indian village. A sign near there said that the road was originally a trail established in 1905 by the Mounties. I tore the leg of my rain suit on my buddy peg during one of my stops when I tried to get the bike on the center stand to oil the chain. The bike was extra heavy with the spare gas and food provisions and I was not as strong as I was when I started, especially on only two hours sleep for the second consecutive night. Actually I had slept very little during the past three nights.

I came across a one-ton pickup with a small utility trailer attached, which was abandoned in the middle of the road. There were three loose wheels with flat tires lying in the rear bed and a fourth flat tire on the rear wheel of the truck. The doors of the cab were unlocked and the window on the passenger side was open. There was a Sanyo tape deck in clear view on the front seat with a full box of tapes. He probably figured if someone had theft in mind, at least his window wouldn't get smashed with a rock in the process of stealing the tape deck.

The mountains were a pastel shade of blue and I wondered if it was the actual color of the stone. At Mile 136 I stopped to rest and to catch my breath from constantly fighting the loose stones. I was huffing and puffing as if I had just run a half-mile sprint and I said half out of breath into my tape recorder, "Stones, stones, billions of stones! When will it ever end?" I transferred the two extra gallons of gas from the Prestone bottles into the tank there. Birds that looked like small swallows would often alight just a few feet from me, apparently unafraid and hungry. The temperature was only in the high thirties and it was raining lightly at the time. In spite of my constant activity of fighting for control, my feet were cold, my hands were cold, and I was getting cold around my shoulders.

When the rain turned to snow I stopped to put on my rain suit top, which was the only thing I had left that I wasn't already wearing. As I was about to get off the machine I saw a huge form on the shoulder of the road and I turned to look. A bear was sitting there on its hindquarters looking back at me. He was about the same height sitting as I was on the bike. He stared at me with a somewhat puzzled look. I restarted the engine and got out of there as quickly as I could and went down the road another mile or two to put on the rain suit top. I recalled what the gas station attendant back at the junction had told me about huge grizzly bears often seen in that area. I wasn't sure what kind of bear it was, but I was not about to wait around to find out. All I knew was that he was big.

A heavy fog settled in near Mile 180. Actually I might have been in the clouds at the time because I was at a fairly high altitude crossing the Continental Divide, which the Dempster Highway does about three times along its 465-mile length. In any case it was cold. Ice had formed on the low bushes on both sides of the road. The road surface had become extremely muddy and only too soon there was a four-inch quagmire of slimy mud on top of the frozen tundra. The thought of turning around crossed my mind several times but I had already passed the point where I would have used up half of my gas, so I had to keep going. I was in first gear, churning through mud for more than eight miles, and a few times I got the bike momentarily stuck in it. I rode mile after mile with both feet skidding along the ground. In some spots where the mud was not as deep I would try to ride with my feet up on the foot pegs, but invariably I would lose it again and have to put one or both feet down.

At around Mile 200 I was surprised to see headlights in my rear view mirror through the snow and dense fog. I was struggling with both feet down at the time and traveling less than 10 MPH. He didn't close the gap very fast but eventually he came up alongside and we both stopped. It was the maintenance superintendent from Eagle Plains in a VW bug. He said he had been trying to figure out what was making those strange tracks. He said he would see three tracks, then sometimes two, and occasionally only one. He laughed and said, "Mostly three." He asked if I was OK. I responded by asking how far it was to Eagle Plains. He said, "Maybe another 30 miles." I answered, "Oh hell. I guess if I've come this far, I can make another 30 miles, as long as it doesn't get much worse." He said if I were not in within an hour or so from the time he gets in, he'd send help. He wished me good luck and slowly moved away with his wheels churning in the mud.

When I finally arrived at the maintenance camp I asked if they knew how long the storm might last. I was carrying food for three days and I was concerned that I may be stranded there for longer. Neither the motel nor the restaurant was open so I asked at the maintenance office where I could pitch my tent. The guy's eyes opened wider before saying, "A tent? In this weather?" I said, "Yes, do you have a campground?" After a pause he pointed to a level spot on the tundra about 400 feet away that was already covered with snow. He said that was the area they had cleared for campers but they never considered tent campers. The blizzard was raging fairly strong at the time and it was difficult to make out where he was pointing.

It took at least a half hour to put up the tent in the frigid winds and blinding snow. The temperature was around 28 degrees with 20 to 40 MPH winds -- and even higher in some gusts, driving the snow horizontally. The wind chill must have been well below zero. I put my spare tire on one corner of the tent, my suitcase on another corner, and I maneuvered the bike around and put the front wheel on a third corner as I worked on getting the tent up. I finally got the ground tarp laid out and the tent assembled on top of it as the wind kept everything flapping all the while. The tundra underneath was frozen, so in spite of my efforts I wasn't able to drive the stakes. The last time I ate, except for a few raisins and a hard roll from my bag, was my 5 AM breakfast in the tent. It was 9:30 PM when I finally got everything set up. I quickly threw the suitcase and spare tire inside to keep it from taking flight until I could crawl in. The tent weighed only a few pounds and it would have gone tumbling across the tundra if I didn't get some weight into it fast. I heated a can of Spam for my dinner. I put the tiny butane stove on my suitcase because the floor of the tent kept billowing up from the wind, which would have knocked the stove over for sure. I crawled into the sleeping bag with all of my clothes on except for the muddy boots and Belstaff jacket. I even wore my balacava to keep my head warm. Fortunately I carried an old woolen Navy blanket with which I covered my upper torso, shoulders, and neck, since my bag was only rated for about 20 degrees. I took a sleeping pill and managed to get to sleep around eleven.

Day 9 - The blizzard raged all night. Snow blew in through the small vent holes in the top corners of the tent. I had zipped up the vents but the wind still forced the snow through. By morning everything inside was covered with a thin layer of fine snow. The walls of the tent flapped wildly all night like a flag in a windstorm. It woke me a few times and sounded so loud and menacing I was afraid the fabric would shred, leaving me to lie out on the open tundra. Wherever there was no weight on the floor it would billow up and snow would pack underneath, much of it between the tarp and the tent. When I got up to urinate during the night I had no bottle to use, so I had to kneel in the doorway. I was glad I had the foresight to put the opening to the leeward side.

While I was crawling around inside the tent I put the heel of my hand down on the only pair of glasses I had with me. My weight snapped the plastic frames at the bridge of the nose. I wasn't carrying a spare so I had to make emergency repairs with a long pencil across the top of the frames. I taped it carefully to both pieces. I wore them that way for the remainder of the trip.

During the night as I lie awake listening to the strongest winds beating fiercely against the side of the tent I thought about my friends at home warning me about the bugs and mosquitoes. I laughed and thought no one warned me about freezing to death. I thought I could probably hold out as long as the tent held out, but it often sounded like the tent was waging a losing battle.

I would lie there and reminisce about the hardships of the previous week and I would actually get laughing about it. I didn't realize at the time that giddiness is one of the early signs of hypothermia. I tried to think about contingency plans but I couldn't concentrate, which is another sign. I thought about possibly needing to be airlifted out by helicopter and I thought about how airsick I would probably get. I wondered what would eventually happen to the bike. Then I wondered what Jeremiah Johnson would do in a case like this; but I thought, "Oh hell, Jeremiah would be out there lying on the open tundra wrapped in a bear skin. He didn't even own a tent." It was like daylight inside the tent at 3 AM, since I was almost on the Arctic Circle.

I heated some breakfast around 6:45 but I stayed in the bag. There was nothing for me to get up for. I couldn't ride anywhere. The snow outside was several inches deep and there were drifts all around the tent. Around noon there was a brief respite from the storm and I figured it would be a good time to head for the rest room in the main building to clean up a little and use the toilet. The guy had told me the previous night that the rest room was there for the use of the campers. As I walked back to the tent I saw someone standing next to it. He had a strange look on his face because I think he had been calling out and no one was answering. When he saw me he said, "Are you the fella' from the tent?" I said that I was and he said he had come out to see if I was still alive. He said the guys down at the camp were making bets and the odds were that I wasn't. He said, "Don't you know it's cold out here?" I said, "Yea, I noticed." He said he had heard about Jack London and those guys but he didn't think real people actually did that crazy stuff. He invited me to come down and have coffee with the crew. I said I would as soon as I got squared away and the wind died down enough so I felt safe about leaving my things for an hour or so. He had no idea how long the storm would last.

I cleared away some of the snow from between the tent and the tarp that was keeping the floor wet. I noticed that the foot end of my sleeping bag and some of my other gear had gotten wet. I tried to arrange the tarp so it wouldn't happen again. By 3:45 PM the temperature rose into the low 30s and the wind calmed down a little, so I walked down to the snack shop where some of the maintenance people were having coffee. We talked for a while and I met some of them. Several of the others were out working. I learned that the temperature had gotten down to 18 degrees during the night. Along with the wind chill factor it was probably well below zero. There was some speculation that it would get even colder that night, and that the storm would continue. I told them I was OK and that I didn't really consider it a problem. I went back to the tent and immediately crawled into the bag, the most comfortable place to be. It stopped snowing for a while around six but the temperature dropped steadily. I had some supper in the tent and "girded up my loins" for another night.

Day 10 - The wind soon picked up and blew under the tent again. Everything that had gotten wet the previous night was freezing up. My boots froze and got like two big chunks of ice near the entrance. The foot end of my sleeping bag froze stiff. The walls of the tent flapped wildly again as the wind increased. I awoke at 1:30 AM from the racket of the thin nylon fabric flapping. My head felt very cold in spite of the balacava so I pulled the woolen blanket over my head, leaving only a small gap to breathe through, and I fell back to sleep. I woke up briefly at three and felt very uncomfortable all over from the cold. Finally I awoke again at four feeling tremors over my whole body. I figured that hypothermia was certainly setting in

68

or that something else serious was happening to me. It was colder than the previous night and the wind was blowing at least as hard. Two inches of fresh snow were on the ground. Fortunately I had the presence of mind when I got the tremors to eat something and make some coffee for myself. I figured that I had better stay awake for the rest of the night or I might slip into hypothermia for sure and never wake up. I heated a can of hot chili beans with meat and had that with the coffee. I continued to have the tremors every few minutes for about an hour. I had a tough time eating with my hands shaking so much, not to mention holding the coffee cup. I thought again about being airlifted out by helicopter and I began to get depressed about the predicament I had gotten myself into.

I stayed in the bag until about 10 AM contemplating my options. There was four inches of fresh snow on the ground with more in drifts. I realized that my body couldn't take much more and I had to do something. I thought about moving into the rest room and taking my sleeping bag with me. I was the only one using the room, there was heat inside, and it was clean. My second thought was to ask the maintenance people if I could find a corner in the garage where I could lay out my sleeping bag or even put up the tent inside the huge garage. The next thought was to go down to the motel and see if they would rent me a room even though the place was closed for the season. I was sure there must be people getting it ready for the first tour group that was due to arrive in two or three days. I went down to check on it at noon and they agreed to rent me the room. The price was $50 a night and I had to be out before the weekend when the first group of 37 people was due to arrive. All of the rooms were reserved from then on. I planned on two nights in the motel and then I would be out of there no matter what condition the road south was in. Mainly I needed a full night sleep that I hadn't gotten for almost a week.

The room was new, modern, and beautiful. I brought all of my wet gear in to dry, most of which I hung around the room. I put my frozen boots near the heater and laid out the tent and the tarp to dry in the garage. I washed out a few things in the sink and hung them up to dry. It was the first time I had my clothes off for five days. I took a long, hot bath and got into bed. I woke up about two hours later in a full-scale depression. By renting the room I had actually surrendered to the elements and like Roberto Duran, the fight was over and I had lost.

It was also Lilli's birthday and I had to find some way to call. If I didn't she would certainly think that something serious had happened. There were no regular telephones but I knew there was a radiophone in the maintenance office. I made the call from there, but I got emotional as I began to talk about my incredible experiences. I tried not to alarm her and I chose not to mention that I might have almost expired the previous night from hypothermia. I tried to tell her a little about my adventures but I couldn't get it out without having my voice waver. Eventually we just talked a little about her birthday and about the family. I felt much better after talking with her.

I heated Spam for dinner again and had it with a sourdough roll and coffee in the room. I took a walk afterward and studied the condition of the road and the sky. The road was covered with snow and it was still snowing lightly, but it was beginning to look brighter in the east. The wind seemed to have diminished somewhat. I began to make plans for the following day as things started to look up. I had a full stomach, a rest, a call home, and the sky was brightening, which was all I needed. The maintenance guys said the road north was in much better shape than the road south, which was still a quagmire of mud, so I told them I would be going north for the day. They said I may have problems getting through the two passes and the Peel River would be a major obstacle because the ice had broken up and they didn't think the ferry captain would start up the ferry and churn across the river through the ice-floes for a single motorcyclist, especially when the road was still officially closed.

Day 11 - I slept for a solid nine hours in the comfortable bed and quiet surroundings. It was my first good sleep in a week. The sky in the east looked slightly dark again, but I could see the sun through some high, thin clouds. The snow had stopped, although the wind was still quite strong. I ate baked beans, the last of my canned provisions. I heated it in the room on my butane stove. The temperature outside was 36 degrees. I thought I probably could have survived in the tent that night or at least it wouldn't have been as bad as the first two nights, although I doubt that I would have gotten as much restful sleep. I left all of my gear in the room except for the clothes I wore and I left the tent spread out to dry in the garage. I topped off my gas for a 180-mile ride into the Northwest Territories. I didn't know exactly where that would take me but since the road south was still in poor condition I decided on the day ride. I left around noon and said if I wasn't back by late afternoon please come and look for me.

The Arctic Circle was just 15 miles north of the maintenance camp. The sign was laying flat on the tundra, probably broken off by the heavy winds of the past few days. I stopped and tried to prop it up for a photo but couldn't get it to stand by itself because the wind was blowing too hard. I tried to pile rocks around the base of the posts but finally gave up and headed north without my photo. The temperature dropped below 30 degrees and the wind blew out of the west at a steady 45 to 50 MPH. I had to lean the bike about 30 degrees into the wind and I tried to keep my head as close behind the windshield as possible to ease the biting pain on my face.

I managed to climb through the passes, both of which were still covered with ice and snow. The crews were there working with huge graders. Ice had built up on the road to a thickness of several feet in a few spots. There was a detour over some grassy tundra for vehicles to get around at the first pass, while they worked on clearing the road. I spun my rear wheel on the ice at the second pass and had to use both feet as outriggers as I inched my way up and over the top. I realized I would have had great difficulty if all of my gear were on the rear carrier.

An even stronger wind blew the snow horizontally at the Northwest Territories border. The NWT border marks the final crossing of the Continental Divide before reaching Inuvik. Drifts along the edges of the road were more than ten feet high. There was less wind north of there and the road was smoother and covered with fine gravel rather than large cut stones. The road was also elevated four to six feet above the rest of the terrain like a causeway, which reduces the amount of snow that accumulates on it. The mountains rise abruptly from the tundra about a half-mile back on both sides of the highway. The scenery was spectacular.

When my odometer indicated that I had traveled 90 miles from Eagle Plains I figured I had burned about half of my gas and it was time to turn around and head back. I was a few miles from the Peel River at that time. I was concerned that the huge drift at the divide could close the road at any time. The strong head winds could also affect my gas mileage. About every ten miles I could see where the sides of the mountains had been dug out to get fill for road construction. South of the divide the crosswinds were still very strong and I held a gloved hand up to my face all the way to shield it from the biting wind. The sun was out at Eagle Plains and the maintenance superintendent said that most of the road to Dawson City was now in pretty good shape. He had just come up again and he said there were still spots where snowdrifts were across the road but a few trucks had been through. He said that by tomorrow morning it should be clear of most of the snow and mud. I had a delicious veal cutlet meal at the restaurant that had just opened for the season. I was in bed by 11 o'clock.

Day 12 - I topped off my gas tank and filled the two Prestone bottles with gas. It cost 59 cents a liter and my fill-up came to $12.00, or about $1.90 a gallon. I left at 8 AM after warm good-byes with my newfound friends who had come out to shake hands and bid me a good trip.

I rode across a few rough sections in the first 40 miles, as well as encountering some fog and cold temperatures at the higher altitudes, but the road was in much better shape than when I came up. When I oiled the chain about halfway down the highway, I had my usual tough time getting the machine up onto the center stand. The clouds obscured the tops of the mountains. The sun broke through around the time I transferred the spare gas into the tank. The temperature eventually climbed into the high forties, which felt good after several days below freezing. I inspected the rear tire and seriously considered mounting the spare. The surface of the tire was completely bald and it was torn up with thousands of cuts from sharp stones. I hadn't realized it was quite that bad. The most beautiful scenery of my return down the Dempster was through the Ogilvie Mountains where I got within 50 yards of three big caribou.

About forty miles from the Klondike Highway it clouded over and the temperature dropped again. Before I reached the junction it was raining. I got gas and provisions in Dawson City before making a beeline for the Yukon River ferry landing. I arrived just in time to see the loading ramp being raised. I watched the ferry leave and had to wait an hour in the rain for its return. It rained all of the way across the Top-of-the-World Road to the US Customs building. There was still a lot of snow at the highest elevations and I had to detour at least three times where snowdrifts blocked the road. One of the detours was very rough with narrow switchback turns, washouts, and steep hills. I was down to second gear a few times, churning through loose stones. The Top-of-the-World Road is still one of the most beautiful and fascinating roads I have ever traveled. It rained about halfway across and I ran into some hail near the customs station.

I stopped at the small village of Boundary for gas. Frank, one of the guys I met at Eagle Plains, wanted me to say hello to Action Jackson who owned the business there. I walked into the bar and snack shop and asked for him. The girl bartender pointed to a real slick-looking guy apparently doing his books at one of the tables. He was a small, thin man; his face was pale white, his jet-black hair was slicked back, and he had a long thin mustache that curled up on the ends. There was very little light in the place except behind the bar and there was a small desk lamp on the table where Jackson was working. I smiled and said, "Hi, are you Action Jackson?" He looked at me like maybe no one calls him that and I thought I might have said something I shouldn't have. Without ever looking up he said, "Who wants to know?" I thought about a guy I had seen in a movie once who had a gun under the table. I would have felt better if I could have seen his hands. I told him I had just come from Eagle Plains and that Frank, who used to work for him, said to say hello. After an uncomfortable pause he said, "Frank who?" I figured it would be a good idea to get myself out of there. As I turned to leave I said, "Well, have a nice day, Mr. Jackson." He didn't answer and I wondered why Frank had ever asked me to stop. Maybe he meant it as a joke.

It rained a little, mixed with hail, between Boundary and the blacktop at Tetlin Junction, which was the first paved road I had seen for several days. The final 100 miles of dirt was extremely rough and twisty, where I was down to 15 MPH several times due to the poor road surface. Occasional hail that stung my already sore face made things worse.

There was still quite a bit of rain around while I searched for a place to camp. I enjoyed the beautiful panoramic views of the mountains southwest of Tok where there were very few signs of civilization. I rode for a long while before finally locating a state-run campground about 14 miles past Glennallen. I got the tent set up by 10:20 PM and crawled in to prepare my evening meal of chuck wagon stew, rolls, and some good cheese. I was about 600 miles of mostly rough dirt roads from Eagle Plains where I started the day. My aching body testified to the roughness of the ride.

Day 13 - After I got into the bag a guy pulled into the campground with a pickup truck and a huge tent. He double-camped in my space, blocking my way out. There were plenty of other spaces around but for some reason this guy liked mine better. I woke up early, ate, and packed. I considered waking someone to move the truck but I spotted a narrow pathway up through the trees. I used it to get around the other guy's tent and out of the campsite. I made enough noise churning on the steep path to wake the whole camp.

The miles seemed to go by much faster than the previous night when I was over tired and every mile seemed like an eternity. It was very cold at Eureka Summit with fog and light drizzle. My feet and hands were cold and I felt cold all over again. I maneuvered the twisty roads through the canyon along the Matanuska River and stopped to view the Matanuska Glacier from a lookout point along the highway. Most houses along there looked like squatter's shacks. I had thought the same thing in 1977 when I saw abandoned cars and other junk and garbage spread around many of the dooryards. Whenever I stopped for gas, food, or lodging I was reminded that the attitudes of many of the people along the highway matched their dooryards.

I rode the last 40 miles into Anchorage under blue skies and warm sunshine with the temperature around 50 degrees. I had completely forgotten about the two-hour time change at the border. I learned when I arrived at the Air Force Base at eight that I actually left the campground around 3:30 AM. I thought about the campers who I probably woke up in the middle of the night. I didn't feel bad about the guy who had double camped in my area though. I arrived at Donna's just as she was getting up and Rey was leaving for work.

It was Saturday and my first chore was to go out and buy a new tire. I tried to find a place to get my glasses fixed, but no one had the right frames. I visited with Donna, Rey, and Asia for the rest of the day and evening. Asia got very sick that day with a fever of 104. She was only a year old at the time. Donna rushed her to the emergency room at the base hospital where she learned that Asia had an ear infection.

I went into town that evening with Rey while Donna worked at the childcare center. Sunday morning Donna and I went to a family restaurant called Flippers for brunch. I had steak and eggs with a huge piece of cheesecake for dessert. I spent Days 14, 15, and 16 with Donna and her family at Elmendorf AFB, during which time I replaced the rear tire and the sprocket, made the very first chain adjustment of the trip, filed and adjusted the points, washed the bike, washed all of my clothes, and stocked up on food provisions. We also visited several interesting sights around Anchorage during my stay. My odometer indicated that I had traveled 5,200 miles since leaving New York, most of which were cold, rough miles.

Day 17 - I left on Wednesday morning a little before eight; carrying snacks for several days, including some freshly smoked salmon that Rey had prepared in his smoke unit. It was partly cloudy and 50 degrees. The skies looked like it would be a nice day but you never know in Alaska. When I stopped to oil the chain about 30 miles past Glennallen it was still 60 degrees with only a few clouds around, but less than an hour later it clouded over and started to rain. I stopped at a small rest area about 30 miles before reaching Tok and ate lunch from my bag. It was a pleasant spot with picturesque mountains all around. I had been nodding off and my back was already sore. After getting back on the road, I rode for another seven-and-a-half hours to the Canadian border, stopping only for gas.

I developed a headache while riding over some really rough and slightly dusty washboard roads in the Beaver Creek area where the temperature was only in the 30s. It sprinkled several times and rained quite hard a few times. The road surface alternated between dusty and slick. A few of the showers were mixed with hail that stung my face. I passed two crowded campgrounds in the rain before finally settling on one about 50 miles short of Whitehorse. It was 660 miles from where I started the day. It was after midnight since I lost two hours due to a time change at the border. I heated a can of Dinty Moore stew inside the tent and ate it with sourdough rolls, cheese, and some coffee.

Day 18 - I was up at seven and on the road in an hour and a half, which was a little faster than usual because the

75

mosquitoes were very thick and they seemed to ignore my Cutters lotion. Hundreds of them would swarm around my head while some would make "Kamikaze" attacks directly into my eyes, where they must have sensed I had no Cutters. I hurried through a can of beans and some coffee for breakfast and got out of there as quickly as I could. My clothes were already full of mud and the bike was covered with it. There was no water at the campsite so I couldn't even wash my face. I had barely enough water left in my canteen to make coffee and rinse out the utensils. I stopped at Jake's Corner for gas and was waited on by an old woman who was just as crotchety as old Jake had been on my first trip in 1977. I concluded that she must be his wife. I had an awful headache at the time.

I dropped the bike about five miles from Jake's Corner in some real slimy mud in a construction area. I had been churning in first gear through some deep ruts when the rear end spun out and I lost it. I got up and tried to lift the bike back on the wheels but I couldn't even stand up. My feet would slip out and I would fall onto my knees or on my side in the mud. The mud was ankle deep and it was raining at the time. I was sure I couldn't lift it with all of the weight piled on, so I began to unhook the bungee cords. A truck driver who had been following me through the construction in an eighteen-wheel rig, climbed down from his cab into the mud to help. As he grabbed one end he turned to me and said, "It sure isn't a very good day for motorcycles. I hope you don't have far to go." I felt a little embarrassed telling him I was on my way to New York. After I said that he looked at me strangely and didn't say anything else. He just stared and lifted.

It was Sunday when I passed through that same area on my way up and truck traffic was much lighter then. The heavier traffic meant I had to be constantly on my guard passing vehicles in either direction. The slick surface made passing much riskier. The wet calcium chloride sections were particularly treacherous, and the roads were very rough, either wet or dry. I had trouble getting the bike to stay on its center stand to oil the chain because mud had packed up underneath so thick that the stand wouldn't go all the way to its park position, causing the bike to roll off the stand. I stopped at a few campgrounds looking for water to take with my Anacin. I finally found some water but then I couldn't find the Anacin. Luckily I got to the dreaded

76

Teslin Lake Bridge between rain showers. Its deep steel grating still gave me the horrors with the poor handling of the bike.

At one of the gas stops the kid who pumped my gas spilled it all over the tank and down onto the engine, causing billows of gasoline vapors to rise from the hot engine. I saw a sign saying the attendant must pump the gas and he was trying to wait on two customers at one time. The price on the pump was set to indicate ¼ of the amount because the total price for some of the trucks and large RVs would exceed $100, which was more than the dial could indicate. The people they hired are usually unable to multiply the indicated amount by four to get the actual price so they would have to go inside to work it out on a piece of paper. Apparently they weren't able to use a hand calculator either. The kid came back and said I owed him $7.78. I said, "Four times $1.92 is $7.68." He looked at me strangely and went back a second time to try it again. He returned to say it was still $7.78. It was only a lousy dime but that wasn't the issue any more. I went in with him to walk him through his faulty multiplication, after which I handed him my credit card. He also made two mistakes on that before finally getting it right.

About a million potholes, a half-dozen rain showers, and one heavy hailstorm later, I was on my way down the Cassiar Highway. Before turning off the Alaska Highway I faced a steady stream of RVs and pickup campers headed for Alaska. It looked like a huge convoy, although it could have been simply an awful lot of traffic on the road. I got to a point where I hated to see another RV or pickup camper. I had to duck constantly to avoid being hit by flying stones. The drivers who I passed almost never checked their rearview mirrors before swerving to avoid potholes. The horrible traffic coupled with the slick road surface combined to make that part of my trip quite unpleasant. The first 40 miles of the Cassiar wasn't much better. It was extremely dusty like it hadn't rained at all. Several short sections of the first hundred miles were paved, although after Dease Lake it was all dirt. Fast moving trucks left a half-mile-long trail of dust. I spotted the peaceful camp area by the lake where I stopped in 1977, but I saw a lot of litter and garbage lying around that turned me off. What a difference four years can make!

I ran into some light rain about ten miles past the lake, which soon became much heavier. I was far enough south by then that it got dark around 10:30, especially with the rain. I had almost forgotten how dark it got at night. I looked a long time for a good place to pitch the tent. After it got dark I searched in desperation for any place to set it up. Finally I settled on a small emergency pull-off area where a truck had recently dumped a huge load of bank-run gravel. I had stopped at a few other pull-off areas before that one but they were all partly underwater. I decided to pitch the tent on top of the pile to keep it out of the mud. I kicked some of the gravel around to level the top and I proceeded to set up the tent on top. It was pouring when I finally crawled in. I was covered with mud so I took off my wet and muddy outer clothes and boots at the entrance. It was the second night in a row I crawled into the tent wet and full of mud. I had nothing with me for a hot meal because the Indian co-op store in Iskut was closed when I went by. I ate smoked salmon, a sourdough roll, some sunflower seeds, and coffee, and I finally crawled into the bag around midnight. I was exhausted from 550 miles of slick mud, heavy RV traffic, and blinding dust on one of the toughest riding days of the trip -- so far.

Day 19 - I had a bowl of instant rice for breakfast with some coffee and cheese. It was still raining in the morning. I rolled up all of my gear and tied it onto the bike in a light rain and fog. Everything was soaked and covered with mud. The fog was so thick when I started I could see for only about 25 feet. I stopped at Meziadin Junction for gas and headed down the final, narrow 92-mile section that I remembered so fondly from 1977. Occasionally a logging truck would come the other way and give me only a few feet of the shoulder to squeeze by. I really had to watch myself with them because they were ruthless.

I rode on alternating sections of new tar, old road, and newly graded roadbed. It was foggy and raining most of the way through the final section of the Cassiar. Some of the new roadbed was slick and the surface was pockmarked with millions of little muddy puddles of rainwater. It was raining hard at the time and the temperature was only in the low forties. My hands and feet hurt from the cold and I was having occasional chills. I rode between 45 and 50 MPH across the wet washboard surface and I felt that if the forks were ever going to give out, now was the time it would happen. The bike shook relentlessly and splattered through muddy water for 30 miles. I thought it was as bad as any enduro I had ever ridden, and with the awful handling characteristics the bike had shown over the previous three weeks, it was a small miracle that I didn't lose it right there. I actually felt a little numb and disconnected from my concentration and I seemed to be charging along on autopilot, just holding the grips tight and staring straight ahead.

I made it through the Cassiar in one piece and stopped for gas in Smithers. I had serious thoughts about giving up before noon because I felt so miserable, cold, and tired. The motel in Smithers looked very tempting but I passed it by. The rain continued for another 30 miles beyond Smithers, after which it was heavily overcast. The temperature rose to a relatively warm 50 degrees, although I was wet underneath and felt awful. I thought about stopping in Prince George too but after cashing a traveler's check in Burns Lake the sky began to brighten a little and I even saw the sun a few times. I figured it was a sign that I should go a little farther and camp again that night.

I stocked up on provisions in Vanderhoof and continued past Prince George without stopping, before beginning the steady, scenic climb toward Jasper Park. I was having a little problem with drowsiness on the smooth blacktop but I managed to ride 650 miles that day, which put me just past Mt. Robson where I found a nice provincial campground in the shadow of Canada's tallest mountain peak. I finally got the chance to wash my face and hands with some nice cold well water from a hand pump. I cleaned up my utensils and had some Spam, sourdough rolls, and coffee for my dinner. It had been an extremely tough twelve-hour day.

Day 20 - I awoke with the sound of rain on the tent again. I had slept really well on a thick bed of pine needles -- much better than the bank-run gravel of the previous night. I woke up dreaming about a white dog. Usually when I dreamt about a dog it meant trouble with one of my boys but I had never dreamed about a white one. I shrugged it off as indigestion from the Spam. I took a Tums and fell back to sleep and slept for a few more hours. I got up at five and heated some spaghetti and meatballs for my breakfast. I waited until just before leaving to pump some fresh water because the noisy hand pump was very close to another guy's tent. It was raining steady and coming down fairly hard when I left at seven.

I was totally dispirited and somewhat depressed that morning as I climbed into the Canadian Rockies in heavy rain and very dark overcast. I was actually wondering if God was still with me. It seemed as though I was having such a terrible time of it with the foul weather and horrible road conditions on this trip. Suddenly a perfectly round opening appeared directly overhead in the otherwise dark overcast and rain. The opening was the size of a football field, exposing a bright blue sky. It was still raining and dark everywhere else, except directly over my head. The hole seemed to get larger as it followed me for almost a mile up the road, drenching me with warm sunshine. I was awestruck, as I took it as a reply from God. Then just as suddenly the huge gap closed, it got dark again, and the rain and darkness returned. I was alone on the road at the time and no one saw it but me. I was really shaken and I broke down and cried.

I turned onto the Icefields Parkway where I saw two large female elk grazing alongside the road. The Icefields Parkway through Jasper and Banff Parks is one of the most awe-inspiring, scenic rides I have ever taken, even in the rain. I spotted several white goats feeding alongside the highway at Athabasca Falls. As I neared Banff Park the rain turned to snow. The snow came down so heavy at one point that it packed against my windshield and fairing, and it began to build up alongside the road atop some old snow left from previous storms. At Columbia Icefields it became a mixture of sleet and hail. Before I left the campground that morning I had packed my mittens and balacava deep in my trunk, thinking I no longer needed them. I would regret doing that all day.

The scenery in Banff Park is even nicer than in Jasper. The mountains are closer to the road and some of the highlights are more spectacular, like the "Weeping Wall" where twin waterfalls cascade down the face of the mountain in two long streams. I developed another severe headache and stopped to dig out my Anacin, which was near the top of the bag this time. I suspected the headache was from my helmet being too tight after having done some maintenance on the inside band in Anchorage. Once when I stopped at a rest area I noticed that the chain was badly in need of an adjustment so I tightened and oiling it there.

I stopped for gas in Banff and noticed that two guys standing by their car while the attendant pumped their gas were staring at me. I must have been a sight to behold. My clothes and the bike were completely covered with mud and it was snowing hard at the time. I hadn't shaved for at least four days, not to mention my glasses with the big pencil taped across the top holding them together. One of the guys walked over behind the bike and looked at the plate, which was barely visible through a thick layer of mud. He said, "Wow, you're a long way from home!" The first thing that came into my mind was, "Not nearly as far as I was four days ago."

A mixture of snow and sleet against my face made it painful and raw. At the lower altitudes the snow gradually changed to sleet and rain, sometimes coming down very heavy. My feet were wet again and I was painfully cold all over. At Radium Hot Springs I saw people swimming in a large steaming pool fed by hot water from the natural hot spring there. It sure looked good to me that day. It continued to rain, sometimes heavy, for the next 150 miles. I would think each time it began again that it was just a shower so I wouldn't stop to put on my rain suit. By the time I would finally stop it would be too late because I would already be wet. I tried to duck behind the windshield to avoid the sleet that continued for hours. The pain on my face from the sleet became excruciating. When I finally pulled into the US Customs station at Eureka, Montana, I was at the very limit of my endurance. The customs guy came out of the building smiling but when he saw me the expression on his face changed. He said, "Are you all right?" I said weakly, "No, I'm not. How far is the nearest motel?"

After a few of the mandatory questions he directed me to a motel about seven miles down the road. It was only 3:15 when I got there. It was the earliest I had thrown in the towel on the entire trip but I hadn't seen the inside of a building for four days and I simply couldn't take any more. I checked in and hung my things around the room to dry. Even the clothes in my suitcase were wet, including clothes rolled up in plastic bags inside the suitcase. I washed out a few pairs of shorts and socks in the sink and I rinsed out a few sweatshirts that were already wet. I didn't wash my jeans because they probably wouldn't have dried by morning. I hung the stuff around the heater and turned it to high. I got into the tub and lay there in hot water for a long time, leaving the very hot water running slowly all the while. I had a snack in the room before going out to see if there was a restaurant within walking distance. When there wasn't I made dinner from my provisions again, which at that time was mainly the smoked salmon that Rey had given me in Anchorage.

Day 21 - It was foggy and overcast when I got up. I left the motel at 6 AM and traveled through mostly farm country over some gently rolling hills. The fog was thick in places and I couldn't see very far. I rode about ten or fifteen minutes in rain early that morning. It was Sunday and most of the gas stations in Whitefish were closed but I finally found a small convenience store with gas. My impression of Montana was that everything is big, including the hills, the valleys, the lakes, and the sky. Polson struck me as a nice little town nestled in a tremendous valley with Flat Head Lake as a scenic backdrop.

It was 47 degrees when I stopped for brunch at a KFC in Missoula. I had originally planned to tour Idaho but I aborted that part of my plan because of the weather. A trip through Idaho would have been anticlimactic after all of my experiences of the past three weeks. I felt I had seen and experienced enough for one trip and it was time I should be getting home to my family. It drizzled in Missoula and continued to rain all the way into Butte. I rode steadily uphill following an eighteen-wheel White Western Star for several miles toward the Continental Divide. He never got below seventy on the fairly steep incline.

About 35 miles from Butte I began to see fresh snow in the fields and on the hillsides. It got very windy and cold as I continued to climb toward the divide. I saw a car coming from the opposite direction covered with snow and a short time later I was in the midst of another snow squall. I decided to skip Yellowstone and the Beartooth Highway for the same reasons I was skipping Idaho. Snow covered both sides of the road at the divide. The roads were wet as I ran through more snow, sleet, and rain on the eastern slope. The sky to the north looked very dark and threatening. I rode through a heavy snow shower in Bozeman and another in Livingston. The showers continued all the way into Billings where I stopped for the day at 4:30. I was too cold, miserable, and tired to continue again. I heard on TV that night that a foot of snow had eventually fallen around the divide and I was glad I got through when I did. I had stayed relatively dry during the day, having ridden all day in my rain suit. If I had a face shield I probably would have ridden for a few more hours. I had long since discarded my last scuffed up shield when I couldn't see through it any more. My face took the worst beating in the crosswinds, especially from the sleet. The temperature didn't get much above 45 degrees all day.

Day 22 - The TV reported that a tornado was predicted for South Dakota, which was along my planned route. The sky looked as though the major part of the storm had passed but it was still quite dark in the east. I left at seven with a strong tailwind pushing me out of Billings. The sun came out after I rode through a brief shower about 15 minutes from the motel. The temperature rose to 50 degrees and it looked like it was going to be a good day. I enjoyed finally seeing the green, rolling countryside bathed in sunlight, as I rode through cattle country in the Flat Head and Crow Indian Reservations. I rode through another two hours of rain and strong winds in some desolate sheep country in northeastern Wyoming where gasoline was available about every 60 miles. In Wyoming I had to oil the chain beneath the overpasses because of the strong winds.

It was still cool when I entered South Dakota with occasional sprinkles and a patch of blue showing through once in a while. Blue skies became more prevalent as I crossed the Bad Lands of South Dakota and broke out onto the open prairie. A few strong wind gusts from the side threw the bike several feet off course. After covering 660 miles that day, all of it in my full rain suit, I checked into a Super 8 in Mitchell, SD and enjoyed my first restaurant feast since leaving Alaska. I "pigged out" at a Bonanza buffet near the motel. I noticed that the bike was getting more than 50 miles to the gallon with the powerful tailwinds. After dinner I dressed the points and added a little oil to the engine.

Day 23 - I ate a light breakfast in my room and later talked with a guy from Duluth in the parking lot as I packed. He was on his way to California with his wife on a new Suzuki 750 like mine. He said he had seen mine when he pulled in the night before and he had watched through the window that morning until I came out. He told his wife he had to talk to this guy who came in on a bike just like his that looked like it had "really been somewhere." They were identical Suzukis except that mine looked like it had been dragged through a swamp and trampled by a herd of wildebeest. My clothes didn't look any better, nor did I. He asked about where I had been and seemed astonished as I related some of my experiences of the past three weeks while I continued to load the bike.

83

I ran through a heavy shower about an hour out of Mitchell, after which I was treated to another spectacular display of nature. I think it was the first time in my life I had ever seen a full rainbow, and this one was huge and very bright. The two ends rested on the horizons to my right and to my left, and the rainbow was exceptionally clear for its entire length. This time I was sure that it was God saying to me that I had endured enough. What an awesome sight! Tears welled up in my eyes as I got closer to the giant arch. A short time later I stopped to dig out a pair of sunglasses and took off the broken pair of prescription glasses. The strong winds didn't let up though, and once when a huge Kenworth came up from behind doing about 75 or better, he hesitated before passing when he saw that I was being tossed all over the road by the wind.

Most of the countryside I traveled through that day was farmland. Some of the corn was eight feet tall. There wasn't a cloud in the sky in central Iowa, where I rode for hundreds of miles without ever losing sight of a cornfield. The wind diminished as the day wore on. I stopped at a KFC for dinner around 4:30 and after eating I rode for a few more hours. I wanted to get within one day of home by nightfall. I located a Motel 6 in South Bend, Indiana after clocking 770 miles.

Day 24 - I was on the road by 5:30 AM on my final day. I must have been anxious to get home, since I left even before first light. For the first time in more than three weeks I was not wearing long johns. It was also the first time since northern Montana that I saw trees on both sides of the highway. I noticed a serious gypsy-moth infestation in central Pennsylvania, as I passed the 10,000-mile point of my trip. I spent most of the day reminiscing my incredible experiences of the past three weeks and making mental notes about how I would improve my next trip. Of the many lessons I learned, the most noteworthy were that I would certainly change the type of clothes I take with me and the kind of motorcycle I ride the next time I head for the Dempster Highway and the Northwest Territories. I was convinced that now I had to do it again and that it had to be better the next time.

ALASKA 3 - THE FAST ONE

I headed for Alaska a third time just two years after returning from "The Tough One." I sold the Suzuki and bought a new 1982 Honda 1100cc Gold Wing. I didn't know a lot about setting up the Gold Wing for a trip to Alaska so I didn't do anything at to it before I left. I figured the trip would show up any weaknesses. My primary objective was to visit with Donna, Asia and Robyn in Anchorage. I toyed with the idea of possibly venturing up the Dempster Highway to Inuvik if everything fell into place, but I knew when I left that it was unlikely; although the Gold Wing seemed like a reasonable bike to do it with since it had a reputation of being reliable and it handled much better than the Suzuki on unstable surfaces, especially with better weight distribution of my gear.

Day 1 - I left a month later in the season than on the two previous trips to avoid the kind of weather I experienced in 1981. The Honda's odometer read 6365 miles when I left Buchanan after lunch on June 28th. My plan was to ride directly to Anchorage and back, traveling a good deal of the way on interstate highways.

I ran into some light rain near the Yonkers Raceway that stayed with me through New York City, making the Major Deegan and the Cross Bronx Expressway fairly slick from the fresh rain on heavy oil drippings. I didn't put my rain suit on until I met the first of several heavier showers in central and western Pennsylvania. It rained sometimes heavy most of the afternoon and evening, and when I reached the Motel 6 near Youngstown, Ohio around 9:45 PM I was a little wet underneath and the bike seat had soaked up some water. I clocked 425 miles on that first half day.

Day 2 - A car belonging to people in the next room was broken into during the night. Police were outside investigating when I got up around five but with little hope of finding who did it. I was relieved when I saw that my bike, parked next to the car that was broken into, wasn't touched.

I was on the road by first light. The mirrors vibrated out of adjustment several times before I realized that the front tire had far too much air in it. It got quite warm along the Ohio Turnpike after the sun came out and the scenery became a little tiresome; so I tried taking a side trip through southern Michigan

85

on US 12, but after only about a hundred miles of that I returned to the interstate. I didn't find much interesting scenery there either and there was far too much traffic. Besides, I was anxious to get on to Alaska.

The weather was fairly good around Chicago although I rode through a heavy thundershower near Peoria. Soon after crossing the Mississippi River at Davenport I saw one of the most unusual and threatening skies I had ever seen. Thick dark clouds swirled through the sky like cars in a demolition derby. I suspected that a tornado was brewing so I pulled into a rest area where many cars had also taken refuge. People stood outside watching the strange show as the sky got darker and the huge black clouds swirled even faster in all directions. Soon it began to rain very hard, accompanied by strong winds, but I didn't see a tornado. I stayed at the rest area until the rain and wind eased up a bit and I left in my rain suit. I didn't get far before the next heavy downpour forced me to find shelter under the nearest overpass. I stopped under several overpasses that afternoon during the heaviest downpours. I reached Des Moines about nine o'clock and found a small motel near the airport after traveling 775 miles.

Day 3 - I located a small cafe about ten miles out of town and enjoyed a full breakfast of sausage and eggs. Most of the fields I passed that morning were flooded from the recent rains. Many of the rivers and streams were swollen over their banks, and corn, soybeans and other crops were underwater in Illinois and eastern Iowa. I explored a few interesting country roads in Iowa and saw several feedlots for cattle and hogs, and I saw a lot of corn. The scenery in the rolling hills and small farms of central Iowa was much nicer than in Ohio and Illinois.

The temperature rose into the nineties in Nebraska where I stopped for a quart of milk, but the milk made me drowsy so I stopped again for a large Pepsi to wake me up. I pulled into Chadron while being chased by another strong thundershower, and I ducked into a small restaurant for a sit-down dinner just as the downpour hit. It stopped raining by the time I left the restaurant and I saw a huge rainbow in the east, so I rode for a few more hours before locating a motel in Lusk, Wyoming where I called it a day around eight o'clock after 760 miles.

Day 4 - After a full breakfast at a small cafe in Lusk I was on the road by 7:30. I noticed a sign that said it I was in

Sioux Indian country. The temperature rose into the seventies by midmorning and I decided to head for Yellowstone Park with the intention of camping that night. I stopped at a deli in Thermopolis to get a sub for lunch and I saw the famous hot spring there, which is a pool of clear, steaming sulfur water that emerges from the ground. Although it was very hot and dry in Thermopolis it was cold, windy, and rainy mixed with sleet in Yellowstone. I rode through Big Horn National Forest, Casper, Buffalo, and Cody on my way into the park.

I hadn't realized it was Friday until I got deep into the park and saw that all of the campsites were filled to capacity. I couldn't even find a spot big enough to pitch my tent. I eventually rode for more than a hundred miles in a cold drizzle with sleet mixed in as I exited through the west end of the park into Idaho. I was beginning to get burned on my face and the backs of my hands from the sun and wind, and I was very tired by the time I got to West Yellowstone. The last two hours of the day seemed like an eternity. I got there well after dark and was lucky to find the last room in town. After checking in I heated some canned stew on my camp stove in the room.

Day 5 - The temperature was in the mid 30s in the morning. I learned that it had snowed a few inches in the park during the night, which made me glad I didn't camp. I was on the road by seven with most of my clothes on my back including my rain suit. I stopped less than two hours later in Idaho Falls to also dig out my snowmobile top. It was very cold, wet, and miserable for my Idaho loop, which was to be one of the highlights of my trip. I had planned to take a lot of pictures there. I saw several elk in the first two hours, I visited Craters of the Moon and Sun Valley, and I rode over Galena Summit where I ran into a brief snow shower. I began to look for a room around Cascade and finally found one in McCall. The proprietor said she had turned down several groups of young people because she was afraid they would tear her place up. I was surprised she rented the room to a biker. It was a reasonably priced room with a queen-size bed. I filled the tub with hot water and soaked my cold, aching body for a long time.

Day 6 - There was thick frost on the seat when I emerged from the room. It had gotten down into the low twenties during the night. I ate breakfast with a couple from Alberta touring with a Yamaha Venture. I spent most of the day taking pictures in scenic areas of western Idaho and Washington State. I enjoyed a beautiful ride along the Salmon River Canyon before heading for Grand Coulee Dam in Washington where I turned north after taking a few more photos. I also stopped a few times for Bing cherries to snack on before entering Canada and I located a motel in Kamloops, BC.

Day 7 - I woke up a few times during the night with cramps in my legs, which is usually a sign of dehydration. I also had a headache and my ears were ringing, which I thought might have been caused by my blood pressure. My face was swollen from sunburn and windburn and I wondered why I was doing this thing that I had already done twice before. Vivid images of my previous trip were beginning to materialize in my memory. I felt lousy and not even well enough to eat breakfast. I rode for about an hour before stopping at a small restaurant in Cache Creek when I felt too weak to go on.

It was a steady climb from there to 100 Mile House. The first forty miles or so was treeless, but I was soon deep into the British Columbia forests. I spent about a half hour at Williams Lake cashing a few travelers' checks for Canadian currency, after which I stopped for lunch in Quesnel. I experienced a few showers between Prince George and Vandehoof and finally stopped in Smithers for the night.

The rear tire that I originally thought would take me to Anchorage was already worn out. I decided to change it before starting up the Cassiar Highway because of the rough roads. It was my first experience changing a tubeless tire on the road and unfortunately I wasn't carrying the proper tool to break the bead. I struggled for almost two hours with the tire change, mostly trying to get the bead loose from the rim. I realized after mounting the new tire that it was low profile, which lowered my ground clearance considerably. Although the marking indicated that it was the same size as the old tire it was definitely the wrong tire for the bike. I felt really beat that evening and had thoughts of aborting the trip altogether after the tire problem. I wondered what ever possessed me to take the trip in the first place. I was totally out of shape for the rigors I would probably face and I wasn't sure I had enough strength to make it all the way.

Day 8 - I crossed the Skeena River into Kitwanga for the start of the Cassiar Highway. The temperature was around 55 degrees and it was partly cloudy. I saw very few cars on the Cassiar that morning, which I was thankful for. The dirt began about 10 miles north of Kitwanga. There was not much left of the original narrow road I traveled in 1977, just six years earlier. Some sections of the road were 40 feet wide while the clearing in the forest was more than 200 feet wide. Most of that part of the Cassiar was only about 20 feet wide in 1977, while the clearance in the forest was only slightly more than that. I averaged between 50 and 60 MPH most of the way. I saw a few trucks disabled with flat tires in the construction areas where there were sharp rocks spread across the road. Many stones flew up under the bike and struck loudly against the bottom. I thought about all of the stones up on the Dempster Highway and figured if I were ever going to attempt it with the lowered ground clearance, I would have problems with the millions of stones.

I saw what appeared to be a pure black mink run across the road. I passed a fire-ravaged area that went on for 20 or 30 miles. I had heard on one of my earlier trips that some of the natives occasionally set fires so they can be hired to put them out. They also find work planting new trees for years after a fire. It rained hard for about ten miles and the road got very slick. I reached the Alaska Highway junction around 7:30 PM and turned east to get a room in Watson Lake just as it was starting to drizzle. I didn't have any desire to camp in the rain that night with memories of the previous trip fresh in my mind. I found a tiny mobile-home-type room for $40. I was tired after having covered 580 miles of mostly rough dirt. I could hear heavy rain beating against the metal roof all night.

Day 9 - It was still drizzling rain when I got up. I decided during the night that I would definitely not make an attempt at Inuvik on this trip. I rode through the drizzle for about two hours. After it stopped I held my speed between 65 and 80 MPH for a long time on the Alaska Highway, since the dirt surface was smooth and firm with very few rocks. I talked with a gas station attendant and learned that he was the father of Toby, one of the guys I had met at Eagle Plains on the Dempster Highway two years earlier.

I cleared US Customs and entered Alaska around 6 PM. Twelve miles beyond the border I rode through a really sloppy eighteen-mile stretch of road construction where the mud was deep and very slick. The cars and RVs were getting stuck all over the place. The construction crew would hook a chain onto a vehicle stuck in the mud and drag it all the way out, sometimes for miles. I had to wait for a half hour for the pilot car. While following it through I was stopped several times as cars and campers would get stuck in front of me. Luckily my low ground clearance didn't cause major problems there.

I lost about an hour in the construction area. I was low on gas when I entered it and when I finally found a gas station beyond the mud I was on my last few ounces of gas. I picked up groceries in Tok around 8 PM and stopped at the same state-run campground I used two years earlier, about 14 miles past Glennallen. I covered 680 miles during that fourteen-hour day, mostly on dirt.

Day 10 - The day began with only a few clouds around. The road was paved all the way into Anchorage but it was rough. I hit a few breaks in the pavement that caused the bottom of the bike to slam hard against the road. I hit one dip doing about 80 MPH and the bottom hit so hard it threw me clear off the seat. I struck another huge dip on a curve traveling about 55 and the side hit the road so hard it threw the bike clear across the centerline. Fortunately the bike was very forgiving, because I traveled very fast during most of the last few days. The low profile tire on the rear made the bottoming problem worse.

The sky became completely overcast by 10 AM and I met a little rain and fog around Eureka Summit as I did on previous trips, and it was also raining at Matanuska Glacier. I experienced what felt like a series of bumps and a strange unevenness in the road. All of a sudden stones began falling from the steep embankment onto the road. I learned later that a 6.2 earthquake had struck the area. It felt really weird and I'm quite sure the road was literally bouncing up and down. I reached Anchorage just before noon on Thursday with my odometer reading 5,800 miles higher than when I left New York. I averaged 650 miles a day for my nine days on the road.

I relaxed at Donna's for the rest of the day and spent Days 11, 12, 13 and 14 visiting. I also serviced the bike and got everything cleaned up during my stay. I learned from talking with a mechanic at the Honda shop that the coolant temperature problem I thought I was having was probably due to a defective gauge, which is the only related part that they've had problems with on that model. I was unable to find Spectro oil or the correct spark plugs for the bike so I chose Pennzoil for my oil change and decided not to change the plugs. Rey smoked up about four pounds of salmon for my return trip and he also made some beef jerky.

Day 15 - I left Tuesday morning in light rain. A drizzle continued intermittently until just before I reached the muddy construction area east of Tok. I got there just as the pilot car and a string of vehicles were disappearing from view and I had to wait for more than an hour for it to return. By that time there was quite a string of cars and trucks lined up behind me. The pilot car driver took one look at the bike and said, "You will NEVER get that thing through here this morning!" She said that most bikes were getting stuck the day before, when it wasn't half as bad as it is now. I told her not to worry about me but she insisted that if I were going to try, it would have to be from the rear of the line. She didn't want me "holding up anyone or getting run over."

After watching 20 or 30 cars, campers, trucks and other vehicles go by I moved in and took up the rear. It turned out to be a real fiasco. Vehicles were getting stuck all over the place, especially the large RVs and cars with trailers. Several vehicles would try to make their own tracks and they would eventually become buried to their axles in mud. Bulldozers and other four-wheel-drive construction vehicles hooked chains onto the cars to drag them out. I remembered that operation from the trip north and mentioned it to a guy in line with a VW bug. He said that no one was going to mess up his front end by dragging him through the mud. I don't know how he ever got through but the last time I saw him he was buried well over his wheel hubs in mud. He was one of those who tried to make his own track.

The entire roadbed began to look like a parking lot, as many drivers would get tired of waiting in line and try to make their own path. I generally kept to the firmest tracks, even though it sometimes meant waiting. I only climbed out of the main rut a few times to get around someone seriously stuck directly in front of me. I almost got stuck once as I squeezed by a guy because it was much softer a foot out from the packed-down wheel track. I paddled my feet in the mud to keep it going and tried to stay very close, because it was obvious that the mud was much deeper farther out and the bottom of the bike was already dragging in it. It took about two hours to get through the

91

eighteen-mile section. When I finally reached the hard surface, about two-thirds of the vehicles that went in ahead of me were stuck far behind. I gave a big wave and smile to the pilot car driver who I think was amazed that I got through at all.

After clearing the construction area I stopped for gas and couldn't locate my credit card. I searched everywhere I thought it might be and I became convinced that I had lost it. The last place I remembered using it was at a Chinese restaurant in Anchorage the previous night where I had dinner with Donna, Rey and the children. The kids were completely uncontrollable there. Asia kept running around and crawling under the tables while Robyn screamed nonstop in his highchair from the time we arrived until we left. I was a little rattled from the screaming, spanking, and yelling. I couldn't remember what I had done with the card, or even if I had gotten it back from the cashier. I called Donna and asked her to look around and check with the Chinese restaurant to see if anyone had found it. I called her again from the Canadian border a half hour later. When it wasn't found, I called an 800 number to have the card canceled out. The whole thing cost me almost three hours and left me without a credit card. Unfortunately I wasn't carrying very much cash and I was out of travelers' checks.

I continued riding for several hours beyond the border and stopped for the night at Burwash Landing on Lake Kluane. A friendly German guy ran the lodge there. I pulled in around 11:30 PM after a very stressful sixteen-hour day. Because of having lost my credit card I was now on a very tight budget for rooms and food. I rented an upstairs room with a shared bath for $25. The cots were small but comfortable. I ate smoked salmon for dinner from my bag. Before turning in I found the card in a pants pocket that I had worn the previous night, but it was too late because I had already canceled it.

Day 16 - I slept until 8:30 and had breakfast at the lodge. I was on the road by ten. The roads were dry and the sky was clear. I took several photos around Lake Kluane, which is one of the most scenic spots along the Alaska Highway. I rode between 70 and 80 MPH most of the day. A few of the sections had soft gravel in spots, which was a little tricky, but for the most part the road was hard-packed dirt treated with calcium chloride and recently graded. I ran through a few light rain showers between Whitehorse and Marsh Lake. I considered myself lucky to cross the dreaded steel-grate bridge over Teslin Lake while it was dry, although the Gold Wing took the grooves much better than the poorly loaded Suzuki. I ate some smoked salmon around six o'clock and kept riding for a few more hours to Muncho Lake, where I camped. I had a little trouble finding a clear spot to pitch the tent and I finally settled for a spot covered with stones near the edge of the lake. I covered about 600 miles in 13 hours.

Day 17 - The day started out clear, breezy, and in the low sixties. I rolled up everything dry for a change and left at eight o'clock. I had a nice ride along the Alaska Highway through the scenic mountains around Steamboat and Fort Nelson. I eventually ran into some rain about ten miles west of Pink Mountain. Just as a downpour was at its peak accompanied by pea-sized hail, I came upon another construction area. I slipped and slid for about 20 miles on the slick road surface. For about three hours after that I rode through several showers before stopping at a motel in Fox Creek, BC around 9 PM.

Day 18 - I started out in a steady rain at 7:30 after eating more smoked salmon with an onion roll and coffee. The temperature was in the low fifties. The sky began to clear around 80 miles out. The sun was out by lunchtime and it was nice for the rest of the day. I stopped for the night at 8:30 in Saskatoon after riding 725 miles. I ate smoked salmon for both lunch and dinner and by the time I got to the motel that night I was getting pretty tired of the steady diet of smoked salmon. I was sure I had consumed too much salt for my blood pressure. I went out to purchase a liter of milk at a convenience store and found a KFC for a late snack.

DAY 19 - I was up at six and out by seven. I had breakfast in the room on the smoked salmon for yet another time with rolls and coffee. A cold front was supposed to be heading my way, but the day started out very clear with a mild 60 degrees. I entered the US at Portal, ND and soon began to see a lot of motorcycles that I assumed were associated with the Sturgis rally.

I had seen many grain elevators in Saskatchewan and I saw even more silos in Minnesota. I had planned to make Au Claire, Wisconsin by nightfall but I ran into rain again and stopped a few miles short of there at a small motel about a mile off the highway. I went out and got some greasy fried chicken after it stopped raining and I carried that back to the motel.

Day 20 - I was up at 5:30 and on the road by 6:15 in a thick fog. It got warm very fast and I stopped around 9:30 to peel off several layers of clothes and my face shield. I rode on interstate highways most of the day through Illinois, Indiana and Ohio. I stopped several times for water, soda, and ice cream as the temperature rose into the nineties. I felt groggy and sleepy several times during the day. I stopped at the same Motel 6 in Youngstown that I used on the way out.

Day 21 - I was up at five and left at first light around 45 minutes later. I rode for a long distance looking for a place to get breakfast. I almost ran out of gas before I finally located a truck stop where I filled up and had a good meal. I opted for Interstates 81 and 84 to get home, and I realized that it was considerably quicker than my usual ride through New York City. It was also cooler in the upper Poconos than it would have been through New Jersey. I traveled 4,450 miles from Anchorage in 6½ days, as I averaged 685 miles a day for my return trip.

SHAKEDOWN FOR THE NORTH SLOPE

I learned from my first three trips to Alaska that to reach the north coast of North America from New York State is a considerable challenge for a motorcyclist. Getting there and enjoying the trip takes good planning and preparation, favorable weather, a good dirt-riding ability, and the right motorcycle, which not only needs to be capable of handling well on loose surfaces, but it must also be comfortable enough to ride the more than 10,000 miles to get there and back.

Soon after returning home from my third Alaska trip I began to look for the right bike for a fourth trip, and I was determined that it would include Inuvik in the Northwest Territories. Modern dual-sport machines were not yet being marketed in the US, but Honda had just made available some leftover 1982 FT500 Ascot single-cylinder machines at a greatly reduced price. Figuring that the bike had promise, I bought one and proceeded to test it. The first thousand miles of local riding proved that the handling on dirt surfaces was adequate although not great, and the engine was certainly strong enough. The real test would be if I could take the stiff ride for more than 10,000 miles, of which about two thousand would be on rough dirt.

I planned a scenic 7,500-mile, two-lane-road tour around the US as a shakedown for it. The Beartooth Highway in Montana, the Cody Museum in Wyoming, and Rocky Mountain National Park in Colorado were the highlights of my plan. When I told my longtime friend and enduro buddy Ralph Spencer in Arizona about it, he promptly went out and bought his own Ascot, paying $300 less in Arizona than I did in New York. We decided on meeting halfway and riding about 3,000 miles together. Ruston, Louisiana was to be our rendezvous point.

After reaching Mt. Jewett, Pennsylvania via remote, scenic byways, I followed US 219 all the way into the Smoky Mountains of North Carolina. On my third day I turned west for a brief visit with an old friend in Ten Mile, Tennessee. The bike handled great and it easily maintained the legal speed limits.

As I approached Loudon, TN I saw a plume of smoke coming from a large barn that was very close behind a two-story, wood-frame house. I got closer and realized the barn was on fire. I stopped and ran around the house calling out as loud as I could but no one answered. There was no sign of anyone around and there were no close neighbors. I felt helpless as I watched the flames grow. It was already too late to save the barn but the house would certainly go next unless I could get some firefighting equipment there in a hurry. A pickup truck stopped and I ran over and asked the driver if he had a way to contact the local fire department. He said the closest one was in Loudon but he doubted they would respond because it was at least two miles outside their jurisdiction. I noticed he had a CB in his truck and I insisted that he try calling. He did and a few seconds later I could hear a fire whistle from a long way off. By the time they arrived, several shingles on the outside of the house had already started to burn as the flames from the barn leaped 30 feet into the air. With only a single 1½-inch hose and about 500 gallons of water on the truck, they managed to save the house with no more than a scorching, but the barn burned to the ground.

Ralph was already in Ruston when I arrived and I found him easily. Actually I spotted his bike at the first motel I rode by. That night as we swapped stories of our experiences getting there we agreed on one common complaint -- that the Ascot seat was hard.

On our first day together we shared an enjoyable ride through some gently rolling hills in the Ozark Mountains of central Arkansas. We reached Dodge City, Kansas on our second day out, where the temperature was an even 100 degrees. Ralph had been dropping back quite a bit during the afternoon and once when we stopped for gas I noticed that he really didn't look very happy. He complained that his butt and the insides of his thighs were so raw that he was having trouble putting his feet down whenever we stopped. It was obvious that he wasn't having fun anymore! That night in Dodge City he was depressed over his discomfort and he said he was heading home in the morning. I pleaded with him to stick with it but he said, "No way!" Although we were more than 900 miles from Sun City, he said it was a lot shorter than the route I had planned via Montana. I learned a week later when we met again in Sun City that, aside from the discomfort of the seat and the heat, he also suffered from a spider bite that gave him a slight fever. He couldn't recall anything about his 900-mile ride home.

I headed northwest out of Dodge City early the next morning riding alone. Although I was sore too I was getting accustomed to the hardness of the seat. I didn't think I was that much worse off than I've been on a few other trips on the fourth or fifth day out. I had already concluded that as soon as I got home I would resume my search for a more suitable North Slope machine. It was in fact a stiff ride and I figured that a few thousand miles of rough dirt roads would certainly take the fun out of it for me too, although I was having fun at that point.

On my first day alone I extended my daily ride to 12 hours and reached Estes Park, Colorado late that evening. While oiling and adjusting the chain at the motel I noticed a nail in my rear tire. I pulled it out and the air began hissing out, so I pushed it back in quickly and immediately went in search of air. All of the gas stations were closed and I wasn't carrying a pump, so I rode around until I found a coin-operated air machine where I proceeded to plug the leak in total darkness with my repair kit.

The temperature in the morning was in the low thirties and frost glistened in the trees. The sky was sparkling clear as I started up the steep, gently winding road into Rocky Mountain National Park. It was still very early and I might have been the first person to enter the park that morning. It was like having the entire place to myself, which is the way I prefer to ride. The Honda was running great and it felt especially good to lean into the mountain curves and listen to the sound of the single-cylinder engine as it climbed effortlessly up the fairly steep incline. I especially enjoyed the spectacular scenery along the mountain roads between Estes Park and Grand Lake, making it one of the scenic highlights of my trip. Riding that little "thumper" up Trail Ridge Road and over Fall River Pass at an altitude of almost 12,000 feet was a truly exhilarating experience.

Near Rock Springs, Wyoming I met a violent lightning storm with heavy rain, strong winds, and hail. Of all the weather conditions I've ever experienced on a bike, western lightning storms are among the most fearful to me. The fierce, long streaks of lightning can be seen for many miles and there is no place to take shelter. The streaks originate at a very high altitude and stretch many thousands of feet to the ground. They seem to dance, shimmy and crackle loudly until they finally break with a powerful, terrifying blast. A few times I actually considered stopping and running for the ditch to hide from the awesome spectacle.

The traffic got very heavy north of Jackson Hole, Wyoming near the Grand Tetons. The road was crowded with slow-moving campers heading into Yellowstone Park for the weekend. I also experienced a lot of road construction that morning. It got so bad that I pulled over and studied my map for an "escape route." I regretted missing Beartooth Pass and the Beartooth Highway again, and also the Cody Museum, but it just wasn't worth a hundred miles or more of stop-and-go traffic. I knew there would be no accommodations in the park, especially without camping gear. I had originally planned on making it all the way to Cody by that evening, but that was already impossible because of the many delays I had experienced so far.

While studying my map I spotted an unimproved secondary road running from near the south entrance of Yellowstone Park for about 50 miles into Ashton, Idaho. I asked the ranger at the park entrance for directions to the road. The ranger referred to it as Grassy Lake Road, but advised me against taking it to Ashton because the road was not maintained as a through road. Campers used it on the eastern end, but the ranger didn't think anyone ever used it to go all the way through to Ashton. A short time later I located the road and gassed up near there. I also asked at the gas station about conditions, figuring they should know. I got essentially the same answer: that it was intended for four-wheel drive vehicles and was not maintained as a through road. That was good enough for me. It sounded like my kind of road and it was in line with my shakedown objectives. Otherwise, I didn't have that many dirt roads planned along my route.

It was in fact a rarely traveled, rough, dirt road with stones, ruts, water splashes and a few fallen trees across it. I stopped for photos a few times although the spectacular views of the Grand Tetons, which I had seen earlier, were barely visible through the dense forest. After about 25 miles, the conditions of the road improved as it widened and straightened, although I had some difficulty with loose gravel. I figured I must have crossed over the state line into Idaho when the level of road maintenance seemed to change. Trees became scarcer and patches of grassy fields came into view on both sides.

Suddenly something moving in a secluded field to my left caught my eye. With a quick glance I saw a sleek, red-and-white helicopter parked in the field with its prop spinning at idle. My first thought was, "What a nice picture!" But as I chopped the throttle and looked again I could see someone carrying

98

something and moving quickly from the helicopter to a waiting Chevy Suburban. I immediately decided it was not a good place for me to be. My first thought was of illegal drugs. I turned the throttle up and leaned forward, hoping that if they had seen me they wouldn't think that I saw them. What they were involved with might determine just how much trouble I was in. I got out of there as fast as I could with the rear wheel fishtailing on the loose gravel. I left a half-mile trail of dust behind. I glanced over my shoulder several times to see if either the helicopter or the Suburban was following. I rode very fast for the 20 miles into Ashton, where I spotted a small restaurant. I parked the bike behind the building and went inside for a late lunch.

That night at a motel in Montpelier, Idaho I heard a news report on the TV about a bank robbery in Texas where the getaway was made with a helicopter. The report said that Texas police thought the helicopter might have headed into Oklahoma or southeastern Colorado. I looked over my maps and doubted that a helicopter could ever make it from Texas all the way to where I saw it in Idaho, which was more than a thousand miles. I didn't think any more about it until two weeks later while sitting in my living room at home when I heard a similar report of another bank robbery in southwestern Colorado where a helicopter was again used in the getaway. I called my local State Police barracks to ask how I might go about contacting Idaho State Police. He asked what it was all about and I described what I had seen. Of course the first thing he wanted to know was what I was doing in a place like that alone on a motorcycle.

I told him the helicopter was white with red trim and it had a sleek nose like an executive jet. He said he would check it out and get back to me. Twenty minutes later he called to say that my description fit exactly with the bank robbers' helicopter and that they might call me if they needed any more information. He also made a few comments about my being lucky, and that it would be a lot safer to stick to paved roads. I didn't take the time to try and explain why I like riding abandoned dirt roads. I never heard any more about the incident.

There was a lot of standing floodwater around Provo, Utah from the spring thaw and recent rains. I also saw some serious devastation from the spring floods along Route 89 in central Utah. The normally peaceful Sevier River took out roads, railroad beds, bridges, and scores of homes as it tore a wide path through central Utah. I ran into the heaviest rain of my trip near Panguitch, where I stopped for the night.

South of Flagstaff, Arizona I visited Jerome, one of the largest ghost mining towns in the west. It has been revived in recent years and is now a thriving tourist attraction, with many artists and hippies selling their wares. The road leaving Jerome was narrow and rarely traveled with very enjoyable, although seemingly endless switchback curves through the mountains.

I spent a few days at Ralph's servicing the bike and resting before heading east. The scenic highlight of my 2,500-mile homeward leg was from Farmington, NM to Chama and then north into Antonito, Colorado, which goes through the San Juan Mountains, via a spectacular and infrequently traveled road over two 10,000-foot passes and through some beautiful high meadows. I stopped briefly at Chama to visit a railroad museum and later I visited Ft. Garland, CO where Kit Carson was once the commandant and a state museum is maintained.

While rounding a tight curve in southern Indiana on a twisty blacktop road I met a guy half limping and half running toward me waving both arms. I barely managed to stop without hitting him. He said he had just turned over his eighteen-wheel gravel truck around the next bend. It was sprawled across the road resting on its side with its cab over one ditch and the end of the trailer over the opposite ditch. A few of the wheels were still spinning and steam was rising from the engine compartment. Luckily it wasn't loaded with gravel. I managed to get around it with some difficulty and I located a small garage a mile down the road, where I asked them to call for help.

I covered a total of approximately 7,400 miles on my shakedown ride, of which 95% was on two-lane byways. My daily average was around 425 miles, while my longest single day was 610 miles, which was the day I rode from Dodge City, Kansas to Estes Park, Colorado. My conclusion from the ride was that the stiff seat was unacceptable and the suspension left a lot to be desired for the thousands of miles of rough roads that I would have to ride up north. I still had a really fun ride. I even thought about having a special seat made and searching for better shocks, but I was quite sure I would eventually find a better machine for my dual-sport purpose. A short time later I sold the Ascot and resumed my search.

BACK ROADS, USA

The summer of 1988 was one of the hottest summers on record. That was when Bud Peck and I took a 40-day, back-road tour of the country that covered more than fifteen thousand miles, of which 98 percent was on two-lane country roads. We visited 29 states, 17 national parks and countless national forests, national monuments, and Indian reservations. We saw this beautiful country from sea to shining sea, from our broad Canadian border to the blistering heat of the Mexican border. We climbed the highest mountains and crossed sweltering deserts as we experienced the extremes of weather from 34 degrees and snowing in Mt. Rainier National Park on the fifth of July to 112 degrees in southern Arizona just twelve days later. One of the highlights of our once-in-a-lifetime tour was crossing the Mississippi River on a tiny ferryboat, where our two cycles were the only fares aboard.

During the trip we saw enough wheat and corn growing to feed the entire world and we saw enough cotton in the fields to clothe a good part of it. We saw beef and dairy cattle in almost every state we visited and to quote Bud, "We never saw a skinny cow." We saw strawberries at 50 cents a basket in California where pickers were harvesting the luscious fruit to sounds of Latin music blaring from loudspeakers, and we ate Bing cherries in Washington's Yakima Valley until we just couldn't hold anymore.

Almost every day Bud or I would say enthusiastically, "Something different every day!" One of the most satisfying things about of the trip was that every new day seemed even better and more interesting than the day before. What a great and beautiful land we live in! From the hustle and bustle of the east, to down-home Americana in the Ohio River Valley, through the rugged cow country of the west, to the giant trees of the far west. God bless America! I wish everyone could see it firsthand the way we did.

It was the trip of a lifetime, for which I had studied the maps and actively planned for 2½ years, and if anyone were to ask Bud he would tell you that he had waited his whole life to do it. I almost went the previous year but I lost confidence at the last moment in the bike I had chosen to ride; consequently, I sold it, put all systems on hold, and set my sights for 1988.

101

Meanwhile Bud saw his opportunity to go and we were able to share the experience.

A major heat wave was already in full swing as we prepared to leave on the 23rd of June. People would ask, "Why now? Why not wait until it's a little cooler?" My answer was usually that this was our window of opportunity. If we waited, it would close, and who knows what would happen next to delay it again. Besides, some of the key places we planned to visit would be inaccessible later in the year due to snow. We really didn't know at the time that it would be one of the hottest summers ever recorded across the country.

I made motel reservations for almost every night and guaranteed them in advance. I planned to meet Lilli at the San Francisco Airport on our sixteenth day and drop her off ten days later at Sky Harbor Airport in Phoenix. Her primary interests were in visiting several ghost towns of the west. Her airline tickets were unchangeable and nonrefundable in both directions. Since we had already canceled her reservations the previous year we made contingency plans for all sorts of things that could arise, but none ever did. Following is a daily journal of our trip:

Day 1 - We rode through a few sprinkles early the first morning and it was overcast when we reached our first scenic highlight, the Delaware River Valley from Hawks Nest along NY Route 97. The weather began to clear soon after we crossed the Delaware via a small steel-grate bridge between Minisink Ford and Lackawaxen, PA. Later we enjoyed a spirited ride through Promised Land State Park and over a series of scenic country roads through central Pennsylvania.

We had our first of several close calls in West Virginia when we came up behind an old truck carrying a huge storage shed. The shed was shaped like a barn and perched on top of the truck bed. It was being hauled down the highway by a really relaxed hauling outfit, and the guy in the truck was obviously having difficulty controlling it in the strong crosswinds. He was driving much too fast for the conditions and the shed was actually rocking dangerously on the truck bed. Approaching cars were forced onto the shoulder as the truck zigzagged down the road and the shed rocked menacingly on top. Bud and I passed the trailing car with the "Oversize Load" sign and one by one we passed several other vehicles until we pulled in behind the truck with the shed. We were just about to pass when one side of the shed rocked way up and a heavy four-by-eight sheet of plywood came hurtling out from underneath. I swerved one way and Bud swerved the other as the huge sheet flew between us. I could hear the screeching of tires behind us.

By the afternoon of the first day we had already passed more than 60 vehicles on two-lane roads. Most passes were perfectly legal and safe with the dotted line on our side, but many others were not. We estimated toward the end of our tour that we probably passed as many as 2,000 cars, trucks, campers, and motor homes during our forty days on two-lane roads. The majority of these vehicles were relatively easy to get by, but others like the truck with the shed presented varying degrees of difficulty. Some drivers intentionally made it difficult for us, including approaching vehicles as well as those we passed, especially when they didn't like the spot we chose to make the pass. There were times when we would go most of the day with the motto: "pass 'em when you get to 'em," which brought on many bold passes.

Our motel reservations on the first night were at the Econolodge in Elkins, West Virginia where they were celebrating a gala opening of a new wing. They served hot and cold hors d'oeuvres, as well as mild and spiked punch. There was also a special wine and cheese tasting bar upstairs next to a newly dedicated bridal suite. We availed ourselves of all of the goodies on both floors and never did go out for dinner that evening.

Day 2 - The day began with a really fun ride between Valley Head and Craigsville, a 50-mile stretch of twisty roads through West Virginia hill country with very little letup. To make it even more challenging there was marble-sized gravel on several of the right-hand turns, probably kicked up by trailer trucks when they sometimes trail their rear wheels beyond the shoulders on sharp right-hand turns. Bud noticed that a flying stone had broken his headlight lens, so we began to look for a BMW dealer to get a new lens. Bud rode his BMW K75 on the trip while I rode a Honda GL1200 Gold Wing Aspencade.

We crossed the Ohio River on a steel-grate bridge near Pomeroy and stopped for the night just outside Middletown. We parked the bikes temporarily on some fresh blacktop behind the motel as we unloaded our gear. A few minutes after checking in we got a call from the desk saying that our kickstands were sinking into the fresh tar. By the time we rushed outside, the bikes were already laying against each other in an ugly heap. Luckily there was no damage to either machine.

I also learned early on the trip when not to use my cruise control, which I had been experimenting with on my new machine. Sometimes while traveling on straight roads I would set the cruise control at a comfortable speed; and later after having ridden several miles with it on, I would forget about it. Once in West Virginia as I approached a fairly tight turn I got well into the turn to the crucial point where the side almost touches the road and suddenly the cruise control decided that I needed a healthy application of throttle. It was pretty scary. That's when I stopped messing with it.

Day 3 - We spent most of our third day in the Ohio River Valley where we saw a lot of wilted corn, some of it severely stunted. It was one of the most drought-stricken areas we passed on our trip. The corn usually looked better in the morning after a cool night gave it a break from the heat. Our ride in Indiana from Aurora to Madison was our scenic highlight of the day. A few of the towns were colorfully dressed for the Fourth of July and I found myself singing lines from "God Bless America" as we rode along. While traveling through some farmland near Lawrenceburg, we smelled a really nice aroma that neither of us recognized at first. When we got closer to the source we began to see huge Shenley and Seagram signs on a few of the larger buildings and realized the smell was coming from grain-mash cooking as part of a whiskey-making operation.

Bud spotted a smoking barbecue at a church in Waverly, Kentucky shortly before we checked into our tiny four-unit motel in Morganfield. After checking in we returned to partake of the feast where people stood eating along rows of makeshift counters. Smiling volunteers kept coming back with platter after platter of delicious barbecue beef, ham, mutton, and a variety of other foods. We learned how friendly the people are there, how good the food is, and how spicy-hot their sauces are. The 105-degree temperature in Waverly at six in the evening was a harbinger of the days to come.

Day 4 - We crossed the Mississippi River on a narrow steel bridge at Cape Girardeau near the southern tip of Illinois. The river seemed much lower than normal and much narrower, which was probably due to the extended drought. All of the

104

roads we traveled that day were excellent bike roads, but our most enjoyable rides of the day were through the Shawnee National Forest and the Mark Twain National Forest. The temperature again topped 100 degrees by mid-afternoon.

We located a BMW shop in Mexico, Missouri, although it was Sunday evening and we had to inquire around to find out who owned the shop. Bud telephoned the dealer at his home and he came out to open the shop for us. Mexico was our planned overnight stop and we were on our evening break when the dealer changed the headlight lens for Bud. Not many dealers would have been that accommodating. I thought it was a sign of Midwestern hospitality, although Bud said many BMW dealers were like that. When I got home weeks later I learned that my own headlight lens was also broken.

Day 5 - We rode through a lot of farm country with hundreds of miles of corn, wheat, and soybeans everywhere we looked. We saw combines in the fields harvesting what was probably the last of the winter wheat. Straw bales on some of the farms we passed were so huge and numerous, it made one wonder how much wheat must have come from all that straw. We traveled through eastern Missouri and southern Iowa to an old but relatively clean tourist cabin in Wahoo, Nebraska.

It had been another particularly hot 100-degree-plus day and we were looking forward to our daily batch of whiskey sours. Unfortunately my supply of dry mix had already run out. I searched all over town that evening for more and I learned that dry mix was not readily available west of the Mississippi. I located a liquor store where the guy remembered having seen a few packages "a few years back." He rummaged through a lot of long-forgotten junk in the bottom drawer of his desk and finally came up with five individual packages that he gave to me at no charge. Much of the printing had been worn off, but you could still read the labels. I brought my treasures back to the motel and Bud proceeded to mix up a 5-bag batch. I'll never forget the look on his face when he took the first sip. He would usually smile, smack his lips real loud, and say, "Boy, that's a good batch!" This time there was no smile and no big smack. He just frowned a little and said, "You know, that's almost a bad batch." We drank it in spite of its off-taste, but from that time on, whenever Bud was asked if he had ever had a bad batch, he would answer no, but he would always mention that one we shared in Wahoo, Nebraska.

Day 6 - After having traveled northwest for a day we turned due west through some of the richest natural farmland we saw on the trip with seven-foot-high corn, healthy wheat, and feeder pens crowded with robust beef cattle and hogs. The contrasting colors of the deep green corn fields, interspersed with fields of golden wheat blanketing the gently rolling countryside gave the impression of a patchwork quilt that stretched to the horizons.

We began seeing large-scale crop watering operations west of the 100th meridian that bisects Nebraska. It's necessary to water most of the crops there, even in normal times. We saw giant watering rigs in many of the western states; some appeared to be a half mile long. Powered by their own water pressure they roll ever so slowly through the fields to keep the crops irrigated.

We stopped for lunch at a hotel-cafe in Hyannis, a small cow town in western Nebraska. A sign posted outside said that the place becomes the rodeo headquarters whenever the rodeo is in town and that real cowboys gather there. We entered through a pair of traditional swinging saloon doors and stepped inside onto a plain wooden floor. After lunch we turned south toward the scenic North Platte River Valley. We stopped briefly at Chimney Rock and climbed onto Scotts Bluff National Monument for a breathtaking view of the area. Chimney Rock and Scotts Bluff were landmarks for pioneers heading west along the Oregon and Mormon Pioneer Trails many years ago.

Day 7 - We turned north again and headed for South Dakota and the Pine Ridge Indian Reservation. Many times during the trip Bud or I would remark jokingly, "Boy, the traffic along here is murder!" We would often ride for a half hour or more without seeing a single vehicle traveling in either direction. We passed very few cars that day. Most of our passing was done near tourist attractions like the national and state parks, and of course later in California where I think there are more cars than anywhere in the world.

Bud had a close call passing an old truck hauling a wood chipper. There were no directional signals on the chipper and we couldn't see the truck's taillights. We didn't know it at the time, but the guy was just about to make a left turn. He shouted obscenities at me when I passed and shook his fist at me. I had no idea what it was all about. He suddenly pulled the wheel hard to the left for a left turn just as Bud started by. Only the fastest reaction on Bud's part avoided an accident. When the guy heard Bud's brakes, he also jammed on his brakes. Bud said later that the truck tires were smoking. We wondered if the guy ever realized he didn't have directional signals on the chipper.

We stopped briefly at Wounded Knee in the Pine Ridge Indian Reservation and read a sign describing some of the events that led up to the Indian massacre that took place there in 1890, when 200 Indian men, women, and children were killed by soldiers ordered there by the Army to "disarm the braves." A lone Indian now stands at the cemetery gate in Wounded Knee; and in exchange for a few friendly words he'll describe the events in much greater detail, and he'll also talk about the more recent "uprising" in 1970 when a church was burned and several buildings damaged in a civil disturbance.

Badlands National Park was our next highlight, followed by Mt. Rushmore National Monument, Crazy Horse Monument, and the Needles Highway. At Mt. Rushmore we saw hundreds of people standing in silence at the foot of the beautifully sculptured granite faces of George Washington, Thomas Jefferson, Theodore Roosevelt, and Abraham Lincoln.

At the Crazy Horse Monument I felt sorry for Sculptor Korczak Ziolkowski, who labored long and hard until his body was bruised and broken in a vain effort to finish what is probably the largest sculpturing task ever undertaken by a man. His surviving wife and family are trying to keep his dream alive, but they need much more support than the paltry funds they collect from the public to view the massive unfinished sculpture of the Indian leader astride his horse. Gutzon Borglum who sculptured the faces on Mt. Rushmore was much more fortunate, having had a great deal of federal funding to complete his task.

At the outset of the Needles Highway the dark clouds that seemed to be following us for days finally caught up with us. Bud and I put on our rain suits as the first big drops fell, and not a moment too soon. The fun was taken out of the 14 miles of switchback curves along the Needles Highway as the rain came in torrents. Most of the cars traveling in both directions drove very slowly, and the twisty road was far too slick for our usual bold passes. The rain stopped as suddenly as it began, and when we pulled into Custer about seven miles from the end of the

107

highway a gas station attendant, seeing our rain suits and wet bikes, asked where we found the rain. Another heavy shower hit Newcastle, Wyoming that evening as we relaxed in our motel.

Day 8 - It was still overcast when we visited Devils Tower National Monument in the morning. Devils Tower was featured in the movie, "Close Encounters of the Third Kind" as the place where the huge alien spaceship touched down. This huge flat-topped butte, which rises abruptly for 867 feet out of the otherwise green, gently rolling countryside, is a strange and impressive sight. It's a favorite spot for rock climbers, as more than a thousand have climbed it each year since 1977.

An almost deserted road to Alzada, Montana was in the process of being paved. The road construction crew was laying down thick, black-plastic sheeting before paving over it. They were putting the huge sheets down in a fairly brisk wind that morning. When we came along, there was no other place to ride except on the plastic, which is where they motioned for us to go. It was a very strange feeling to ride on these huge billowing sheets that resembled ocean waves.

We stopped for coffee in Alzada, where our first choice for a snack was pie or Danish pastry; but when all they had on the menu was cinnamon rolls, we each ordered one. When the waitress returned with the heated rolls we were amazed to see that they were almost two inches thick, and each roll covered an entire dinner plate. At future western coffee breaks we ordered a single cinnamon roll between us but we never got another one nearly that large, or quite that good.

We rode through the Northern Cheyenne and Crow Indian Reservations and Custer National Forest on our approach to Custer Battlefield National Monument on the banks of the Little Bighorn River. We toured the battlefield and its adjoining national cemetery, which contains the remains of servicemen from many Indian wars as well as recent foreign wars. Most of the 200 7th Cavalry soldiers who died with Custer are buried there. General Custer's remains were removed several years ago and are now at West Point. Various myths surround Custer's encounter with the overwhelming force of Indians at the Little Big Horn River. The version we heard at the site debunks the fierce hand-to-hand combat version that is usually shown in dramatic recreations of the battle. Although Crazy Horse and Chief Gall led direct attacks against the group as shown in the movies, it is said that most of the cavalrymen died from many hours of Indian gunfire from concealed positions. Stone markers have been erected at the exact spots where General Custer and each of his men died.

Day 9 - The stepping-off point for one of the most beautiful and inspiring days of our entire trip was Red Lodge, Montana, the beginning of the Beartooth Highway. This seldom-used, spectacular road leads over Beartooth Pass to the northeastern entrance of Yellowstone National Park. Charles Kuralt, CBS's special "On The Road" correspondent once called it the most beautiful roadway in America. I had intended to go over the pass on several earlier bike tours, but reports of fresh snow usually changed my plans each time. This time we were confident that snow would not stop us.

Above the 10,000-foot level we realized what Jeremiah Johnson from the movie of the same name must have found so enthralling about the high country. Alpine meadows, sparkling clear lakes and streams, and a few rugged mountain trees that cling eagerly to life are all part of this spectacular setting that sparkles vibrantly during the brief summer season. The high meadows are filled with red, white, blue, and yellow mountain flowers and the grass is a lush, deep green. We saw whitetail deer, mule deer, moose, and several smaller wild animals as we got our "Rocky Mountain high" riding through this beautiful setting. As we stood gazing from one of the highest viewpoints, I said to Bud, "This is what I came for." The Beartooth Highway ranks near the top of my own all-time favorite roads.

In Yellowstone National Park we saw hundreds of buffalo grazing on Blacktail Deer Plateau. Words like huge and tremendous best describes the area of Yellowstone between Tower Junction and Mammoth Hot Springs. These giant fertile meadows are several miles wide and the buffalo herds that graze there appear like clusters of tiny dots, even through binoculars. We avoided Old Faithful and the area around the main village and camp areas because of the expected congestion, and we opted for the northwest exit near Gardiner, Montana.

While getting gas in White Sulphur Springs we asked the attendant where a guy might get some lunch. Without hesitation he said, "Take a right, then another right and it's right there," like he's said it countless numbers of times. By following his directions, we found ourselves directly outside what appeared to be a bar. The building had no windows, only a plain, white door. We figured it must be the place, so we stepped inside and I asked the bartender if he served hamburgers and soft drinks. He said, "Sure, how would you like them cooked?" It was the best lunch we had on the trip.

In sharp contrast, our dinner that night in Conrad was the worst. I ordered fish, which I returned because it was raw inside. It was a thick chunk, probably taken directly from the freezer to the deep fryer and dipped for a very short time. When I got it back the second time it was cooked so hard I couldn't eat it. Bud said his meal wasn't much better. That dinner in Conrad became our comparison standard for the remainder of the trip. Weeks later, if I ever complained that something didn't taste too great, Bud would always ask if it was as bad as what we had in Conrad. He said, "The moral of that story is, 'never order seafood in Montana.'"

Day 10 - Most of the barley used for beer malt in this country probably comes from Fairmont, Montana. A sign there says that 83,000 acres of barley for malt are grown in Fairmont, and that more barley for malt grows there than anywhere in the world. We saw a tractor pulling a 20-foot wide set of disc harrows in a barley field where I couldn't see the end of the field, which faded into the horizon. The tractor probably ran in a straight line for several miles before turning around.

Glacier Park was one of the most beautiful and spectacular parks we visited. We stood at a few of the highest viewpoints on the face of Garden Wall, where the road is cut into the face of the mountain; and we stared in awe across the huge ravine called Avalanche Creek. On the far side was a tremendous panorama of beautiful mountain peaks and glaciers. It was like standing in a huge amphitheater. Bud's remark seemed to fit perfectly: "Kinda boggles the mind, don't it?" The road is called the "Going to the Sun Road," and is another of Charles Kuralt's favorites. It winds for 50 miles over Logan Pass, past St. Mary Lake, and through McDonald Valley into the town of West Glacier.

Montana is one of the few states we visited where small white markers are erected along the highway at sites of traffic fatalities. The crosses are about a foot high by seven inches wide. We saw several clusters of these crosses, and at one point I saw as many as five in a single cluster. We saw so many singles, doubles and clusters around Libby that it gave the impression of riding through a cemetery.

From Eureka, near the Canadian border, we rode along scenic Lake Koocanusa Reservoir, south to the Libby Dam, and then along the Kootenai River and through the Kootenai and Kaniku National Forests into Idaho. A forest fire had destroyed large sections of the Kootenai Forest and another section was ravaged by a bark beetle infestation; but in spite of the devastation, it was a beautiful ride. Our overnight reservations were at Sandpoint, a tourist town on Lake Pend Oreille.

Day 11 - We entered Washington via Route 20 and followed it all the way across the state. We had no idea when we started that day just how spectacular it would be. From our scenic entry near Newport we proceeded west through Colville and Okanogan National Forests into the desert-like terrain of the Okanogan Valley, and then through the beautiful Northern Cascades National Park and Mt. Baker National Forest to our motel in Burlington near the western end of the state. The scenery all the way across Washington was outstanding.

The terrain in the Okanogan River Valley is naturally dry, and for anything to grow there the soil needs to be cultivated, fertilized, and constantly irrigated. The main crops are cherries and apples. We had lunch in Omak near the Colville Indian Reservation and later stopped at a fruit stand where we ate our fill of delicious Bing cherries at a price half of what one might pay at the local supermarket back home. The road from Winthrop to Rockport through Northern Cascades National Park has got to rank near the top of beautiful roadways in America. The high craggy mountains on both sides, with glacial streams, patches of snow, and deep blue lakes were all part of an outstanding panorama. Magnificent Douglas firs and giant red cedars dominated the forests.

We saw many motorcycles on the road in and around Winthrop. We learned that Winthrop is a favorite spot for motorcyclists from British Columbia as well as from our own northwest, especially on the Fourth of July weekend, which it was. The spectacular scenery around Diablo Canyon is another favorite spot for bikers. We walked across the breathtakingly high, see-through bridge that spans the canyon and saw the rushing water and raging waterfall hundreds of feet below.

111

Day 12 - Not having a ferry schedule, we were lucky to arrive at Port Townsend Ferry just before it shoved off at 7:45 AM. The next scheduled run would have been an hour and a half later. It takes the ferry 30 minutes to cross Admiralty Inlet to the Olympic Peninsula. About ten miles from there a large female deer crossed the road in front of me while we were traveling about 65 MPH. She hesitated momentarily as I went for the brakes, but I also glanced in the mirror to see how much room Bud had before I locked them up. Then both tires screeched for what seemed like an eternity. Bud said I waited so long he thought I didn't see the deer. About six times on the trip we had to brake for deer but that was the closest I came.

There were many small fishing boats at Neah Bay in the Makah Indian Reservation. We could see Vancouver Island, British Columbia from there, across the Juan de Fuca Strait. The road from Neah Bay to Port Angeles was a great bike road that twists through a forest of cedars and Douglas firs with extremely dense underbrush. In Port Angeles we saw the trunk of a Douglas fir that measured at least twelve feet across.

We rode through a rain forest in Olympic National Park where thick green moss hung from the tree branches. The rain forests consisted mostly of Douglas fir, Sitka spruce, western hemlock and western red cedar. We saw one huge red cedar tree with a trunk that was about eight feet across. The forests appeared almost tropical with their thick, lush undergrowth of ferns and other jungle-like flora. Hundreds of varieties of wild flowers were in bloom everywhere we went and giant Piper bellflowers grew wild along many of the roadways.

A dusty gravel road near Neilton led us out to the Pacific Ocean where we rode the bikes out onto the white beach sand. Many weather-beaten and surf-beaten logs were strewn all over the beach. Storms probably claimed them from the thick forest that grows right out to the high water line. Once the ocean claims a tree it proceeds to beat the fallen giant until all of the bark and limbs are gone. The surf-beaten wood eventually turns white from the salt water and the weather. The temperature was in the fifties most of the day and it drizzled occasionally while we were on the peninsula, which is very common for the area.

Day 13 - We started our thirteenth day in rain suits for our visit to Mt. Rainier National Park. Although the rain stopped just before we entered the park, heavy fog prevented us from seeing the tops of the mountains. We did see the magnificent Douglas firs, beautiful lakes, streams, and waterfalls. Most of the fir trees were at least six feet in diameter at the base, with their first branch as high as 125 feet above the ground. The trees were so dense in some areas there seemed to be as many as a hundred of these magnificent specimens in a single acre. It snowed lightly at the higher levels, where there was still an 80% snow cover from the previous winter. The temperature was 34 degrees and we were wearing most of the clothes we packed for the trip. It was hard to believe it was the fifth of July.

The weather cleared for our descent into the warmer Yakima Valley via Chinook Pass and Snoqualmie National Forest. We rode in desert-like terrain between Yakima and White Salmon where we crossed the Columbia River Gorge into Oregon. The Yakima Valley is heavily irrigated, making it a very fertile fruit-growing area. We stopped and treated ourselves again to some delicious Bing cherries. Most of central Washington is normally dry from the "rainmaker effect" of the Cascades, which extracts moisture from the clouds before they reach the valley. From north of the Columbia River Gorge in Washington, where we saw several people wind-surfing on the river, to Bennett Pass in Oregon only 40 miles south of there, the weather changed from sunny and pleasant to cold rain and sleet. We were unable to see the top of Mt. Hood because of the rain. In Washington and Oregon we experienced the most abrupt weather changes of anywhere in the country.

Day 14 - There was a thick frost on the bike seats in the morning when we checked out of our motel in Bend, Oregon on the 6th of July. We took a long, cold ride from there to Crater Lake. Along the way we saw another serious bark beetle infestation in Deschutes National Forest, affecting primarily lodge-pole pine trees. Millions of dead trees for about 40 miles along US 97 were gradually being removed.

Crater Lake National Park is nestled high in the Cascade Range in southern Oregon. There were patches of snow along the rim of the now-extinct volcano. The lake for which the park is named, which has no inlet or outlet, is inside a volcanic crater that was formed thousands of years ago. The blue water of the lake is two thousand feet deep in some areas and approximately six miles across. A volcanic cone in the center, which rises from the floor of the lake to above the surface, is called Wizard Island.

Lassen Volcanic National Park was a pleasant surprise. Lassen has beautiful meadows, sparkling deep blue lakes, cinder-cone peaks, pumice fields, magnificent Ponderosa pines, and other huge trees. Ponderosas were growing even at the 8,000-foot level to more than two feet in diameter. The park road that we traveled was built over the 8,500-foot rim and leads right through the mouth of the volcano. Lassen is considered to have one of the only active volcanoes in the continental United States. Several eruptions have occurred there during the 20th century. We saw bubbling hot springs and steaming mud pots along the roadway. It was one of the most scenic and most interesting national parks we visited.

The weather was cool and clear and the roads were free of congestion for our twisty descent from Lassen Park through beautiful Lassen and Plumas National Forests to the town of Sattley in the Tahoe National Forest. There we met the northern end of California Route 49, the famous "Forty-niner's route." We saw people swimming, wading, fishing, panning for gold, and just sitting leisurely on the rocks as we rode alongside the Middle Fork River. We saw Ponderosa pines, Douglas firs, mountain mahogany, western juniper, and many other varieties of trees in the spectacular forests.

The first 70-mile section of Route 49 was a terrific bike road that climbs out of Sierra Valley with tight turns, switchback curves and light traffic. We hadn't had that much fun riding since West Virginia, and there were no loose stones or gravel anywhere. We enjoyed our lunch in Downieville, which is a restored gold-rush town on the North Yuba River.

Just before reaching Nevada City we ran into hordes of California traffic and our special kind of fun was over for the day. From Auburn to our motel in Sonora we passed hundreds of cars for almost three hours on two-lane roads, almost all with double-yellow lines. The trick was to get by without appearing too reckless and without offending anyone, but many motorists we passed let their displeasure be known by honking their horns as we went by. The temperature was 100 degrees and I think many tempers were running thin. Bud's usual relaxed comment was, "No problem." We stopped briefly at Sutters Mill where gold was first discovered, but otherwise we pressed on because it was late and it was one of the few places we had no advance reservations.

Day 16 was not only our day to meet Lilli at the airport, but it was our High Sierras day. Her plane was due at 3:11 so we had plenty of time for a 200-mile rambling loop through the Sierra Nevada Mountains. The ride included Sonora Pass, Monitor Pass, and Ebbetts Pass. The special thrill we experienced earlier on the Beartooth Highway could also apply to the Sierras. It was one of the most enjoyable rides of our trip with spectacular scenery and tight switchback curves around huge volcanic rocks and through the beautiful high forests.

After stopping for lunch at Angels Camp we headed for the airport across the northern end of the San Joaquin Valley, which is famous for its produce; although it seems that the only way anything will grow in that area is with heavy irrigation. We saw apricots, nut trees, tomatoes, lettuce, and many other crops at various stages of maturity. Some of the corn was more than seven feet tall and we saw Spanish onions as big as softballs bagged and waiting to be picked up.

Hundreds of spinning wind generators covered several square miles of the dry, brown hills along a section of interstate highway near Livermore. It looked very strange to see all of these contraptions on the high ridges for miles in every direction, with almost all of them turning. Of the many different types of strange-looking contraptions, some had giant pear-shaped blades perched horizontally atop vertical shafts. A fairly brisk wind was making everything turn at roughly the same speed. It was a very strange sight.

After 16 days of two-lane roads, the interstate highways seemed foreign and dangerous. Traffic was moving four abreast at 65 and 70 MPH, very close together. It was obvious how California freeway accidents can involve hundreds of cars. The temperature got noticeably cooler as we neared the coast. It was foggy where we crossed San Francisco Bay via the San Mateo Bridge. Lilli's plane arrived on time and soon after loading her luggage onto the Gold Wing we called it a day in Sunnyvale.

Day 17 - We rode from Silicon Valley to Big Basin Redwood State Park over some dramatic earthquake rifts and hills in the coastal range. We rode through a redwood forest where the trees were more than fourteen feet in diameter. They are said to be the world's tallest trees, growing to a height of 360 feet. Some are estimated to be 2,000 years old. They are found only in this narrow strip of land about 20 miles wide by 500 miles long near the Pacific coastline. The road through the redwoods is very twisty because the trees are protected and are never removed for road construction.

Between Santa Cruz and Monterey we took a side trip from our planned route into some local farmland, as we were curious to see what was growing there. We saw thousands of acres of artichokes, strawberries, lettuce, cabbage, avocado, and other crops. Huge fresh strawberries were selling at nearby fruit stands for 50 cents a basket and medium-sized artichokes were four for a dollar. We saw a large group of migrant workers picking strawberries to Latin music blaring from loudspeakers. All of the crops were irrigated, even though the area seems to get a lot of rain.

Spectacular 17-Mile Drive along the Pacific Ocean from Monterey to Carmel goes by Pebble Beach and Cypress Point. This beautiful drive was to be one of the highlights of our trip. I traveled it once by car but never by motorcycle. To our surprise and dismay we were turned away at the tollhouse and told that motorcycles are not allowed because "the noise distracts the golfers." It was a ridiculous argument against our quiet road machines, but it is a privately-owned road and there wasn't much we could do but turn around and find an alternate route.

Just before pulling up to a traffic light near Carmel on our four-lane detour, I noticed a young guy in a car behind us hanging out of the driver's window screaming obscenities. He jumped out at the light and ran toward me, yelling and using the foulest language imaginable at the top of his lungs. He kept getting angrier and louder as he screamed something about my cutting him off. It was a real bad scene at the crowded intersection. I couldn't remember what I had done to bring on his tirade. I figured the best thing to do was to calmly say I was sorry; but that only seemed to enrage him even more, and I thought at any moment he was going to take a swing at me. I was wearing an open-face helmet with both hands on the controls and Lilli was on the back. I felt if I were alone at the time and 40 or even 20 years younger, to quote the famous mayor of Carmel, he would have "made my day."

After we got out of there, I asked Bud what I had done. He said, "Nothing. Didn't you see his eyes? He was strung out on something." I was watching his hands more than his eyes. I recalled reading about California motorists who had been shot in similar confrontations. The single hour we spent around Carmel included that ugly scene, the rejection at 17-Mile Drive, a mediocre four-dollar hamburger, regular gas at a price higher than high-test anywhere else, and a strange new gas nozzle that prevents topping off the tank, not to mention the crowded four-lane detour. I thought, "Welcome to California."

The Coastal Highway from Carmel to Morro Bay is said to be another of the most beautiful roadways in America. While we were there the fog was so thick we couldn't see the famous bridge at Big Sur. At times we couldn't even see the ocean. What we did see certainly lived up to what we had heard, although it was crowded with traffic. It was the Saturday of a Laguna Seca Motorcycle Race weekend and there were hundreds of motorcyclists on the road, in addition to the hordes of cars.

During our short ride from Morro Bay on the ocean to Atascadero, 16 miles inland, the temperature rose from 65 to 95 degrees. We were scheduled to meet Ralph Spencer from Sun City, Arizona there on his new BMW. He had planned to accompany us for a week, back to his home in Sun City. When we couldn't find him, I called his home and learned that he had burned himself pretty bad and was in the hospital. Although we were disappointed that he couldn't join us, we still planned to visit with him the following week in Arizona.

Day 18 - From Atascadero we headed east on a road that I thought was our route; but about a mile out of town the road took a sudden left turn without warning, and we charged straight ahead onto some soft dirt. It took almost two hundred feet to stop. Realizing that a road without signs couldn't possibly be the state highway, we went back into town to find the right road.

It led us through several miles of tight curves and some of the strangest terrain I had ever seen. It twisted and turned through miles of high grassy mounds and ridges. There was a sign at the end saying that late movie idol James Dean, who loved to maneuver his Porche along that road, was killed in a high-speed car crash near there. Later we saw another mile-wide strip of the same odd terrain extending north and south for many miles, and we learned that it was the San Andreas Fault line.

Bud left us near Lemoore for a few days on his own side trip to Kings Canyon and Sequoia National Parks while Lilli and I went in search of ghost towns, which was her interest. As we got gas in the San Joaquin Valley I asked the attendant what was growing on both sides of the road for the past 15 miles. He said it was cotton, and then he went on to tell us enthusiastically where to look for pistachios, figs, apricots, raisin grapes, wine grapes, walnuts, and other crops.

I think the "turnout law" in California is a great idea, but all drivers don't observe it. The law apparently says it's unlawful to delay five or more vehicles on two-lane roads. Several times we were crawling along in a string of more than a dozen cars, campers and trailers for miles, led by someone moving at a snail's pace. Turnout areas are provided for slow vehicles to pull over so others can pass, but it doesn't always happen.

Yosemite National Park was a beautiful spot. It was also the most crowded park we visited. The tremendous solid granite peaks impressed me the most. They say that El Capitan is the largest single chunk of granite in the world. We chose to skip a possible side trip inside the park to Glacier Point because our stomachs told us we were already late for lunch; so we went directly to Yosemite Village rather than delay lunch two or three hours with a side trip. Yosemite Falls and Ribbon Falls were much thinner than normal due to the lack of rain. A heat wave in the valley brought the temperature to an unusual 95 degrees for several days.

We exited the park through the east end along Tioga Road, where some of the scenic highlights included Tolumne Meadows, several mountain climbers scaling the steep granite inclines, several deep-blue lakes, and finally Tioga Pass at an altitude of 9,945 feet. Our reservations were at Mammoth Lakes, one of the largest ski resorts in the far west. I tested the motel pool and it was disappointing to find that the water temperature was about the same as my body temperature. I went in but it was much more refreshing when I got out and felt the water evaporating in the gentle breezes.

Day 19 - The most outstanding highlight of the tour for Lilli was Bodie, California. Bodie is probably the best all-around ghost town in the west. It has been made into a state park, which brings with it a discipline that reduces vandalism. A hundred years ago it was a sinful and lawless gold-mining town. "Good-bye God, I am going to Bodie" was an evening prayer recited by a little girl whose family was moving there. A preacher once called Bodie "A sea of sin, lashed by the tempests of lust and passion." Bodie had 65 saloons and countless brothels in its heyday. We rode over a few miles of loose gravel to get there and later we rode eleven miles of terrible washboard dirt road to exit a different way. Although a large percentage of the buildings were destroyed by fire, set by vandals earlier in the century, about a hundred buildings remain, including a church, a school, the jailhouse, several stores, and many residences. Lilli and I enjoyed walking through the town for about two hours and we also visited an interesting museum there. Some of the buildings in town were adorned with fancy metal siding made from patterned, Victorian sheet metal. Other buildings owned by less affluent people had flattened tin cans for siding.

We tried to reach Gilbert, Nevada, a small ghost town west of Tonopah. It was 101 degrees in the surrounding desert at the time. After about a mile of churning through deep, loose sand, the bike's coolant temperature rose higher than I had ever seen it. I was hot too and exhausted from struggling to maintain control riding double. We eventually decided to skip Gilbert rather than risk overheating the bike and myself. A flagman on nearby US 95 told us later that he once got his four-wheel-drive truck stuck several miles up that road and never did find a town.

Day 20 - Our search for ghost towns and partial ghost towns continued with a visit to Belmont, nestled in the hills 47 miles northwest of Tonopah. Belmont was the county seat of Nye County in the 1860s, as well as a prosperous silver-mining town with a population of about 2,000. A large, brick building that served briefly as Nye County Courthouse is one of the only buildings remaining. Efforts by the State of Nevada were underway to restore the courthouse as a historic site. A deserted cemetery that we visited there contained the graves of many children, which was evidence of an arduous lifestyle where only the strongest and healthiest survived.

In Manhattan, another former mining town, a tiny, abandoned Catholic church sits high atop a hill overlooking a few occupied buildings and several abandoned buildings that probably hold many memories of a prosperous and colorful past. Round Mountain, north of Manhattan, was another gold boomtown that we visited. It seems to be reviving to some degree with renewed mining activity. Later we searched in vain for signs of Hannapah but found only jeep tracks leading to deserted mines, but no buildings.

After our 2-day tour of the ghost towns, we returned to Tonopah to rejoin Bud. The mining museum there has an interesting historic display of central Nevada mining operations and of the people who lived and worked there. There was also a large display of old mining paraphernalia around the outside of the building. The museum features mostly the towns of Goldfield and Tonopah. We also visited Goldfield, once Nevada's second largest city, with a population of 40,000. Only a few hundred people still live there.

Day 21 - We saw a sign as we left Tonopah saying that the next gas was in Caliente, 196 miles away. At one point we were delayed a few minutes by roadwork and had to wait for a pilot car. The girl who stopped us there said that she had been at her post for an hour and a half and had seen only three cars. Cows grazed in the desert on whatever they could find to eat, which wasn't much. I didn't see any sign of water for miles. I assumed that the cattle probably "tank-up" in the morning and graze all day in the scorching heat. The natural flora consists of scarce range grasses, tumbleweed, and several varieties of sagebrush. We saw a few spiny Joshua trees and occasionally we saw scrawny cedars and juniper bushes. Central Nevada is mostly hot, desolate terrain of sagebrush and sand, with ranches spaced many miles apart.

West of St. George we saw alfalfa, hay, and potatoes growing, helped along by much watering. Nearby Snow Canyon State Park has picturesque scenery with brown and white sandstone outcroppings interspersed with fields of black lava. The afternoon temperature in St. George was 102 degrees. The sun blazing in my face felt like a sun lamp too close to the skin.

Day 22 - We located Grafton, a ghost town near Zion National Park, although we were unable to find an entrance to the town. We tried several possible accesses, but they all had signs like "No Trespassing", "Keep Out" and "Not the road to Grafton." Eventually we viewed it from across a stream in a farmer's field where we settled for looking at the old buildings through binoculars. Zion is a small although beautiful national park, the highlights of which include spectacular sheer cliffs, canyon landscapes, and sparkling streams. A road with several switchback turns leads up to a mile-long tunnel; beyond which, we traveled the scenic Mt. Carmel Highway. Most roads in Zion Park have a reddish tint, probably from having been made from crushed native stone. The highlight of our day was Zion Canyon Scenic Drive where we enjoyed spectacular close-up views of the colorful mountains.

Bryce Canyon is a fascinating national park with very strange rock formations, most of which are salmon-colored or white. We stopped at several viewpoints for more than 20 miles along the canyon rim and took photos. Hiking along the many trails down in the canyon between the odd rock formations seems to be a favorite activity of many visitors, but we were content with our views from the rim.

Dixie National Forest and Cedar Breaks National Monument offered other unique scenic highlights. From Panguitch, Utah we climbed steadily from the Sevier River Valley through a beautiful aspen, spruce, pine, and cedar forest to the 10,300-foot level where we found huge alpine meadows filled with red, white, blue, and yellow mountain flowers. A huge flock of sheep was grazing in one lush meadow near the 10,000-foot level. We saw much more of the salmon-colored rock formations from the Cedar Breaks overlook, which afforded a panoramic view of the countryside.

As we sped along one of the highways I kept noticing a strange feeling on several of the turns. Both wheels would squirrel a little as if there were ridges along the road surface. When we stopped by the high meadows for a photo, I noticed that the road underfoot felt very strange. Although the tar wasn't sticky, my feet moved on the road surface and left a half-inch-deep footprint wherever I stood. After learning of this unique road hazard we were extra careful on the tar roads in the area.

Day 23 - We rode to the north rim of the Grand Canyon from our motel in Kanab, Utah. The temperature dropped several degrees as we neared the rim at the 8,000-foot level. The brisk, clean air felt refreshing after the heat of the past few days. I thought the scenery along the Kaibab Plateau on the northern approach to the canyon was far nicer than the scenery along the approach to the south rim that I had used on earlier trips. We saw aspen and pine trees, beautiful meadows, and we saw deer grazing. There appeared to be very little water running in the Colorado River. I had heard that the river was getting smaller every year because of increased water usage for irrigation and recreational use upstream, but seeing it was still a surprise. At the distance we were from the river it would probably appear small, although it was definitely narrower than I remembered.

Along US 89 we got a spectacular view of Echo Cliffs and the huge Painted Desert in the Navajo Indian Reservation, with its layered shades of salmon, gray, white, brown, and blue. The temperature rose to over 100 degrees near Cameron and hours of dry heat and dehydration eventually got to Lilli. She said, "Please stop the bike. I think I'm going to faint!" She was very pale and weak and had to lie on the ground while I quickly put together an ice pack with ice from our cooler. She sipped ice water while I filled one of my clean tube socks with ice. I tied it at the top and used that with more ice water to cool her head, face and neck. She rode with it around her neck, and every twenty minutes or so I would find a way to get out of the sun so we could refill the sock, as the ice melted very quickly. We stopped for lunch and stopped again for a fresh bag of ice and cool drinks. Near Black Canyon City the temperature was 105. We rested for about 20 minutes in the shade before descending into Sun City, where I said to Lilli and Bud that it would get much hotter. Bud said, "How could it possibly get any hotter than this?" An hour later in Sun City it was 111.

Day 24 - Our Sun City stop was the first I had scheduled for servicing my bike. We did the service in Ralph's garage in 112-degree heat. Although we had covered 9,000 miles so far, my plan called for merely changing the oil and filter, inspecting the machine, and making minor adjustments. I had mounted two long distance tires a few days before we left, with the hope that they would go the distance. We spent much of the day visiting with Ralph and Trudi. Riding in 112 degree heat is like standing in front of a blast furnace. Some people who have never felt 112 degrees might say, "Yes, but you don't feel it because it's dry heat." This common myth became a joke between us. People who never rode in that kind of heat might also think that the breeze on the bike would make it feel cooler. Actually it has the opposite effect. Whenever the air temperature exceeds body temperature, it tends to raise the body temperature above its 98.6 and actually dehydrates the body much faster. To compound the problem, the air behind the fairing is at least 5 degrees higher than the ambient temperature because of the heat from the engine. The pool water at the motel was also more than 100 degrees, and it wasn't even refreshing to take a shower because the water from the cold-water tap was around 90 degrees.

Day 25 - The heat doesn't let up at night either and the temperature at 6 AM was 91 degrees. After seeing Lilli off safely at the airport we headed southwest toward Gila Bend and Why, where it was already over 100 degrees by 10 AM. We saw a lot of irrigated cotton west of Phoenix. I mentioned to the woman proprietor of a small general store in Why, "It gets pretty warm around here, doesn't it." She looked at me as if I had insulted her with my understatement and she enunciated loudly, "It gets HOT here!" We saw giant saguaro cactus and an abundance of other strange flora in the Papago Indian Reservation that grows only in the hottest deserts.

I had one of my closest calls of the trip when a huge vulture that had been feeding on a small carcass on the opposite side of the road took flight directly across my path. At the speed I was traveling, nearly 70 MPH, he would have shattered my windshield and in all likelihood knocked me clear off the motorcycle. I ducked and braced for the impact that never came. Bud said the huge creature made a spectacular evasive move, missing the top of my windshield by less than an inch. It's a good thing I ducked!

We stopped briefly at Bisbee to peer down into the Lavender Pit Queen Mine, which is a 950-foot-deep, open-pit copper mine where 380 million tons of ore were extracted before it went out of operation in 1976. The nicest scenery of the day was through Coronado National Forest near Huachuca City. We saw a lot of yucca and a few century plants blooming in the sun. Contrary to popular belief the 12-foot-tall century plants actually bloom more than once in their lifetime.

Day 26 - The Morenci mine near Clifton is one of the largest open-pit copper mines in the world. Billions of tons of ore have been extracted from Morenci, which is still an active mine. Trains that haul copper ore from the mine look so small you have to look carefully to spot them, even through binoculars, as they move around in the tremendous pit.

US Route 666 from Morenci to Alpine has more turns and tight switchback curves than any road I have ever traveled. We noticed one S-curve sign in the mountains that said "10 MPH - Next 6 Miles." There was no traffic at all on the road and the scenery through Gila National Forest was the best of the day.

A brief rain shower with a little hail at the 9,000-foot level couldn't dampen our spirits, although one might actually get tired of seemingly endless switch-back curves after a while.

In Petrified Forest National Park there were thousands of petrified logs and pieces of logs lying around on top of the sand. It is said that they were buried under mud, silt, and volcanic ash as long as 200-million years ago. The lack of oxygen prevented them from decaying and the original wood fibers were gradually replaced with silica deposits from the soil. Later the area rose far above sea level and natural erosion eventually exposed the petrified logs. We visited several viewpoints in both the Petrified Forest and the Painted Desert. It's said to be bad luck to take any of the petrified wood as souvenirs

Canyon de Chelly National Monument is a beautiful spot in the Navajo Indian Reservation. This canyon, which typifies colorful southwestern Native American culture, once served as an ancestral stronghold for the Navajo. Many ruins of prehistoric dwellings can be seen perched precariously along the canyon walls, which drop 400 to 700 feet straight down to the canyon floor. Indians still live and farm in the canyon, as well as on the high ground above the canyon.

Monument Valley Navajo Tribal Park in Utah is owned and operated by the Navajo Nation. Every spectacular freestanding butte and rock formation in the valley is unique. Many early western movies were made there, including "Stagecoach" and "My Darling Clementine." Nearby Valley of the Gods and Mexican Hat are equally colorful attractions with buttes, huge mesas, and desert landscapes that seem to change color as the sun moves across the sky. Except for the San Juan River, which flows through Mexican Hat, north of Monument Valley, no perennial streams flow in the valley and very few people live there because of the harsh, dry climate.

Day 28 – Ancient Indian ruins at Mesa Verde National Park in southwestern Colorado make this the most interesting and educational of all the parks we visited. The Anasazi, meaning "ancient ones," who lived and farmed there between 1100 and 1300 AD suddenly abandoned their cliff homes for no apparent reason. We viewed the spectacular Cliff Palace, Spruce Tree House, and several other cliff dwellings from viewpoints on Chapin Mesa. We also browsed through the archeological museum before taking a scenic, 21-mile drive with sharp curves and steep grades to many of the viewpoints along the mesa.

US Route 550 from Durango to Montrose, Colorado is another of my own favorite roadways. We climbed through beautiful San Juan National Forest, over Coal Bank Hill Pass (10,640 feet), Molas Divide (10,910 feet), and Red Mountain Pass (11,018 feet) to the mining town of Silverton, nestled in the mountains at an altitude of 9,318 feet. Scenic highlights of the day included many spectacular snowcapped peaks, abandoned gold mines around Red Mountain, and later our canyon descent past Ouray into Grand Junction.

Day 29 - After arriving at Bud's sister Posey's home in Grand Junction we enjoyed a full day of socializing. She took us in her station wagon on a tour of Colorado National Monument with its red-rock formations and sheer cliffs. We had a picnic lunch in an aspen grove atop one of the mesas. Western Colorado has the largest mesas we saw anywhere. That evening we had a delicious home-cooked meal of steak and sweet corn at Posey's home. Bud changed his rear tire there with one he had shipped earlier.

Day 30 - From Grand Junction we returned into the Rockies alongside the Colorado and Roaring Fork Rivers on a spectacular climb through the high mountain country toward the Continental Divide and Independence Pass (12,095 feet). We rode through spruce and aspen forests with steep, rocky cliffs and rushing white-water streams close to the road. I met a car towing a house trailer on a steep uphill curve as we approached the divide. He was apparently being pushed much faster than he cared to be by his heavy load. If I had been in a car he would certainly have knocked me clear off the road into the Roaring Fork River. I swerved toward the shoulder as far as I dared as the car and huge trailer took the entire road.

East of the divide we had another spectacular view of snowy mountain peaks and beautiful alpine meadows. We scaled the divide again at Freemont Pass and were almost to Loveland Pass on our "Rocky Mountain ramble" when a state highway employee rushed out to stop us. He said a truck was afire on the east side of the divide and traffic was backed up both ways on the narrow, cliff-edged highway unable to turn around. We detoured through Eisenhower Tunnel, from where we headed south for Pikes Peak on a gravel road over Guanella Pass

(11,665 feet). It was a disappointment to miss Loveland Pass, which I had been very impressed with on an earlier tour.

Our ride up to the 14,110-foot summit of Pikes Peak was an exciting experience. It was the highest altitude we reached on our trip. The last 15 miles was a steep gravel road without railings that was smooth to the edge, with sheer drops of several hundred feet. Following very close on too many dirt roads finally took its toll on Bud's air cleaner. He had to stop to rap out some of the dirt before he was able to reach the summit. Later we descended side by side because of the thick dust.

Day 31 - At Royal Gorge Bud took the aerial tram ride across the 1,100-foot gorge and back while I took a more sedate cable railway car ride down into the gorge. Later we walked out onto the bridge together and peered over the rail at the river far below. We recalled seeing on TV where people jumped off the bridge with long bungee cords tied to their waists. They would drop most of the way to the Arkansas River before reaching the end of the cord's stretch. The wooden planks on the bridge clattered loudly as we rode the bikes across later.

US 50 from Royal Gorge to Poncha Springs is a 50-mile stretch of very scenic, twisty bike road along the headwaters of the Arkansas River where we saw many people white-water rafting, fishing, and camping. We turned south over Poncha Pass into a beautiful 10-mile-wide valley, which got progressively wider and more scenic as we rode south. While getting gas at a small general store in Villa Grove I commented to the attendant what a nice day it was. The guy turned to me with a smile and said, "It's always nice here."

Route 17 from Antonito to Chama, New Mexico is yet another of my personal favorite roadways. It goes over La Magna Pass and Cumbres Pass into a beautiful alpine meadow with blue, white, lavender, and yellow wild flowers. The surrounding grassy hills are accentuated with occasional deep-green evergreen trees and cattle grazed in lush green meadows. A small steam-powered train that carries passengers on round-trip excursions from Chama chugged up through the valley.

A spectacular western lightning storm struck as we neared Antonito. A long and almost transparent curtain of rain draped all the way to the ground from the bottom of a huge dark cloud more than 10,000 feet up. Suddenly a huge bolt of lightning streaked down through the thin curtain all the way to

126

the ground. The fierce looking bright streak shimmered and crackled for a full second before it cracked very loudly and disappeared. Similar long bolts of lightning flashed several times close around us as we rode into the valley. It was one of the most awesome and terrifying displays of nature I had ever seen and it made me feel very small and insignificant.

The road through Carson National Forest in New Mexico between Tierra Amarilla and Tres Pedras was another exceptionally scenic ride with wide, sweeping turns, high meadows, and spectacular views of the San Juan Mountains where we saw lightning storms and rain showers in the distance. From Questa to Eagles Nest past the Red River Ski Area was another highlight, as was our ride through Cimarron Canyon State Park near the Philmont National Boy Scout Ranch.

Our original plan was for the two of us to visit Bud's brother John in Amarillo for 2½ days, but when I heard during our trip that Big Bend was one of the more spectacular national parks I decided to split for a few days on my own to visit there. Bud and I needed a break from each other for a few days after having spent so much continuous time together, especially since we were unable to replenish our supply of whiskey sour mix, which helped us to relax in the evening and relieve the tensions. Before reaching Raton, I put together a three-day revision to my route sheet.

Day 32 - The 107 degrees in Carlsbad made me wonder if I was doing the right thing by heading south into the heat again. It began to get to me after several hours of exposure, in spite of stopping often to drink ice water and put water into my shoes and my helmet. I experienced lightheaded spells several times, which was at least partly due to the buildup of tensions after having lived together for more than a month.

The long ride alone afforded me with hours of reflection on the trip, including an awareness of the greatness of this land, and I thanked God for my opportunity to see it all. I thought about the many things I had learned about earth sciences, geology, anthropology, volcanology, agriculture, and other things. We saw where the earth's plates buckled, shifted, split, rose thousands of feet, eroded, and exploded; and we saw where it rained a lot and where it hardly rained at all and we learned the reasons why. We saw where gold, silver, copper, molybdenum, lead, oil, and other minerals were extracted from the ground; and we learned where many crops, trees, and other flora thrive and where others barely cling to life or are unable to survive at all. The temperature reached 108 in Pecos, Texas where I stopped for the night.

Day 33 - I left Pecos before first light in an attempt to avoid the heat, but by the time I got to Big Bend it was 105. Many areas of the park reminded me of the surface of the moon. Big Bend is a volcanic park with lava rock, pumice, and large craggy volcanic outcroppings everywhere. The flora that grows there consists mainly of cactus, creosote bush, yucca, sotol, and mesquite. Whatever rain falls in Big Bend falls in the Basin, an area where green leafy shrubs, mountain mahogany, and other small evergreen trees seem to thrive. Signs posted in the Basin warn of mountain lions. I saw where the Rio Grande River cuts through the massive, picturesque Santa Elena Canyon, which is the familiar scene often featured in promotional photos of the Rio Grande Valley.

Farm Road 170 from Big Bend to Presidio is one of the most scenic roadways in Texas, affording spectacular views of the Rio Grande Valley. Rain sometimes washes sand and water across low areas of the roadway as flash floods rush toward the river. I rode over 16 percent grades, off-camber turns, and several deep dips where an inch or more of soft sand covered the road. Taking it easy was the order of the day, while hot was a good name for the day. I welcomed the light rain showers late that afternoon as I headed for Fort Stockton. I didn't stop to put on my rain suit because the cool rain felt so good.

Day 34 - On my return north to meet Bud I passed through Delaware Basin, probably one of the richest oil fields in America. I saw hundreds of pumps operating to draw the heavy crude oil from the otherwise dry, mesquite-covered wasteland north of Monahans, Texas. After rejoining Bud in Amarillo we passed many miles of field corn that seemed to be eight feet tall, planted along the southern edge of the Great Plains. We also saw massive grain elevators and huge, beef-cattle feeder pens.

Day 35 - We enjoyed the least expensive meals and motel room of the trip in southern Oklahoma, where we paid $24 for our double room at a motel in McAlester, and I enjoyed a full, baked-chicken dinner in the motel dining room for $1.99. The people were outgoing and friendly everywhere we went in Oklahoma. We saw several old abandoned houses of dirt farmers who probably migrated west during the big drought and dust storms of the 1930s, but otherwise we saw many fertile, abundant farms.

Day 36 - We stopped to visit with Jack Piner and longtime enduro rider Leroy Winters at his Honda cycle shop south of Fort Smith, Arkansas. He took us on a tour of his place and showed us his more than 30 species of ducks, white swans, and rare black swans. He also showed us his homemade ultra-light helicopter and his collection of 1960s Hondas. The ducks and swans occupy an area of his backyard where he once had a luxurious swimming pool. Later Leroy took us out in his old Cadillac stretch limo and treated us to lunch. We talked about the old times we shared at bygone enduros like the Jack Pine, Little Burr, and the Berkshire International.

Day 37 – The three of us inspected my rear tire before we left Leroy's shop. We agreed that in spite of its 14,000 miles, it should have at least another 1500 miles of rubber left to get me home; but after riding only 80 miles of Ozark Mountain curves between Ozark and Eureka Springs, followed by another 80 miles of rough road from Bakersfield to Doniphan I checked it again and saw that it was already bald all the way around. Only a few hundred miles of really spirited riding had done the tire in. About 60 miles consisted of an extremely coarse surface that made the tires roar, and probably also made it wear much faster.

Our approach to the Mississippi River was over several scarcely-traveled Missouri farm roads through seemingly-endless fields of corn, sorghum, soybeans, cotton, and rice. We found the Dorena Ferry landing and watched the tiny ferry as it plied its way across the river with a single car aboard. The ferry landing consisted of a gravel road on the levee with a few planks laid out to support the ferry's steel ramp. The attendant told us that one car or two motorcycles was the minimum load for a crossing. The fare was three dollars per bike, so he collected a total of only $6 for that crossing.

As soon as it backed away from the levee, the tiny tugboat section pivoted around to a pushing position while the barge section remained steady. It took only about ten minutes to cross the river to Hickman, Kentucky, a typical, small river town, where we landed against the eastern levee. The attendant said the river was ten feet below normal. There were no cars waiting as we rode the bikes up and over the dirt levee into

Hickman. A short while later I located a new rear tire at Abernathy's Honda and Harley-Davidson shop in Union City, Tennessee. I changed it at our motel in Clarksville that evening.

Day 38 - From Clarksville to Bland, Virginia we enjoyed a full day of twisty roads through scenic farmland and national forests that epitomized our trip. It was one of our most challenging days from a riding standpoint. We had very little letup from thousands of curves and hills past countless corn and tobacco fields in northern Tennessee, through the backwoods country of Kentucky, and finally through the hill country of southwestern Virginia near Cumberland Gap. We covered 475 miles, which included a great deal of passing on two-lane roads.

Day 39 - One of my all-time favorite country rides is in western Virginia where a series of seldom-used county and state roads run parallel with the West Virginia state line for about 280 miles from Benhams to Harrisonburg. The valley is neat and clean and our route took us through scenic landscapes with small farms, silos, barns, homes, and picturesque churches. Cows grazing on the steep, sloping hillsides and crops growing among the green rolling hills accentuated the beauty of the ride.

Day 40 - Every time I plan a trip I experiment with a different route across Pennsylvania. This time we began our final day in Chambersburg and passed many colorful farms between Doylesburg and New Bloomfield. We saw many Amish farmers driving horse-drawn buckboards along the country roads. We passed the Pennsylvania National Race Course for horses, Indiantown Gap Military Reservation and the Flying Dutchmans Motorcycle Race Course before traffic began to get heavy around Pen Argyl. We crossed the Delaware River at Portland Bridge into the heavier traffic of central New Jersey.

Before we split for our respective homes we had lunch at a small country diner in northern New Jersey where we reflected on the trip. One of the things we talked about was why people go to foreign lands to ride when there are so many outstanding things to see right here in our own beautiful country. Even though we saw a great deal on our 40-day trip, there is still so much more out there to see; and even though Bud seemed reluctant to make any commitments for next year, I could tell that his appetite for long tours had been whetted.

COPPER CANYON WITH A GOLD WING

My annual Daytona pilgrimage usually provides me with an excellent opportunity for a late winter tour. I remember being at a motel once in Fort Stockton, Texas on one of these pre-Daytona tours when a guy noticing my license plate said, "Boy, you're a long way from home. Where are you headed?" I said, "I'm on my way to Daytona Beach." He hesitated for a moment and then he laughed and said, "You must have taken a wrong turn somewhere." On a few occasions I would meet my friend Ralph Spencer there. He would ride in from Arizona and together we would tour scenic areas like the Rio Grande Valley, the hill country north of San Antonio, and visit the Nimitz War Museum in Fredericksburg. Eventually I would turn east for Daytona Beach and Ralph would head back to Sun City.

This year I decided to visit Barranca del Cobre, or Copper Canyon, in the Sierra Madre Occidental Mountains of southwestern Chihuahua province in Mexico. When I told Ralph about my plan he said he wouldn't travel in Mexico on a bet. Having already made up my mind, I proceeded to prepare for taking the trip alone. In the months leading up to it I got lots of advice from friends about not drinking the water or eating vegetable salads, and I heard horror stories about people disappearing, never to be heard from again. "You are not really going to Mexico alone!" was a typical comment.

The day after leaving on my tour I realized I had forgotten my birth certificate. Although thousands of people enter Mexico every day without birth certificates, one is required to visit the interior. I wondered whether I should return home for it, ask Lilli to send it to Presidio, Texas by express mail, or should I take my chances and put together a Plan B just in case I don't make it across the border. I chose the latter and decided on Carlsbad Caverns as my Plan B.

I arrived at the Mexican immigration building ready to give it my best shot. As I stood in line at the counter I felt a strong urge to head for the men's room. I couldn't have become afflicted already! -- I was in the country for all of five minutes. On the contrary, I was pretty sure I had acquired my problem in Texas. I suspected a small greasy-spoon restaurant where I had stopped for breakfast. I broke from the line and hurried for the door with the silhouette of a man and the sign "Hombres." To my dismay there was no seat ring on the commode, no paper on the roll, and no water in the sink. I improvised the best I could and thought, "Welcome to Mexico!" Thank goodness for the extra napkins I usually help myself to at restaurants.

I returned to the line where a pretty senorita behind the counter motioned that I was next. I told her briefly of my plans and the first thing she said was, "I see your birth certificate, please." I said, "I was born in New York and I have my New York State driver's license here that tells you how old I am. What else would you like to know?" She slowly turned her head side to side and said she must see my birth certificate. I proceeded to show her my Medicare card, my retirement ID card, my Golden Age Passport for the national parks, my AARP card and my Blue Cross card. I even showed her pictures of my grandchildren and an honorary New York State Police PBA card. When all of that seemed to be in vain, I appealed to her good nature and told her how I had just traveled 3,000 miles to be a tourist in her beautiful country and how I would hate to have to go to Carlsbad Caverns instead. That did it. She shook her pencil at me and said, "Next time you no forget."

I had read about Mexican vehicle insurance requirements and I asked where I could get the insurance. "No need insurance" was her answer and I was directed to another counter for my vehicle permit. As the next agent was finishing up I also asked him about the insurance. He pointed back to the previous counter and said, "Get insurance there." I explained that the senorita just said I don't need insurance, upon which they exchanged a few words in Spanish across the room. He turned to me and shrugged, saying, "No need insurance." I learned later that you only need insurance in case of an accident, in which case you BETTER have it.

I located a bank in Ojinaga where I got an exchange rate of about 2700 pesos to the dollar. It took me a while to get used to the pesos and dividing by an odd number like 2700 in my head. It cost about 40,000 pesos per night for a hotel room, 15,000 pesos for dinner and about 9700 pesos for a gasoline fill-up. I figured that comes to about $14.80, $5.50 and $3.60 respectively. The gas was the best buy, although it was only about 81-octane in the remote areas. I estimated gas to be less than 80 cents per gallon. Higher-octane gas is available only in the larger cities.

As I left Ojinaga for the hinterlands I noticed that the government apparently doesn't spend much time or money cleaning up along the highways. It looks like all of the trash that gets thrown out or dropped there, stays there. If an animal is killed on the highway it lays there until scavengers finish it off. During my visit to Mexico I saw some of the biggest "road kills" I had ever seen, including a full-sized cow, a horse, and several dogs in various stages of decomposition. You could smell some of them for long distances. Much of the trash looked like it was there for quite a while. It was a real mess around Ojinaga.

I was stopped about 20 miles from the border at a Mexican immigration check in the mountains. A uniformed official asked where I was going and he asked to see my permit. Upon producing the permit, he looked around my windshield and said, "Schticka, where schticka?" As he continued to walk around the bike I tried to explain that I didn't know anything about stickers, but I would go back to Ojinaga to get one if that was necessary. After a few more minutes of studying my permit and looking at me like I was in real trouble, he handed it back and said, "No. No need schticka." I had the distinct impression that a few thousand pesos would have been accepted. I thought about the senorita at the customs desk and wondered if I would have gotten the sticker if I had shown her my birth certificate. Maybe that's also why she said I didn't need insurance. She may have assumed I would never get by the security check.

The highways were easy to follow in the open country but in the cities and towns the route signs were scarce. I missed a sign in the town of Aldama, a Chihuahua suburb, and got into some back streets that were rough dirt with quite a bit of mud. I stopped and asked for directions to get back on my route. I learned early that I could make out better with my limited vocabulary of Spanish than by trying to get someone to understand my English. They seemed to feel more comfortable with me in the disadvantaged position of struggling with their language. I found very few people in the interior who spoke as much English as I did Spanish, and I don't really speak Spanish.

My rear tire slipped out a few times on sand traces on the mountain roads and I had to dodge a few wandering farm animals and big loose stones; but otherwise I had no problem traveling on the numbered highways. The drivers were generally courteous and most signs are clear enough, although I couldn't translate all of them. At one place I saw a sign, "Topes 500m." As I was trying to figure out what topes were, I saw another -- "Topes 300m," followed almost immediately by "Topes 100m." I thought it sounded a lot like something to eat and I was looking around for a roadside stand when I suddenly hit the first huge speed bump. The front forks bottomed, followed by the frame smacking the 18" wide by 6" high bizarre bump in the road. Fortunately I was going about 25 MPH at the time. I hate to think of the consequences of hitting one of those at 60 or 65.

Once as I was cruising along on a fairly good two-lane highway I saw a sign with an arrow pointing to what looked like a narrow dirt road to my right. I think it said something like "Divisero." I thought it was saying that there was a town in that direction called Divisero. About half a mile farther down the road I realized I was driving on the wrong side of a divided highway with trucks coming at me. The sign apparently meant that a divided highway was coming up and I should have switched over to the other side at that point.

The first time I got gas I pumped until my tank was full and handed the attendant a 10,000-peso note. As I waited for my change I got a really strange look that I didn't understand and his hand was still out. My first thought was that I hadn't given him enough, so I started to hand him another 10,000-peso note as I glanced over at the pump. It registered 9160, so I quickly pulled back the second 10,000 and held out my own hand for change. Finally he dropped about eight heavy 100 peso coins in my hand with an unfriendly grunt. I figured out later that each of those big coins was worth less than four cents and that my total change was around 30 cents. Obviously they don't like making change for small amounts.

I found most of the eating places to be relatively clean. Of course I passed up many where I didn't have the courage to try. I also steered clear of the fancy places to avoid inevitable delays. I learned that most restaurants in Mexico begin cooking the food after it's ordered. I figured that's why enchiladas and burritos are so popular -- because they're quick. Restaurants in Mexico range from the fanciest down to some real cockroach havens. I don't know if they have government health controls.

Luckily I spotted a sign pointing to a bypass of downtown Chihuahua. I wasn't ready to get lost in a major city, so I took it. I had some difficulty following the bypass until I finally spotted a sign for Cuauhtemoc, which was my next town. Once in Cuauhtemoc I looked for the road to San Juanito. I carried three different maps from three different sources, all of which showed a direct road to San Juanito. I asked several people for directions and learned that the road I was looking for simply doesn't exist. The only way to get to San Juanito from Cuauhtemoc was by way of La Junta. None of my maps showed a continuous route going that way. I didn't have much confidence in Mexican maps after that.

As I was picking my way through some rough cobblestones in San Juanito at about 10 MPH, a squad of Mexican soldiers stepped out into the road and blocked my way with automatic rifles and pretty serious looks. The first thing that crossed my mind was the incident a few years earlier when some nuns were murdered and buried in shallow graves in El Salvador. I was glad I was in a town. One of the young soldiers, who appeared to be the leader, said something nervously in Spanish. Just as nervously, I answered, "No comprendo." A different soldier pointed his gun at the camera bag hanging from my belt and said in halting English, "You got gun?" I answered, "No -- no. No gun. Camara. Fotografica." Two of them walked around to my side and looked at the holster-shaped bag on my hip. They exchanged a few words in Spanish, studied the bag a little more, and finally allowed me to pass. I was not about to reach for the camera.

The road from San Juanito to Creel crosses the Continental Divide at least once. I guessed that the altitude at the divide was about 8,500 feet. The bike gave me no problems at that altitude, even with the low-octane Mexican gas. I had anticipated a problem by carrying octane booster in a can but I never had to use it. There was some snow in the woods at the higher elevations, but not very much. The altitude at Creel, where I stayed for two nights, is about 7,650 feet. Altitudes in Mexico are stated in meters.

The city of Creel is in Tarahumara Indian country in the heart of the Copper Canyon region. The Tarahumara retain many rites, laws, and customs from ancient times, and they are friendly to tourists. Barranca del Cobre is a national park near Creel that attracts visitors from Chihuahua and other parts of Mexico as well as from the United States. A scenic tourist railway passes through the entire length of Copper Canyon.

135

Trains carrying motor-home caravans on flatcars stop at Creel and lay overnight there. I heard that the tracks cling precariously to the edges of the steep canyon walls as the train winds slowly through the scenic mountains. Most of these motor caravans originate in the United States. Early one morning I spoke with a few tourists sitting in their motor homes on the train. After two days in Mexico it felt good to hear English spoken at me again.

It was apparently the off-season at Creel. I was one of the only guests registered at the hotel. My room could best be described as rustic. Temperatures dropped to the mid twenties at night and the only heat was from a tiny wood stove in the corner when it was lit. I searched the area in vain after dark for some kindling wood to start a fire. The only wood provided was 2" diameter pieces that needed help to ignite, so I went without a fire the first night. I learned the next day that the big Pepsi bottle near the stove was filled with kerosene for lighting the fire. I had plenty of heat the second night.

The floors were bare wood with scatter rugs and the bed was very uncomfortable. The corners of the thin mattress rose when I sat on the bed, while the corners of the flimsy, fitted sheet pulled off at the same time. The mattress under the fitted sheet was covered with a moisture-proof plastic cover that crinkled every time I moved. The blanket was like a heavy braided rug. When I got under it I had trouble breathing, so I decided to put on my hi-tech long johns and socks, and sleep with just the sheet and bedspread. The temperature inside the room in the morning was about 50 degrees. The entry door to the bathroom was only about 5' 10" high. Every time I entered with my 6' 4" frame I banged my head, which was particularly annoying at night when I was half-asleep. The hotel brochure described the rooms as "without luxury, but clean."

Breakfast was served at the hotel restaurant starting at 8:30 AM. From the time I usually got up I had two hours to explore the town before breakfast was served. The town was pretty rustic too, if not shabby. I left on my first full-day loop a little after nine, much later than I would have liked to leave. From a small hand-drawn map in the motel brochure I learned that there are actually several canyon accesses in the Barranca del Cobre area. I decided to head for La Bufa in the Canyon de Batopilas, 75 miles south of Creel, which is said to have the nicest scenery.

The two-lane macadam road leading south from Creel was well-maintained and scenic. The macadam consisted of crushed red stone similar to roads in our own Zion National Park. Much of the scenery reminded me of central Arizona. Twenty-four miles south of Creel the road changed to two-lane dirt with loose stones, potholes, and a rough washboard surface. It gradually descended for another 20 miles, where I located the turnoff for La Bufa. The La Bufa road soon narrowed to a single lane and continued downward through the Indian village of Kirare, where the Tarahumara inhabitants have one of the most primitive cultures in the Sierras.

I stopped briefly in Kirare and was immediately surrounded by children who acted like they had never seen a big motorcycle before. Everyone was friendly and smiling. I didn't try to use my limited vocabulary of survival Spanish because I figured they probably had their own language or dialect and I'd probably get along better if I just smiled. Less than a half-mile beyond the village the road dwindled to two tire ruts, which began to descend at a much steeper angle. It led to the edge of the canyon, an ideal spot for photos. I could see for many miles up and down the canyon and I could see a bridge across the Rio Urique at the foot of the canyon. It was a long way off and I wondered if it was on the same road that I was on.

I checked my watch and my gas and I did some quick figuring to estimate if I could make it all the way down and back to Creel before I ran out of gas, daylight, or both. I decided to go for it, at least until two o'clock when I would reassess the situation. There were several partial washouts in the road and many loose, round stones. At times it looked like even a four-wheel-drive vehicle would have a problem with traction on the steep descent, not to mention coming back, which concerned me a little. Certainly I would have a problem in a few spots if I met someone coming the other way. On one steep descent I had to apply both brakes as much as I dared on some loose stones because I kept gaining speed. Both wheels skidded for several feet before I was finally able to regain control and stop the bike. I looked down between my forearm and my leg and I could see several hundred feet down a rocky cliff. That brought a few cold chills down my back and a lump in my throat, but I continued.

At one viewpoint where I had a panoramic view of the canyon I could see several hairpin turns below me. By then I was quite sure the road was taking me to the river. I got to the bridge across the Rio Urique at two o'clock sharp. I took a few photos there, peeled off a few layers of clothes, turned the big bike around, and started back up the hill. I estimated La Bufa to be another several miles from there over similar gravel roads. The temperature at the foot of the canyon was in the mid-eighties. The ride back to Kirare was more than 8 miles from the river, for which I used first gear all the way. The rear wheel broke traction several times on the steep climb, but for the most part I had enough traction to get back out as long as I was careful with the throttle. The 8-mile climb to Kirare took about an hour, which included stopping a few times for photos.

I met an Indian with two cows about a third of the way up. The bike frightened the cows and they lunged for the sides. I shut off the engine as quickly as I could as one cow turned toward the cliff side of the narrow road and the other cow climbed the embankment. The first cow stopped, avoiding a tremendous drop off the cliff, but the other cow climbed to a precarious ridge about 15 feet above the road. I held my breath when he came to the very edge and the unstable bank began to give way under his hooves. I didn't think the Indian would be very happy about losing one of his cows so as soon as the cow turned briefly away from the edge I started the motor as quietly as I could and churned my way out of there. I figured he could deal with the problem better if I wasn't around.

Near the top I met a four-wheel-drive pickup coming toward me on a very narrow section of the road. It was the only vehicle I met going in either direction. I figured I could probably back down a little easier than he could back up the hill, due to poor traction on the loose stones. Holding my front brake as it occasionally skidded, I backed down very slowly for about 50 feet to a shoulder on the cliff-side of the road. I had to lean the bike toward the edge so his side mirror wouldn't hit my arm on the way by. I could see down the scary edge of the cliff again between my forearm and my leg.

I made it back to Creel at around 6 PM on my reserve gas. When I pulled into the only gas station in town there was a line of four trucks and two cars waiting. An old one-ton pickup being served when I got there was getting several 55-gallon drums in the back of the truck filled. I didn't know how much gas the place had left or what time they closed, so I stayed in line for about a half hour rather than returning to the hotel first.

I arrived at the hotel hungry, tired, and covered with a thick layer of dust. I hadn't eaten since my 8:30 breakfast. After a quick shower I was ready for dinner but the restaurant was closed. I went down into the small general store and found the woman who had cooked breakfast for me. I said, "Quiero algo comer, por favor," which means I would like something to eat please. She rattled off something in Spanish. I recognized the word espere, which I knew meant wait, and I also recognized ocho y media, which means 8:30, the time her store closes. By 8:30, I was ready to eat anything. She suggested pork cutlets, which consisted of several tiny pork chops cooked well done in a frying pan. She served them with fried potatoes and a large serving of refried beans. I usually drank bottled soda in Mexico, which they call refresca.

The water at Creel looked very clear and had no odor, but I still didn't drink it because of stories I had heard about Mexican drinking water. Since I got diarrhea from something I had eaten or drank in Texas, I used my purifier pills in the Texas water that I carried in my cooler. It turned the water slightly yellow and made it taste and smell pretty bad. I used it mostly for brushing my teeth, and I drank only the refresca while I was there. The tap water was probably pure in the mountains, but I didn't care to risk it.

I expected my return trip to be very easy, but I was unable to locate the Chihuahua bypass that I used on my way down. Consequently I bumbled right into the city. I stopped for gas and asked the attendant in Spanish for directions to Ojinaga, which is like asking someone in the center of Washington, DC for directions to Philadelphia. With the general directions that he rattled off in Spanish I only got deeper into the city. I saw a motorcycle cop giving a guy a traffic ticket so I stopped and asked him, hoping he spoke English. He was a clean-cut looking young guy wearing a neat, new uniform and a shiny new helmet. He rode a small displacement Yamaha Virago with no tank emblem and a Harley sticker on an after-market fairing.

He spoke much too fast in Spanish for me to understand and after I answered a few times with "No comprendo" he looked a little annoyed. He got on the radio with his home station and exchanged a few words on the mike that I was also unable to translate and he motioned for me to follow. I was hoping for the best but I must confess that visions of the legendary Mexican slammer did cross my mind. My police escort through Chihuahua went right through the heart of the city, passing big churches, statues and large department stores. It is actually a very beautiful and clean city. After about ten minutes of riding very fast through city traffic, he finally stopped, got off, pointed down the road, and said, "Ojinaga." I thanked him with "Gracias por todo," shook his hand, and headed in the direction that he had pointed. I wondered if I should have offered him a few thousand pesos. In hindsight I probably should have.

This young cop was typical of most of the Mexican people I met on the trip. Everyone I met along the way was friendly, helpful, and polite. They were nothing at all like the stereotype that is usually projected in the movies. I would have no hesitation about returning for another visit. A moderate vocabulary of survival Spanish is very helpful, particularly in the restaurants and for directions. The more words and phrases one knows the easier it is to get by. I did double lock my bike at night but I could think of many other places where I would double and triple lock it and still feel much less than sure of finding it in the morning.

A RETURN TO NEWFOUNDLAND

Ed McIntyre suggested the trip when he, Bud Peck, and I stood near the ferry slip in North Sydney, Nova Scotia on an earlier tour of the Maritime Provinces. The highlight of that earlier tour was the Cabot Trail around Cape Breton Island. We rode the twisty coastal highway all the way around the island and saw many quaint villages whose economy is based primarily on trapping lobsters and fishing.

Remembering the two years I spent in Newfoundland in the early 1950s my immediate reply was, "What would anyone want to go to Newfoundland for? It's rainy and cloudy all the time and the wind blows constantly." I recalled from my Air Force tour there that on the rare occasions when the rain lets up and the wind stops blowing, you couldn't see for the fog.

Actually it rained for a total of only about four hours out of the seven days we spent on the island and we experienced strong winds only once while we were there, which was near Stephenville. I saw a road sign near there during our trip that warned motorists of wind in excess of 200 kilometers (125 MPH) having been measured along that section of highway. We saw fog only once too and that was miles out at sea on the Grand Banks off the southern tip of the Avalon Peninsula. We heard from several native Newfoundlanders that it was the most extraordinary summer they had experienced in 30 years.

We arrived at the ferry slip in North Sydney in the early evening of the day before our reservations. We allowed plenty of time for loading, although space for a few motorcycles would usually be easy to find. The huge ice-breaking bow of the seagoing ferry was raised up and out of the way as cars, trucks, campers, and motorcycles entered through the gaping bow section onto two vehicle decks. On our return trip we loaded in a similar fashion but from the stern. The total fare for a bike and rider at the time was $30 (Canadian).

Ferry rides have never been my idea of fun, especially seagoing ferries, but the MV Caribou made the 4½ hour trip from North Sydney to Port-aux-Basques as pleasant as any sea voyage could be for me. Having extreme inner ear sensitivity I took medication both ways, in spite of advance reports of a calm sea, because I remembered the rough crossing I experienced in 1953 on a much smaller predecessor of the Caribou.

141

After riding up the steep loading ramp onto the ship we were directed to a rear corner of the top vehicle deck. They provided more than enough tie-down straps to lash the bikes to the deck. One strap would have been sufficient in a calm sea but because of my recollections of the earlier trip we used four straps on each machine and tied them securely. Due to concerns about seasickness I also declined the ship's dinner menu, which appeared tempting and the prices reasonable. Bud and Ed reminded me often about how good the food was. The onboard theater presented a double-feature movie while a musical group sang "Newfie" folk songs in a well-stocked lounge. Many passengers strolled the decks keeping an eye out for whales, while others just snoozed in plush reclining chairs. Staterooms were available at an extra charge, primarily for night crossings, but a few hours sleep is the most anyone would hope to get.

I was sure my predictions about the weather had come true as we approached Port-aux-Basques. We could barely make out the rocky shoreline through some light rain and mist. The captain did an expert job of piloting the huge ship into the tiny harbor as it cleared the craggy rocks on both sides with only a few feet to spare. After slowly entering the harbor through the narrow channel, the captain turned the huge ship completely around and backed it in toward the dock in an area so small you had to see it to believe it. Disembarking went smoothly in spite of a very steep decline on the wet-steel ramp. Our motel reservations were nearby in the town of Port-aux-Basques, so when we arrived we had less than a ten-minute ride in light rain to reach our room.

Traffic on the ferry crossing is said to be up 30 percent from the previous year and growing at a phenomenal rate. The population of many towns in Newfoundland has increased several times since I was there in the early 50s. Growth has been due primarily to the opening of the Trans-Canada Highway across the island in the mid 60s. The highway begins at Port-aux-Basques near the southwestern tip of the island and goes through the forests of western Newfoundland with its marshes, bogs and hills past Corner Brook and Deer Lake. It then crosses the sparsely populated northern expanses past Gander Airport and through Terra Nova National Park to the more populated and scenic areas of the rugged Avalon Peninsula where it ends at St. John's, the capital of the province. I remember making that trip on a narrow gauge railway with my family, aboard a steam-powered train affectionately dubbed the "Newfie Bullet". It was the only way to get across the island in 1953. Our car and 35-foot house trailer were loaded aboard the same train on a flatcar.

The Trans-Canada Highway consists of mostly two lanes across unpopulated areas with an extra lane for passing on most long hills. It becomes four lanes in busily traveled, populated areas like between Stephenville and Corner Brook, and also nearing St. John's. It was being upgraded in several areas while we were there and might be four lanes most of the way in a few years. The speed limit in most areas was 90 kilometers (56 MPH) and the traffic was light.

Our first stop was Stephenville where I spent most of my Air Force tour. The US Air Force is gone now and Ernest Harmon Air Force Base no longer exists. All US military personnel pulled out in 1966 after a 25-year occupancy as part of our defense and early warning (the DEW line) during the Cold War. I recognized many of the main buildings, although the base chapel has become a Zion Pentecostal Church and the officer's club is now a popular local lounge. The base hospital where Donna was born now houses the Harmon Corporation. The airstrip, one of the longest in eastern Canada, is still in use but most of the parking aprons and taxi strips are wide-open, paved expanses. We drove in across a large area of concrete where painted lines now mark the vehicle travel lanes. The town of Stephenville has grown at least tenfold since 1955. It now apparently derives its economic dependency from a large modern newsprint mill operated by Abitibi-Price. Fishing still accounts for a portion of the economy but not as much as other smaller towns we visited.

Our next stop was Gander Airport, once called the "Crossroads of the World" because of the massive amount of air traffic that passed through there before jet planes with longer travel ranges bypassed this once-essential refueling stop. After checking into our motel and having dinner, we rode to the airport and saw a single 45-year-old Catalina flying boat fire up its engines and taxi out for takeoff. In spite of its civilian colors, seeing and hearing the old PBY brought back memories of flying in the lovable old birds during my Navy days in World War II. Local residents told us that several eastern European airlines, including the Russians, still use the airfield regularly.

From Gander we rode north to Musgrave Harbor on the Atlantic Ocean where the coastline is very rugged and barren. Bud's rear tire went flat from hitting a rough break in the pavement on our way to Cape Bonavista. After Bud quickly plugged the hole, we used my "onboard" compressor to fill the tire, and in just a few minutes we were on our way. A few days later when Ed's rear tire went flat after having hit a similar road hazard, we again realized the benefit of the compressor.

The old Bonavista Lighthouse has been converted to a museum so visitors can see how the lighthouse keeper and his family lived and how the light worked in bygone days. A mechanism of heavy weights and reduction gears that slowly rotate the light is similar to an old clock mechanism, only much larger. This mechanism requires manual rewinding every two hours. Cape Bonavista is where John Cabot landed in 1497 and declared to the King of England that he had discovered the "New Founde Lande". Although the Vikings preceded him by more than 500 years, that didn't seem to affect Cabot when he promptly claimed the land for the king and was later rewarded ten pounds of sterling for his deed.

St. John's is the oldest city in North America. It has endured for half a millennium and has thrived as a major seaport -- first for the fishing industry, with visitors from many seafaring nations of the world, and later for Newfoundland's offshore oil industry. As recently as 90 years ago the city burned to the ground but was rebuilt and has grown many times larger with homes spread out over the generally treeless hills for miles.

Signal Hill stands high above the city, overlooking the harbor and the famous Narrows that provides access and shelter from the Atlantic Ocean. The old cannons, which once guarded the Narrows in battles between the British and French, still point menacingly toward the harbor entrance. Cabot Tower, one of Newfoundland's oldest and most famous landmarks, stands majestically on the summit. It houses a museum with an interesting exhibit that shows Marconi receiving the first transatlantic wireless message. The gun emplacements on Signal Hill, built in 1796, were once called the Queen's Battery.

North of St. John's we visited Pouch Cove, one of the highlights of our tour. We stood high above the tiny cove and watched fishermen unloading their morning catch. We watched them fill a huge net with a few hundred pounds of fish from deep, flat bottom fishing boats, and we saw the bulging net filled with fish as it was hoisted 50 feet to the fishery level, emptied, and lowered again. A waste drain from the fishery spewed discarded fish parts out onto the rocky cliff where hundreds of hungry, screeching sea gulls fought for every morsel. The scene epitomized Newfoundland's fishing industry.

From there we rode over a rough, gravel road with ruts, holes, and loose stones to the lighthouse at Cape St. Francis, perched precariously on the edge of a cliff. Two workers were painting one of the steep sides of the building using high ladders on a narrow ledge around the building. The older of the two clung to his ladder so tight it was a wonder he could swing the paintbrush. I asked if he ever looked down and his face seemed to turn a little pale as he answered that he tries not to.

The area around Conception Bay near Portugal Cove and St. Phillips is one of the most beautiful spots on the island, with its magnificent view of Bell Island surrounded by bright blue, crystal-clear waters. Local legends abound that pirate treasures are buried near there. The Bell Island ferry runs frequently for travelers visiting the tiny island.

When we stopped for gas near Trepassey Bay on our southern loop around the Avalon Peninsula, we learned that the main herd of 2,000 caribou had been sighted recently near St. Shotts. We rode the 18-mile round trip into St. Shotts in hopes of seeing the herd, to no avail, but we spotted it later midway between there and Peter's River. With our excitement running high, I quickly put the bike on its side stand and ran with my camera across the muskeg-like terrain hoping to get close-up photos of the herd. At one point I had caribou all around me. The largest rack I saw must have been four feet high with many points. I got several pictures with and without my telephoto lens. The animals didn't seem to mind my presence as they continued to graze, and only occasionally looked up to see what I was up to.

On our return across the island we visited Twillingate on the northern coast and the lighthouse at Crow Head where we stood at the edge of a vertical cliff hundreds of feet above the ocean to look for whales. Most visitors were content to stand behind a tall fence and look from there, but Bud and I walked out to the very edge, which gave me a rush from the excitement. A voice yelled, "Whale," and sure enough one of the large mammals surfaced directly below us and blew water far into the air from its spout.

We visited St. Anthony, which is near the end of the Great Northern Peninsula and the northernmost city in Newfoundland. It is the home of the famous Grenfell Medical Mission, where we saw a helicopter swoop in toward the large modern hospital as we rode through town. The hospital supports a large surrounding area including remote Eskimo communities on the mainland as well as other islands much farther north. We encountered the only significant rain of the trip in St. Anthony and decided to skip a side visit to L'Anse-aux-Meadows, site of the first Viking settlement in North America.

On our return down the peninsula near Eddies Cove along the Viking Trail we saw a group of huge icebergs in the Strait of Belle Isle as they drifted near the Labrador coast on their way to the open Atlantic. We passed through Gros Morne National Park on our way to and from St. Anthony. The park offers some of the most magnificent scenery on the island with its many majestic fjords, lakes, and mountains.

Our last night in Newfoundland was spent at a motel at Plum Point on the northern peninsula, where we enjoyed the best food of our trip in the small motel dining room. Aside from many identifiable items they served a full menu of traditional Newfoundland dishes such as fish 'n brewis, cod tongues, cod-au-gratin, scrunchions, Atlantic salmon, and others. A major difference we noticed with the food in Newfoundland was with over-easy eggs and breakfast sausages. The eggs were usually served over hard and the sausages were always bland. Once during the trip we stopped for breakfast at a McDonald's, hoping to get spicy sausages. Instead they served the blandest sausages we ever tasted at a Mickey D's.

As we stood on the dock in Port-aux-Basques a small musical group stood nearby singing Newfie folk songs like "I'se the Bye" and "The Squid Jiggin' Ground". Their music sounds a lot like a mixture of the Highland fling and the Irish jig. It seemed a perfect end to a perfect visit. Most people there were outwardly friendly and hospitable toward us. It was normal for someone to come up and start a conversation. Whenever we asked for information it was given with a smile. They laugh at the traditional "Newfie jokes" and will tell you a few right back. Newfoundland is aptly called "The Happy Province."

ALASKA 4 - SAGA OF THE AILING BMWs

Five members of the RAMS Motorcycle Club traveled to Alaska together in 1991. The group consisted of myself, the oldest at 66 on a GL1200 Gold Wing; Jake Herzog, a 52-year-old head of a specialty welding business supporting the petroleum industry around Albany, NY on a BMW R100GS; Ed McIntyre, a 61-year-old retired mailman from Somers, CT whose friends in the Postal Service said at his retirement party, "One thing you can say about Eddie, he's steady," on a 1983 BMW R80RT; Bud Peck, a 61-year-old stone mason and staunchly conservative Yankee from Stow, Massachusetts who my wife says is "The Salt of the Earth" on a BMW K75; and the youngest member of our group, John Thurber, a 48-year-old building contractor from West Dover, VT who has been just about everywhere including a bike tour of the Soviet Union. John rode a new Suzuki VX800 on this trip. A few of the things we shared in common besides belonging to the same motorcycle club are that we are all longtime dirt riders and we are all Type-A personalities. We had a combined total of almost 200 years of motorcycling experience. Ed was our token bachelor.

Our first of several disagreements arose even before we got started when John said of my planned route, "I wouldn't ride through Kentucky, Arkansas, and Oklahoma in July on a bet. Don't you realize the temperature reaches 110 degrees down there?" I tried to convince John that I had chosen the best bike route across the country and that a spirited ride through the Ozarks would make him forget about the heat. That didn't cut any ice with John, and eventually Jake and Ed sided with him after he laid out a route across Ontario, Upper Michigan, and Minnesota. This conflict served as a harbinger of some of the trials and tribulations we would face as our individual idiosyncrasies surfaced. Following is my journal of the trip:

Day 1 - Bud and I left Buchanan on the morning of July 8th. It was a comfortable 74 degrees with cloudy skies. Light showers were forecast. Bud was put on his toes early when a car pulled out in front of him at the Seven Lakes Drive traffic circle only eleven miles from my house. I heard the loud screech of tires as Bud barely missed the guy. Temperatures dipped slightly as we rode through some light showers in northern New Jersey. We crossed the Delaware River on a narrow steel-deck

147

bridge north of Easton, followed by a series of scenic two-lane country roads through eastern Pennsylvania. We stopped for lunch at a Hardee's near the Susquehanna River. It didn't rain at all after lunch and the temperature rose into the low 80s.

We crossed the Potomac River into West Virginia over a very low, single-lane wooden bridge, with 8-inch-high wooden side rails, similar to the infamous bridge at Chappaquiddick. We then rode about eight miles of scenic and scarcely traveled dirt roads through C&O Park in West Virginia. The scenic highlight of our first day was WV Route 55 between Petersburg and Elkins. We reached the Econolodge in Elkins around six, just ahead of a heavy thundershower. We shared a batch of whiskey sours before walking next-door to the KFC. We wondered how the rest of the group fared on their first day, having left around the same time from Jake's house.

Day 2 - It was heavily overcast and 68 degrees when we left Elkins after a complimentary breakfast of fruit, donuts, and coffee. The weather held for the first 40 miles although we ran into some thick fog. It was so thick in spots we had to slow down to 10 MPH to see where we were going on the extremely twisty road. We also rode through a few light showers between Valley Head and Webster Springs. It all cleared up before we reached Webster Springs and by 10 AM the sun was out. We stopped for a second breakfast at Hardee's in Summerville.

One of the highlights of the day was a remote secondary road I had chosen between Belva and US 60 in West Virginia. The south side of the Kenawha River was also interesting although a little congested. We had lunch at a Dairy Queen in Kermit before entering Kentucky where the temperature rose to around 86 degrees. It was also congested for the first five or ten miles in Kentucky and a real mess through Manchester and a few other small towns. We saw where many poor Appalachian mountain folk live in dilapidated hovels and we saw several areas overrun by Kudzu weed.

Day 3 - It was barely first light when we left at 5:30, which was only 4:30 Central Time just a few miles down the road. We left early to allow extra time for our Mississippi River crossing, where we planned to use the same tiny ferry across the river that we used in 1988.

The fog and haze that hung over the mountains didn't prevent us from seeing some really nice scenery during the first

60 miles. Route 100, which we took most of the way across the state, was an excellent two-lane bike road. We saw rice, tobacco, corn, milo, soybeans, and other crops. Western Kentucky didn't look nearly as poor as the eastern part, although I did see one guy working with a hand plow behind a mule.

In Fairview we saw a monument to Jefferson Davis that looked a lot like the Washington Monument, only smaller. It seemed strange to see this huge spire in a farmland setting. When we reached Hickman we learned that our ferry had stopped running two years earlier, so we had to detour for several miles into Tennessee to cross the river. The temperature climbed to 100 degrees in northern Arkansas before we stopped at the Rolling Hills Motel in Hardy.

Day 4 - The roads became very congested around the vacation areas of Mountain Home and Eureka Springs. It was much better west of there on the steep and twisty descent into Oklahoma. There was practically no traffic through the gently rolling hills and remote ranches of eastern Oklahoma, although it got very hot. We had lunch at a small convenience store, after which the heat became somewhat uncomfortable.

West of Severy, Kansas the skies appeared threatening. When the wind became very strong we stopped and sat on the grass in front of a cemetery to see what it was going to do. It actually looked like a tornado was brewing. Eventually we concluded that most of the lightning and the heaviest part of the storm was north of us. When the strong winds subsided we left, but a few minutes later the rain came in torrents. By the time I found a spot to pull over again it was already too late to suit up. We stood in the heavy downpour and got drenched. We reached the Star Dust Motel in El Dorado about an hour later, checked in, and wrung out our wet clothes. After having a whiskey sour in the room we walked next door for a steak at the Golden Corral.

When I called home the previous evening I had asked Lilli to check on the progress of the other three guys. She reported back that Jake had figured out a way for Arlene to meet us in Billings for our planned Montana loop where Lilli was already planning to meet us. Arlene had wanted to go, but when Jake chose to ride his dual-sport BMW rather than the Harley, Arlene said "No way!" Jake's new plan was to rent a car for the Montana loop so Arlene could join us there. Bud had been resting on the bed and when I told him about Jake's latest plan

149

he looked at me with indignation over his half-empty whiskey sour glass and yelled, "Jake is going to rent a WHAT?"

Day 5 - There was a lot of lightning around when we got up at 5:15 and the sky in our direction looked very threatening. It began to rain soon after we started. We put on our rain suits as we neared Council Grove and rode about 20 miles in a strong thundershower. There wasn't much wind with it but there were several close lightning flashes. We saw a sign in Cassoday proclaiming it to be the "World Capital of the Prairie Chicken." I learned later that a prairie chicken was a small grouse.

Most of the two-lane roads we traveled in Kansas had fairly nice scenery with no traffic. We rode through a lot of gently rolling prairie and we saw a lot of corn. The winter wheat had already been harvested and the beans were about ankle high. The rolling hills eventually gave way to the flat lands of western Nebraska and eastern Colorado, where we saw a huge trainload of coal coming out of Wyoming. We didn't see many sunflowers, which is one of the popular crops in western Kansas. We had lunch at a small cafe in Stockton, Nebraska and dinner at a KFC in Sterling, Colorado, our overnight stop. The temperature rose to the mid 90s by early afternoon, although it eased off later in the day to the high 80s.

Day 6 - We decided to try McDonald's promotional burritos for breakfast and we agreed they were awful. With the temperature at a cool 55 degrees, I wore two jackets and used my Hot Grips for the first time. We saw mostly corn, wheat, onions, beans, and a lot of sugar beets on the prairie between Sterling and Ft. Collins where we stopped for a better breakfast at Hardee's. Our view of the Rocky Mountains and other scenery north of Ft. Collins was spectacular. The scenery got even more spectacular as we climbed through Medicine Bow National Forest to the 10,000-foot level, where the road from Laramie to Walcott was our scenic highlight of the day. It was also excellent through the Wind River Canyon between Riverton and Shoshoni. We saw several pronghorn antelopes grazing with the cattle near Muddy Gap. We stopped for lunch at a McDonald's in Rawlins, which was very crowded. We began to see a mysterious crop with yellow blossoms and light green leaves that for the lack of a better name we began to refer to as "the yellow shit." It would be ten days before we finally identified it. The temperature again reached 100 before we stopped for the day.

During the afternoon Bud's rear shock blew its seal and lost all of its fluid, causing the bike to lose all damping action in the rear and of course affecting the handling. After trying to contact the listed BMW dealer in Billings, who we learned had gone out of business three years earlier, Bud contacted his son George in New Hampshire and asked him to call Razee's shop in Rhode Island to work out the details for shipping one to Helena via 2nd Day Air. George called back a half hour later to confirm that it was on its way. Bud also blew a fuse that afternoon when the wire to his Hot Grips shorted against the fork. He changed the fuse at the side of the road and taped the bare wire. His K75 had 88,000 miles on it at that point.

We stopped at Thermopolis to view the hot spring where clear water and sulfur gasses emerge from the ground at more than 130 degrees, creating a deep, 20-foot diameter pool. The crystal-clear water is piped from the spring into the local hotels and health resorts where it is used for hot mineral baths. Our final 300 miles that day consisted of rangeland with a backdrop of scenic mountains, typical of central Wyoming.

Day 7 - After breakfast at a truck stop we were on the road by 6:30. Our ride through Shell Creek Canyon was spectacular, with steep, rock-canyon walls on both sides of a twisty road alongside a fast-running creek that flowed through the canyon. At the 10,000-foot level in Big Horn Forest a huge herd of sheep wandered onto the road for almost a mile. We eased our way through and later I surprised two young elk in the road. A twisty 9-mile descent took us to the Big Horn River.

It was our day to meet Lilli and Arlene at Billings Airport for our planned one-week loop through Montana, Wyoming, and Idaho. We arrived in Billings at 10:30 AM and had an early lunch on our way to the airport. We looked around to see if Jake was there before taking a short ride to kill time. The plane arrived at noon, after which Arlene rented the car and I transferred some of my stuff into the trunk – like my tent and sleeping bag -- to make room for Lilli's luggage on the bike. Jake, John, Ed, and Ralph Spencer were waiting for us at the motel in Red Lodge. Ralph had come from Sun City, Arizona to join us for our scenic loop. We did some laundry, had a few batches of whiskey sours to celebrate our rendezvous, and we all had dinner together at the Round Barn. It sprinkled a little on the way, but we managed to stay dry.

Day 8 - Ed phoned our room at six to make sure we were up. We had donuts and coffee in the lobby and talked about having a full breakfast as a group in Cooke City. It was about 50 degrees when John took off up the mountain at 6:30 while the rest of us were still getting ready. Jake & Arlene left 10 minutes later in the car, followed a minute or so after that by Ed. Finally Bud, Lilli and I started up the mountain at 6:45. Having learned of a problem at home, Ralph headed back to Sun City.

We came across Ed on one knee removing his headlight bulb near the 9,000-foot level. His BMW started to act up after the generator went dead and weakened the battery. After we removed all of the bulbs, Bud followed him back to Red Lodge where he hoped to get it fixed. Lilli and I continued up the mountain. The Beartooth Highway was spectacular in the crisp morning air and the temperature at the pass was only 40 degrees. We took a few pictures there and continued on to Cooke City. We met the others just as they were leaving the restaurant. So much said for the group-breakfast plan. Lilli and I decided to skip the full breakfast and we all headed for Yellowstone Park.

Inside the park we saw bison, elk, a lot of beautiful scenery, and a lot of burned-out forest where fires had ravaged a huge area a year earlier. I just missed a big pothole that John hit dead center, bending both wheel rims. Our scenic highlights inside the park included Yellowstone Falls, which we viewed from Inspiration Point, and Old Faithful where we arrived a few minutes before it blew hot water and steam high into the air. Traffic in the park was moderately heavy with many slow-moving RV's and campers.

We took photos at Grand Tetons and later noticed a lot of lightning as we approached Jackson Hole, our overnight stop. The skies had been looking progressively darker and more ominous during the afternoon. John passed us as we neared the motel. Jake and Arlene were already there when we pulled in at 4:20. Bud arrived about 45 minutes later, having left Red Lodge the same time as Ed, who got his generator fixed, but Ed travels a lot slower. The brushes hanging up in their slides had caused Ed's generator problem. He got in around 6:15 and we all went downtown to the Sizzler for dinner. Bud's bike had been running poorly and it smoked a lot during the day. John managed to straighten his bent rims a little that night. Of the four bikes, we had problems with three on our first day together.

Day 9 - It was cool when we left the motel for a few days of visiting ghost towns. Lilli and I had muffins from the Mini-Mart next door with tea from the lobby. Four of us rode together for the first time as we climbed the 10% grade toward Targhee Pass, followed by a steep and twisty descent down the west slopes into Idaho. Bud's bike spit and smoked a lot during starting but performed well all day after a fill-up with high test.

We stopped for a full breakfast at the Old Bank Restaurant in Victor, Idaho. The service was slow but the food was good. Jake & Arlene arrived a little later in the car and skipped breakfast, having had a complimentary breakfast where they stayed. The ride over Targhee Pass was beautiful, as was the scenery through the lush farmlands in Idaho. We saw potatoes, oats, summer wheat, and a lot more of the yellow shit. We saw cattle feeding in lush fields of alfalfa and we saw a bark beetle infestation that affected the lodge-pole pine trees.

Virginia City, the first ghost town we visited looked more like a tourist town with its many gift and craft shops. Most buildings were occupied, so it wasn't much of a ghost town. Nevada City was better with more interesting exhibits and several unoccupied houses, but it was still not a true ghost town.

On our way to Bannack that afternoon we ran into a sudden, fierce thundershower with strong winds and heavy rain. Jake and Arlene were directly behind us in the car at the time, so I pulled off the highway and Lilli and I quickly got into the car. John and Bud stopped earlier to put on rain suits but Ed ran into the heaviest rain as suddenly as we did and got soaked. We watched him pass from our dry haven of the car, where we stayed until the storm passed.

Lilli and I went directly from there to Bannack while the others checked into the Super 8 in Dillon. We were happy to find that Bannack was a true ghost town, much like Bodie, California, where we visited three years earlier. We parked outside and walked through the historic town, once the capital of Montana. We were allowed to enter and inspect many of the abandoned houses and other buildings. We got to the motel at 5:30 and had a batch of whiskey sours with the group before we all went to dinner at a nearby Pizza Hut. The service was terrible but the pizzas were pretty good. My $6 senior-citizen discount on the combined check prompted someone in the group to suggest that it partially made up for the poor service.

Day 10 - It was quite cool when we got up, so we ate a leisurely breakfast and left late. We rode on a narrow, unmarked country road with a lot of potholes near Anaconda. I could see where the area had been strip-mined for copper ore. Otherwise it was a scenic ride that included a section called the Pintler Scenic Route. We stopped in Drummond for gas and a cinnamon roll, which served also as our lunch, since we went directly from there into Garnet, our next ghost town. We rode ten miles of fairly rough gravel to reach Garnet, the last two of which were steep and twisty with washouts. We all made it without incident, after which some of us strolled through the ghost town for about an hour. Bud and Ed didn't care for the sightseeing part, so they waited in the parking lot and watched the bikes. Garnet is an authentic ghost town, smaller than Bannack but at least as interesting. We left via an easier northern exit as it rained lightly for about a half hour. We kept our rain suits on all the way to the motel. Heavy cloudiness discouraged taking pictures around Flat Head Lake where the scenery is usually superb.

Day 11 - It began to rain just as we entered Glacier National Park. We rode through several miles of construction in the rain, including areas with slick mud. We were unable to see the high peaks through the heavy overcast as we climbed the steep approach to Logan Pass along Garden Wall. At one point near the summit we rode through a very thick cloudbank where we could barely see the double-yellow line in the road. Heavy fog and snow banks up to 12 feet surrounded the parking lot at Logan Pass. It was barely 40 degrees and very windy. It cleared up by the time we reached St. Mary on the eastern end of the park. Although it is one of the most spectacular national parks, we were able to see very little of it during that visit.

The road from St. Mary to Browning was a great bike road with smooth macadam and long, sweeping turns that were slightly banked. We had lunch at a small burger shop in Browning that was run by Blackfeet Indians. We were the only Caucasians in the place. The terrain between Browning and Choteau consisted of rolling hills through cattle country where we saw hundreds of head grazing in the fields. After the ground leveled a bit we saw wheat, barley, alfalfa, and a lot more of the yellow stuff, which by then some were saying could be mustard. The wide-open country between Choteau and Helena was very beautiful, and typical of Montana.

We got to our motel in Helena about 4:45. Bud's new shock had arrived so he went right out and replaced it in the parking lot. Later we had a batch of whiskey sours and went next door to Ralph's Family Restaurant for dinner. The service there was worse than Pizza Hut. It took a half hour to get the salad and at least another hour to get the food. They ran out of prime-rib special, meaning that a few of us had to change our orders. When the meal finally came, my alternate roast beef was dry and tasteless. We didn't get back to the room until after nine o'clock. Ralph's Restaurant epitomized some of the eating conflicts we experienced on the trip. I personally get very little pleasure from pseudo-epicurean, so-called full-service restaurants and I dislike eating late in the evening. I also get irritated with bad food, bad service, or both. When we left Ralph's that evening I was quite irritated, although it didn't seem to bother most of the group.

Day 12 - Lilli and I had breakfast at McDonald's while the others returned to Ralph's for the more traditional breakfast. Elkhorn, our next ghost town, was about 12 miles up a rough gravel road. It was once a mining town where silver, gold and lead were extracted. Now it was mostly private property where visitors were allowed to walk amongst the buildings, but there were signs saying to stay away from certain homes. We didn't see anyone, although we saw several places that were obviously lived in. Sportsmen may have rented the houses during the hunting season. We saw a young elk and a few deer while we were in the town. We explored the abandoned hotel, saloon, barbershop, mining fraternity hall, and a few of the abandoned buildings that were open. Lilli and I located the cemetery about a mile from town and saw almost a hundred graves, mostly children between the ages of three days and 11 years. The founder of the mine was also buried there. I almost lost the bike when I stopped on a steep incline at the cemetery gate and the front brake wouldn't hold on the loose gravel. We were on the bike together as it slid backwards down the hill faster and faster with the front wheel locked and dragging all the way. I managed to hold it upright with both feet also skidding backwards. The bike finally stopped without falling over, which seemed like a small miracle on the rutted, washed out terrain.

From there the group rode 156 miles along Interstate 90 to reach our motel in Columbus. Bud, John and Ed continued on to Red Lodge to change oil and service their bikes, while Lilli and I stayed behind and checked in early. I changed my left-front brake pads in the parking lot. I had a slight sore throat and an irregular heartbeat so I took an extra blood pressure pill and rested. I knew that part of my problem was caused by the buildup of stress from trying to keep our tour running on an even keel for the past five days. Bud and Ed returned by 5:30 while John, Jake, and Arlene remained in Red Lodge on their endless pursuit of gourmet eating-places. Bud found a huge nail in his rear tire that needed two plugs to seal. We shared a batch of whiskey sours at the motel to relax and went next-door to the Town Pump for dinner.

Day 13 - I woke up with a sore throat and my sinuses totally clogged after having spent a rough night. I felt sick and almost decided to head for the emergency room in Billings for antibiotics but I took two extra-strength Tylenols instead. I soon felt a little better although weak, and my heart was still acting up. The four of us had breakfast at the Town Pump.

The road to Red Lodge afforded panoramic views of the Beartooth range. We rejoined John, Jake, and Arlene and left immediately for Cody, Wyoming over some exceptionally scenic roads. We located the museum and spent three hours browsing the exhibits and having lunch at the snack shop. The museum had a great cowboy section, an Indian section, an art section including both cowboy and Indian art, and the largest small-arms exhibit I have ever seen. On our return to Billings via another exceptionally scenic route, the temperature rose to above 90 degrees. Lilli and I had a relaxing dinner alone at Perkins during an evening rain shower. I retrieved my sleeping bag and other gear from Arlene's trunk because the guys were heading for Alaska in the morning.

Day 14 - I slept much better, having taken two 12-hour Sudafed caplets and a Sominex. My sore throat was gone and it seemed as though my cold was breaking up. We had breakfast at Perkins and returned to the motel, where Lilli packed for her flight home. Arlene's flight was the following day. The four guys left early for Whitefish, figuring that if they waited for me it would get too late. I left immediately after taking Lilli to the airport. I rode faster than usual and looked for them along the way, especially in Helena where I thought they might be having lunch. The view of Helena from an overlook fifteen miles west of town was spectacular. I had a great ride the entire day, especially along one route where I spotted a private buffalo herd. Ed said later he saw a bear near Flat Head Lake.

I got to Whitefish at 4 PM and the others pulled in 45 minutes later. They said that after having a problem locating gas in the morning they decided to wait for a station to open while having midmorning coffee. As we gassed up that evening Ed noticed a puddle of oil on the ground dripping from his fork. He said he changed the oil before leaving on the trip but didn't know exactly how much he had put in it, which is typical of Ed. He said he was quite sure he didn't overfill it and he wanted to visit the BMW dealer in Kalispell in the morning to have the seal replaced.

Day 15 – The sky was clear although it was quite cool. After breakfast Jake and Ed headed for Kalispell to locate the BMW dealer while the rest of us headed for the Canadian border. The dealer had other on-the-road customers with more serious problems than Ed's and he wouldn't be able to get to Ed's fork seals for quite a while, so Ed bought some stop-leak and left. Meanwhile the rest of us topped off our tanks in Eureka with the last US gasoline available before crossing the border.

We climbed steadily into the Canadian Rockies in British Columbia where we spotted five huge male bighorn sheep about 5 miles out of Radium Hot Springs. We took a 38-mile unscheduled side trip into the town of Banff to exchange currency, since we didn't know of any other banks along our route. John wouldn't eat at McDonald's there with the rest of the group, opting for a few pieces of fruit and other "healthier food" at a nearby grocery store.

The scenery through Banff and Jasper Parks was spectacular. John split off for a side trip to Lake Louise while Bud and I continued on the planned route. We saw a large herd of mountain goats near the gas station in Banff Park and later we saw four white longhaired goats. We took only a few pictures in Jasper Park because of having consumed too much time in Banff where we stopped to view Crowfoot Glacier, Bow Glacier, and Columbia Icefields. The weather was excellent all day with a crystal-clear sky and temperatures in the low 70s. John passed us along the way and got into Hinton, our overnight stop, about 20 minutes before Bud and I got there. Ed and Jake arrived a little after nine. Jake had gotten a speeding ticket from a British

Columbia provincial cop as he stepped up his pace to catch up. Ed's fork mysteriously stopped leaking without using the stop-leak.

Day 16 - The temperature was only 42 degrees when we started, as it was getting progressively cooler every day. We were wearing long johns for the first time, and I wore most of the clothes I brought with me. We stopped after only a few miles, where I also put on my rain suit to break the wind. The 86-mile ride from Hinton to Grand Cache was over a nice, winding, two-lane tar road through thick conifer forests, where we saw a few deer and a coyote.

That was followed by a 100-mile stretch of very rough gravel into Grand Prairie. Freshly applied calcium chloride made the first 15 miles wet and slippery, after which we traveled 85 miles of loose, dry gravel where the bikes raised a half-mile trail of dust. We had to spread out to avoid fouling each other's air cleaners. John was carrying a spare tire on his rear carrier that he lost somewhere along the way. Ed dropped his bike on the loose gravel, which fortunately happened at slow speed. I reached the tar and waited as the others arrived a few minutes apart, except for Ed who motored in about an hour later. While waiting for Ed, John went back to search in vain for his lost tire. We had lunch in Grand Prairie where we finally learned that the "yellow shit" we had been seeing for the past 10 days was actually canola, the predominant crop around Grand Prairie.

It was a warm 86 degrees when we stopped in Dawson Creek for Ed and Jake to exchange currency. We got to our motel in Fort St. John earlier than expected, which gave us time to hose off some of the calcium chloride and share a batch of whiskey sours. The family suite there cost the least of any accommodations on the entire trip.

Day 17 - Sunlight streaming through the window woke me at 4:15 AM but I didn't wake the others until our usual 5:30. We ate at a classy inn nearby and were on the road by seven. Meanwhile the temperature had climbed to around 60 degrees. I mentioned to the group before leaving that we had to get gas near Mile 171 because there wasn't much gas along that section of the Alaska Highway. When we got there I saw a small sign directly across from the gas station, "Next Gas 123 miles." John saw it, but Jake was looking the other way at some interesting equipment and sailed right on by. We yelled and waved our arms to no avail. Fortunately Bud and Ed saw us and stopped.

Jake must have assumed we were flying because he took off very fast. As soon as I got my gas I went in hot pursuit, averaging about 80 MPH for the next 50 miles. I was eventually stopped by road construction where I asked the girl at the flag if she had seen someone fitting Jake's description. She said he was in the group that had just left with the pilot car but I would now have to wait for it to return. As several vehicles lined up at the flag I walked back through the line to see if anyone was carrying spare gas. I found a guy from California in an old VW wagon who had a full 2½-gallon can in his trunk. I explained our problem to him and asked if he would please stop when he saw us stranded alongside the road.

I finally overtook Jake about 30 miles beyond the construction. By then he was traveling only 40 MPH to conserve what gas he had left. I calmly pulled up alongside and said, "Hi Jake. How are you doing on gas?" He turned to me with a forlorn look and said, "Terrible!" I said that the next gas was only about 20 miles ahead, and he said that he was quite sure he couldn't make it, having already been on reserve for 35 miles. Confused because his bike usually had a much longer range than mine, he asked how I was doing on gas. I smiled and said, "Pretty good." At that point I explained what had happened and said that he was about to be rescued by a guy from California.

We followed the Good Samaritan into Ft. Nelson where Jake refilled his can and thanked him again. The scenery beyond Ft. Nelson was much nicer, especially around Summit Lake, Toad River, and Muncho Lake. Our reservations were at the old Muncho Lake Lodge where the rooms were very reasonable. John took a quick dip in the lake, where I think the water temperature was barely above freezing. His rear tire was showing significant wear and he began to worry that he wouldn't make Anchorage with it. We shared a batch while Ed, Jake and John also had a beer, after which we had lasagna for dinner in the dining room of the lodge. We also had our RAMS club portrait taken beneath a huge, stuffed ram's head on the wall.

Day 18 - We had breakfast at the lodge next door and were on the road by seven. John left for Whitehorse at 5:45, hoping to find a tire. We met a road crew about 80 miles out, just starting work for the day. I slipped through before the flag

159

station was set up and noticed that Bud got through behind me; but when I got to the other end of the construction I saw that Bud wasn't with me. Ed came through and said that Bud had stopped along the road and he didn't know what the problem was. I tried to get back to him but flag stations had been set up in the meantime, blocking my return. Jake learned when he came through that Bud's bike had stripped its drive-shaft spline, so he returned to where the vehicles were lining up at the flag and found a guy with a pickup truck, escorting a large modular home on a tractor-trailer. The guy agreed to carry Bud and his bike 125 miles into Watson Lake, although they had a problem with the girl at the flag when she insisted that an escort vehicle was not allowed by law to leave the vehicle it was escorting. After a lengthy argument she agreed to let the pickup go out and get Bud and his bike, but everyone had to wait there for its return.

They were afforded extra time to load the bike because the pilot car was still at my end of the construction area where the driver, a pretty blonde, had jumped out and run for the bushes saying to the girl at the flag, "Oh, I gotta pee like you wouldn't believe!" She was several feet short of the bushes when she suddenly stopped and pulled down her tight jeans right there. When she came running back, pulling up her jeans, she said to the other girl, "I didn't make it! I peed all over myself!" The other girl just said calmly, "Next time don't wait so long!"

When Bud arrived at Watson Lake he made a quick assessment of his mechanical problem to determine what parts he needed. He made a call to Gordon Razee in Rhode Island, who had the parts in stock and would ship them immediately via Federal Express. Jake stayed with Bud to make sure the parts were on their way while "Steady Eddie" and I started out for Whitehorse. Bud hoped to catch-up in a few days.

Ed and I got to the hotel in Whitehorse at six, after riding through several light showers. I didn't bother putting on my rain suit, although Ed did suit up. The scenery around Teslin Lake and Marsh Lake was beautiful. Ed got a few white knuckles on the infamous steel-deck bridge over Teslin Lake. John, having been unable to find a tire in Whitehorse, was at the hotel when we arrived. Our rooms there cost $80 (Canadian) each, which was the highest price we paid for lodging on the trip. We delayed dinner until Jake arrived around 8 PM, after which we enjoyed the salmon steak special.

Day 19 - I slept well in spite of the late dinner and I woke up at 6:15, the latest on the trip so far. We ate at a hotel across the street where my breakfast cost $7.20 and Jake's came to more than ten dollars. It seemed as though prices on food and lodging had gone up considerably in the area since my last trip through the Yukon ten years earlier. We gassed up and were on the road by 7:50, having suited up and headed out under a very threatening sky. We rode through a few cold showers about 40 miles up the Klondike Highway as the temperature dropped several more degrees. The poplars, balsams, and other trees were getting slimmer and shorter as we headed farther north. We gassed up in Carmacks and again at Stewart River Crossing where we had lunch and removed our rain suits.

About 12 miles south of the Dempster Highway junction we saw a smashed Honda CB1000F parked against a tree. Its front wheel was pushed back more than a foot, apparently from hitting the ditch. We saw the rider's gear piled up neatly against a tree. His tank bag was still there as was his sleeping bag and saddlebags, which had been torn off in the accident. It appeared that he had left the road at a fairly high rate of speed, possibly forced off by an oncoming vehicle or by one he was passing; or he could have fallen asleep. It was on a relatively straight stretch of road. We made inquiries in Dawson but couldn't find out anything about the accident. We assumed that he survived because there appeared to be no obstacle for him to hit after apparently going over the handlebars, unless he hit another vehicle. The bike bore a Swiss plate. That scene and a few of our own breakdowns brought home some of the risks of traveling alone in areas where there are hundreds of miles between small pockets of civilization.

We stayed at the Dawson City Bed & Breakfast where our host insisted that everyone remove his shoes at the front entrance. His wife probably did most of the cleaning and cooking while he was the gracious host. After checking in, we strolled through town and visited a museum. We ate salmon steak at a hotel in town and telephoned Bud in Watson Lake. He hadn't received the parts yet but still had high hopes of joining us in a few days. John noticed oil dripping from somewhere in the rear of his Suzuki but couldn't determine the exact source. The second half of Ed's air-filled seat cover ruptured and lost all its air. The first half had ruptured several days earlier.

Day 20 - I had requested that our breakfast be ready by 6:30 and our host obliged. He served strawberry rhubarb short cakes, cheese scones, cereal, muffins with butter and jam, bananas, orange juice, and coffee, all of which were great. We had packed the motorcycles before breakfast, so as soon as we finished eating we headed for the ferry landing. Our host told us about a stubborn forest fire burning between the Yukon River and the US border. Due to the inaccessibility of the area they were letting much of it burn out. It had been burning for more than a month in spite of water being dumped on it occasionally by helicopters. The Top-of-the-World Road was shrouded in a thin cloud of smoke, but in spite of the smoke the road was still one of the highlights of our trip. There were sheer drops off unprotected edges, where at one point we saw the remains of a pickup camper over the side. The dirt surface of the 60-mile Yukon section was fairly smooth, having been graded and treated with calcium chloride. The Alaskan end consisted of 115 miles of dry, loose gravel with a rough washboard surface. We stopped near Chicken, Alaska to explore a large abandoned gold dredge that had been there since Klondike-gold-rush days.

As we neared Tetlin Junction I figured that Ed wouldn't be there for quite a while because of the loose gravel, so I pulled into a turnoff area and changed my oil, oil filter, and spark plugs. I took considerable heat from the group for polluting the environment, but they often oil the turnoff areas anyway to keep the dust down. The gas station at Tetlin Junction had gone out of business, but we still had enough gas to reach Tok, 14 miles farther; where we also had lunch at a small corner cafe. We encountered a few light showers later between there and Fairbanks. I got a speeding ticket from a state trooper for doing 70 in a 55 MPH zone, but he didn't bother the others.

Fairbanks hadn't changed much since I stayed there on my first Alaska tour in 1977. Arlene had gotten the names of two motels through the triple-A and we chose the better of the two. I wouldn't say it was in the seedy part of town only because most of Fairbanks looked seedy. One of our two run-down rooms was on the third floor while the other was on the second. The first floor seemed to be occupied by welfare people. Athabascan Indians operated the motel and most of the guests and people hanging around the lobby were Athabascans. The streets were full of them. We ate at a small cafe across the street, which was filthy and the food was the worst we had on our trip. I ordered fried chicken and the others had hamburgers. Ed's bike fell over while we ate, when the side stand sank into some soft tar. We took a short walk after supper and were panhandled, propositioned, and generally pestered by hordes of street people. I washed my jeans, shirt, and socks in the sink. They were dry by morning.

Day 21 - I don't think anyone got more than a few hours sleep. The Indians prowled the streets and talked all night, which caused me to be a little anxious about the bikes. It finally quieted down around 5 AM, but when I looked out I realized it had started to rain, which merely made them find temporary shelter. We began the day in the rain. The road out of Fairbanks had some nice curves and rolling hills that we enjoyed in spite of the weather. The temperature dipped into the 40s around Denali Park. We stopped at the Visitors Center and took in a slide show. It rained until we got to Trappers Creek, where we stopped for a deli lunch at a large general store.

It was more comfortable after lunch as the temperature rose into the 60s. We decided to bypass Anchorage and go directly into Palmer where we had reservations. No one seemed interested in visiting Anchorage, which was influenced somewhat by our stay in Fairbanks. We learned that the bed and breakfast that Arlene arranged by phone had two double beds for the four of us, so we canceled that and went to a motel instead. We felt sorry for the woman at the B & B who probably bought all of the food for our breakfast. We had a batch of whiskey sours at the motel before walking six blocks in the rain to the Valley Hotel for a roast-turkey dinner. After returning to the motel we had an interesting talk with a guy who worked on a mining job nearby. It rained steady most of the evening.

Day 22 - I heard heavy rain when I woke up in the morning so I didn't wake the rest of the group until six. John left for Anchorage at 6:30 to get a new rear tire mounted and his bike serviced. He planned on getting to Anchorage long before the place opened so he could wash the bike and be their first customer. We returned to the hotel for breakfast before leaving in the rain. It rained steady for the first two hours, during which time we stopped briefly at Matanuska Glacier for a few photos from the highway. The roads between Palmer and Glennallen were very twisty with steep rock embankments to our left and the Matanuska River Valley on the right. I was disappointed that we had to ride that section in the rain, which made the pavement slick. It dropped to the low 40s at Eureka Summit, where the fog was thick and the rain became mixed with sleet.

It sprinkled a few times between Glennallen and Tok and heavy clouds hung over the mountains, which were barely visible through the overcast. We got to Tok early because of having skipped Anchorage. We inquired at the Visitor's Center about the best motel deal and they directed us to the motel across the street, where a two-room family suite cost $120, or $30 each, which we thought wasn't bad when split four ways.

Jake also canceled the bed and breakfast reservations in Tok after learning that they intended to put us in one king-sized bed, a queen, and a single. Jake and Ed replaced spark plugs in front of the motel. Jake's BMW had been cutting out again and he hoped that new plugs might help. John got in at six with his new tire mounted, his bike fully serviced, and the rims banged out a little better than they were. We ate at the same corner cafe where we had lunch a few days earlier. The young girl who waited on us was high on something and she seemed to float around the dining room and smiled a lot.

Day 23 - The temperature was 41 degrees when we left Tok, our coolest start of the trip. We stopped to put on rain suits to break the cool wind. The roads from there to Canadian customs were in fair condition with occasional gravel breaks. It was rougher from customs to Kluane National Park in the Yukon with severe dips that made the Gold Wing's center stand slap the road a few times. One of the dips on a turn actually threw me a few inches off the seat when the bottom of the bike slammed the road. It rained a little before reaching Lake Kluane, where we had lunch at a small cafe on the lake. It was quite expensive: $5.75 for a thin ham sandwich and $1.50 for a coke. The proprietor was a surly guy in his 50s dressed in construction clothes. When I asked if he had a little water, he motioned toward the window and said gruffly, "Sure, I got a whole lake full of it." He didn't bring any, which took care of his tip.

It was very scenic from there to Whitehorse and the last 50 miles of pavement was wide, straight, and smooth. The temperature never rose above 55 all day, although the crisp air felt refreshing. We stayed at the same hotel that we used on our way up. We also had salmon steak for dinner again although this time we ate at the hotel next door, which was much less expensive. We called Bud and learned that his parts had been held up in Vancouver because they were trying to figure out how to get them to Watson Lake. He now expected them on a 4:30 PM bus the following afternoon, and he hoped to meet us between Teslin and Watson Lake in a day and a half.

DAY 24 - We had breakfast at a McDonald's, where Ed complained loudly about the plastic flatware and polystyrene container; the same as he usually did whenever we stopped at a fast-food place, but he was also getting more and more irritable every day. The temperature was 49 degrees and raining lightly when we left in our full rain suits. The road to Skagway was paved, although there were occasional breaks in the pavement with gravel patches. Beyond Carcross the scenery got very nice, especially around White Pass. The fog was thick in some areas, but we were able to see the craggy snowcaps and other scenic highlights. We cleared Canadian customs just before reaching the 3,292-foot pass. US customs was eight miles from there on the south side of the pass. It was overcast and windy at the summit, which cut down even more on the visibility. We were barely able to see the small ponds, tundra, and the strange lichen-like moss that was growing on the rocks.

Skagway was six miles beyond the US customs station via a twisty descent through a spectacular gorge. Two cruise ships were in port at the time, and small planes and helicopters kept taking off and landing from a grassy area near the dock. A narrow-gauge railroad took people up through the gorge on sightseeing excursions to White Pass. The auto-road clung to one wall of the gorge, while the railroad tracks clung to the opposite wall. The auto-road actually looked wider and safer than the railroad. We walked through town, visited the bank and the museum, and we ate some delicious pie at a restaurant. The town was filled with tourists.

We gassed up and left Skagway around 10:45, stopping only for a few photos on our way back up through the canyon. On a loose gravel road between Carcross and Jake's Corner, I chose the wrong way around a road grader and got held up for a few seconds. Meanwhile Jake and John crossed a nine-inch berm, passing both the grader and me. By the time I got by I noticed that their speed had increased considerably. I turned it up to 75 MPH and realized that they were still moving away like it was a race, so I grabbed a big handful of throttle and went after them in earnest. At one point I got into some soft sand on an inside corner and the big machine squirmed around a lot, but when I reached a firmer surface I was able to get by clocking about 85 on some loose gravel. Jake kept his head and decided that it was getting a little ridiculous at that point. He just laughed as I fishtailed by the both of them. John resumed the chase but when he got close to my back fender he decided I was already out of control and he figured if he attempted a pass, one of us might end up getting hurt.

We stopped at Jake's Corner for about a half hour and inspected the machinery. There were two right-hand-drive 1940 Ford trucks, a V8-driven snow-blower mounted on the back of a six-cylinder, four-wheel-drive truck, an old snow-track vehicle, and several other interesting pieces of equipment. I learned that crotchety old Jake who originally owned the place had sold out to the guy who is there now.

We got to the Northlake Motel in Teslin around 4:30. It drizzled quite a bit during the day and the temperature only rose to the 50s. We had dinner at Mukluk Annie's Salmon Bake where the food was excellent. Their salad bar had homemade macaroni and potato salads, baked beans, sourdough rolls, and a variety of vegetables. I ordered sweet-and-sour ribs and had a huge blueberry turnover for dessert. The friendly woman proprietor came by our table during the meal and asked if we would join them singing "Happy Birthday" to her daughter Nicki who was nine years old that day. She had composed a song for Nicki that she sang as she played the piano. After the birthday song she sang another older song that she had written about Mukluk Annie's and the Alaska Highway. We left in the midst of the songfest that I thought was great and typical of the Yukon Territory. John didn't think much of all the fuss. After calling three different radiophone numbers trying to reserve lodging in Iskut for the following night, I was finally able to contact the Tatogga Lake Resort by regular telephone and reserved two small cabins.

Day 25 - We had breakfast at the motel, which was expensive and the food wasn't that good. As we were packing to leave a couple of drunken Indian teenagers drove up in a beat-up old Datsun truck and barely missed running into the bikes. They were still reeling from the previous night and were anxious to tell some of their "Newfie" jokes. Ed was trying to fix his fairing bracket at the time and having trouble getting the screw started when one of the kids volunteered to help. He promptly dropped the screw and lost it behind the fairing, which made Ed grumble and grunt a few times. The motel management must have called the Mounties because before we left they came by and took the kids away in handcuffs. It was one of the only times I saw the Mounties all the time we were in Canada.

We left Teslin across the long steel-grate bridge at seven. About two hours later our BMW jinx struck again when Ed's alternator stopped working and his battery went completely dead. Bud was supposed to meet us not far from there so I continued on to look for him while Jake and John stayed to check the brushes and connections. I would also look for a gas station to get a piece of wire with which to charge Ed's battery if they couldn't fix it. The first gas station I found was at the Cassiar Highway junction, 53 miles away. I didn't see Bud along the entire stretch, so I bought a piece of wire and headed back.

I met Jake and John coming the other way. They had checked everything and decided that a pickup truck was the best answer. I got to Ed and immediately wired my generator to his battery. After removing my headlight fuse I ran my engine at 2500 RPM for about a half hour. That and a push start with all of his fuses removed was enough to get him the 65 miles into Watson Lake. We met the pickup truck about 10 miles before reaching there and I turned him around. I bought a battery charger at the local NAPA store for $75 and gave Ed another charge there, after which the two of us headed down the Cassiar. Bud's new part, which missed the bus the previous day, was now definitely due on the 5 PM Greyhound. The others would follow Ed and me as soon as Bud's bike was fixed.

Ed was very slow on the dirt sections of the Cassiar but the charge lasted four hours into Dease Lake where we caught the gas station just before it closed at nine. I thought the others should have caught us by then, but there was no sign of them. I charged Ed's battery for another 30 minutes as we got a sandwich "to-go" at a small cafe. His battery must have gotten much less current with my headlight fuse in. In hindsight, it would have been better to find an electrical outlet and set the charger on high during that time. We left Dease Lake at 9:30, just as it was getting twilight.

We were soon on dirt again and it started to rain. Darkness settled in around 10:15. Ed's night blindness, his recent cataract operation, and his lack of a headlight all gave him a sizable handicap. I tried to provide light for him by riding alongside, but he went so slow a few times I had to slip my clutch in first gear to stay with him. Consequently his battery died in less than two hours. The blackness of the night, the pouring rain, and the muddy road, combined to make this our darkest hour in more ways than one. Tatogga Lake was still 12 miles away and I suspected our hosts had already gone to bed. I had given up hope on the other guys by that time.

I wired my generator to Ed's battery in the dark, trying to contain my frustration. It seemed like Ed had given up because he just stood there. Several trucks and cars passed, but no one stopped to offer help or even find out what our problem was. Finally as we stood waiting for the battery to charge, three single lights came bobbing over the hill. I was never so glad to see anyone. Bud stayed with me to provide more light for Ed while Jake and John went ahead to locate and secure the cabins. John had brought only dark glasses and a dark face shield on the trip, never intending to ride at night, so he was essentially night blind too. Ed did a little better with the extra light shining on the road and we finally reached the cabins. They were very rustic but had warm blankets and space heaters. I set the battery charger on low for an overnight charge before we turned in. We had ridden only 40 miles of dirt that day but it felt like much more. If we only had the makings for a batch of whiskey sours to relieve the tension, but I had run out weeks ago. We got to bed at 1:15 AM.

Day 26 - The people at Tatogga Lake were friendly and we had a good breakfast before taking on the rest of the Cassiar in the rain. Road construction near Meziadin Junction created a real mess. The mud was slick with deep ruts in some places. A few times I had to skid my feet on the ground to control the Gold Wing. Ed got through OK but he fell when he stopped too close to a ditch to park the bike for a pee stop. I think he was getting over-tired. The bike fell over into the ditch, pinning him under it. When I stopped, I sat on my bike and yelled, "I've fallen and I can't get up!" When I didn't immediately jump off and run over to free him, a guy in a pickup truck stopped, looked at Ed, and then looked at me and said, "Is he a friend of yours?" He got out and helped me lift the bike off of Ed. The only damage was that his left mirror snapped off. Ed wasn't hurt.

Since Bud had missed out on the rest of Alaska, he followed my original route sheet into Hyder from Meziadin Junction, an 83-mile round trip. Hyder is a small town on the extreme southern tip of the Alaskan panhandle. The road into Hyder passes three active glaciers where the scenery is spectacular. The rest of us skipped Hyder because of Ed's battery problem and we continued south on the Cassiar after lunch. I got permission to plug the charger in for a quick charge while we ate. The scenery along the Cassiar was great, as was the first 50 miles of the Yellowhead Route into Smithers, where the temperature rose into the 70s. We stayed at the Aspen Motor Lodge there, ate at Smitty's Restaurant and washed a lot of dirt and calcium chloride off of the bikes at a nearby car wash. We rode about 380 miles that day, of which 120 were on dirt with some slick mud. It felt good to be back to civilization.

DAY 27 - We got up later than usual at six. We gassed up after breakfast and left with a full charge in Ed's battery. We ran into a few sprinkles and a few messy detours before the weather finally cleared and it got warmer around Vanderhoof. We stopped at a KFC in Prince George and found a 110-volt outlet for the charger behind the building. The young waitress wouldn't sell Bud the specific pieces of chicken that he wanted, saying he could only order one of the combinations from the menu board, which didn't please Bud at all. He was beginning to get quite irritable, especially following the frustrating week of waiting for his parts in Watson Lake.

We were entering a long holiday weekend for British Columbia Day, and all of the BMW shops in Vancouver and Kamloops would be closed; so we decided to take Ed all the way to Lewiston, Idaho, where according to Bud's dealer directory there was a BMW shop in Clarkston, WA just across the Snake River. That would be five days from where Ed's alternator died.

The temperature rose to the mid 80s by the time we reached Williams Lake. Bud, Ed and I located our motel and unloaded our gear. An hour later Jake and John still hadn't shown up, so I started back to look for them. I stopped at a small cycle shop just before it closed to arrange for a pickup truck in case we needed one. I thought Jake's BMW had broken down for sure, since he had been having progressively more trouble with it cutting out during the previous nine days. Just as I started up the long hill out of Williams Lake, Jake came flying down. I turned around and tried to catch him, but after pushing it up to 85 and 90 MPH, I decided it would be far less frustrating if I just followed him until he stopped.

He said later that he worked on the bike for more than an hour and when he got it going, the only way to keep it going was to run at high speed. We rented the Queen's Suite at the Super 8, which gave us three beds rather than two beds and a rollaway. The room included a small kitchenette, a living room area, a queen bed, an extra-long double bed, and a large pullout couch. The price was almost the same as a double with a rollaway. Bud and I ate at a family steak house called Mr. Mike, while the others opted for the "finer cuisine" of the Pub next door. I set Ed's battery on a slow charge for the night.

Day 28 - Jake woke us at 6:15 when I overslept again. The sky was crystal clear and the temperature was 57 degrees. His bike started and ran good all day. We passed through some nice, green farmland until about 15 miles out of Cache Creek, where we descended into a huge dry valley. The terrain around Cache Creek is dry and hilly. We continued to descend into Thompson River Canyon where we saw several large white-water rafts and a few kayaks coming down through the rapids. A short time later on a twisty road along the Fraser River Canyon, we watched a cable car being raised slowly out of the canyon.

We had lunch at a busy tourist restaurant in Hope called Rolly's while we charged Ed's battery at a motel next door. Later we rode 48 miles of super highway to Abbotsford before crossing the US border at Sumas, Washington. Bud filled out the necessary forms at Canadian customs to recover the duty he paid on his drive-shaft parts. We enjoyed a pleasant ride through some lush farmland in a fertile valley below Mt. Baker. The temperature rose to the low 80's before we stopped for the day in Burlington. Jake used my first-aid kit to treat his arm, which he had burned while working on his machine the previous day. We had dinner at a restaurant near the interstate, the same one that Bud and I used in 1988 on our back-road tour of the US.

Day 29 - There was a chilly ground fog around when we started the day. We stopped at the steel-grate bridge over Diablo Canyon where we took photos of the waterfall upstream and the raging creek 500 feet below the bridge. We stopped for photos several times in the Northern Cascades during our climb to Washington Pass. The scenery was outstanding for the entire distance. It was 80 degrees in Winthrop, so we peeled off several layers of clothes there. It was very dry around the Chief Joseph and Grand Coolee Dams.

We saw a lot of wheat fields in eastern Washington between Paternos and Lewiston, and a sign that said it was the largest wheat-producing area in the country. The view of Lewiston from the highway north of the city was spectacular, giving the impression of coming in by airplane. It was easy to find Mac's Cycle Shop in Clarkston but their mechanic had the day off. Jake took a chance and bought a voltage regulator for his bike, hoping it would cure his cutting-out problem but he soon learned that it didn't. We made arrangements for Ed's bike to be worked on in the morning before we re-crossed the Snake River to locate our motel in Lewiston. We ate across the street at Spencer's Restaurant where the service was slow. We finally got back to the motel around 9:30. Bud called his sister Posey in Boise to say that we would be there the next day to pick up the tires that the three of us had sent before leaving home.

Day 30 - A strong thunderstorm passed through during the night, although everything was dry by morning from the steady breezes. We ate breakfast at a nearby cafe and left by 6:45 in a comfortable 64 degrees. We left Ed after discussing the options of how he might catch up when his bike was fixed. We knew he would have to wait two hours for the shop to open and we figured that it could take another three to four hours to fix the electrical problem, change his tires, and road test the bike. If the problem involved a part they didn't have in stock, Ed might be there for a few days.

We saw beautiful, hilly countryside as we left Lewiston via some treeless, rolling hills for about 60 or 70 miles. Golden wheat swayed in the breezes over the tops of the hills. After cresting White Bird Pass we entered a huge valley and saw White Bird Battlefield, a historic area of Nez Perce Indian fighting. Our next canyon descent was nine miles of twisty roads with several runaway ramps. We enjoyed yet another spectacular ride through Payette River Canyon and later through some high meadows from Grangeville to the town of Meadow, where we saw thousands of head of cattle grazing in the tall green grass. We stopped at a fruit stand for a basket of peaches

171

and spoke with a guy from Oklahoma at one of our stops who was traveling with his wife on a GL1500 Gold Wing.

We got to Boise at three o'clock, unloaded our gear at the motel, and looked for Posey's house to pick up our tires. Jake was the only one to change a tire there. Bud's tires weren't worn enough because of his full week in Watson Lake, John had gotten his changed in Anchorage, Ed was getting his changed in Clarkston, and mine weren't worn enough to change. I had shipped two tires to Posey's house, which I would now have to carry on the back as luggage until they were needed. I used the extra time to wash my jeans and shirt at the motel. I draped them over the bike to dry in the 94-degree sun.

Bud got back from Posey's about 6:30 and we had dinner at Denny's. I had a bad dizzy spell and a few momentary blackouts that afternoon. I knew it was from stress, as the extended periods of interacting with the group and dealing with all of the problems began to take their toll on my nerves. Our evening "batch" usually helped to relieve a lot of that tension and we could have used it now more than ever, because the irritations in the group were running high. Ed got in around 8:45 with his bike fixed and a new rear tire mounted. His generator problem turned out to be a bad rotor, which they had in stock.

DAY 31 - I didn't sleep at all, which might have been partially due to anxiety about my bad spell, although the two cups of tea with dinner certainly contributed. It was my turn to sleep on a rollaway and it had a bar across the middle of my back. I tried moving the mattress onto the floor but it didn't help. Once when I began to doze off, Ed turned the bathroom light on, bringing me to full consciousness again. Finally I got up at 4 AM and went down to the lobby to have a few cups of tea, hoping it would keep me awake for riding that day.

We rode through more grassy hills followed by a thick Ponderosa pine forest with very twisty roads for about 60 miles. That led us up into the high meadows, where I stopped to view a few huge wild turkeys through my binoculars. We also saw five elk on our way through the forests. We went over Galena Pass into Sun Valley where the traffic was heavy, and we enjoyed excellent sandwiches for lunch from a convenience store there.

We visited Craters of the Moon where Bud and I rode the scenic loop through the lava fields and took several photos as the others waited at the Visitor Center. It was difficult for me to

172

stay awake between there and Idaho Falls due to my lack of sleep. After checking into our motel, Bud and I had an early supper at Smitty's, after which I fell asleep at 7 PM and didn't wake up for anything, while the others watched TV and talked for a few hours.

Day 32 - I got up at 4 AM and tiptoed down to the lobby for some tea. When I returned around five I started to draw water from the sink for our cooler, but for some reason the water pipes were full of air and the sound of air blasting through the pipes woke Ed and Bud. Ed soundly cursed me out for waking him up "in the middle of the night," even though it was only about 15 minutes earlier than our usual wake-up time.

In addition to all of the bike problems, our personal idiosyncrasies were beginning to wear on each other. Innocent offhand cracks and criticisms that would normally be taken good-naturedly were being taken as slurs. Ed was having more than his share of bike problems and he was on edge most of the time. Sometimes he would vent his frustrations at the desk clerks, saying that as a senior citizen he should not have to climb stairs to a second or third floor room; and he would also vent his anger at us when someone charged the room before he got there because he wanted a chance to use his own credit card.

When I left the motel that morning, I noticed the starter on the Gold Wing turned over very slowly. The bike took me to breakfast and back OK, but a quick check of the battery revealed that the water was low. I added a quart of water and it snapped right back. I figured it must have boiled out when I ran several days in Alaska and the Yukon with the headlight fuse removed.

Our route from Idaho Falls to Alpine Junction was very scenic, as were a few roads in Wyoming through beautiful fertile valleys in cattle country. We had lunch at Arby's in Evanston and used Interstate 80 for about 25 miles, which was also scenic. Our scenic highlight of the day was through Utah's Flaming Gorge country, followed by our steep descent via many switchback curves into Vernal, where it was over 90 degrees. John had already checked into the Econolodge an hour before the rest of us arrived and he wanted to know what took us so long! His innocent comment only added fuel to the tension. Jake changed his front tire that evening, giving him two fresh tires.

Day 33 - The road from Vernal through Dinosaur to Craig was desolate, rough, and narrow. Dinosaur is a tiny,

173

ramshackle western town surrounded by huge, sandy mesas and dry desert. We gassed up in Steamboat Springs and had a snack before heading into the high Rockies. The first 30 miles was a beautiful climb, after which we crossed a high desert for another 50 miles where the hardtop was covered with a thin layer of sand. The 50 or 60 miles we rode east of the Continental Divide was spectacular. It included a steep, twisty descent through the Poudre River Canyon where some of the vertical rock walls were 60 and 70 feet high, with a swift running, white-water river cascading down alongside the road.

Bud wanted to stop in the high desert for lunch but no one else seemed interested in stopping. Bud never liked having to make his stomach wait and he was also getting very irritable. Most of us were already uptight and after this latest difference of opinion with Bud, everyone seemed to drift apart and we rode down through the canyon on our own to give the emotions time to settle down. The exhilaration of flying down the twisty road for an hour helped to heal some of the irritation; although when we met at the bottom, Bud said he had decided to take a side trip through Estes Park to Fall River Pass in Rocky Mountain National Park. John and Jake started out with him, but went only as far as Estes Park, where they turned back because of heavy traffic. Bud continued on alone, which I believe is the way he wanted it in the first place to help him cool down. Ed and I headed directly for the motel but we got separated in one of the small towns. Later he spotted my bike at a rest area on the interstate where I had stopped. I parked the bike so he could see it since he really didn't know exactly where we were staying.

The Winterset Inn in Greeley was not the easiest place to find but we finally managed to regroup there. Before the others arrived seemed like an opportune time for me to change my rear tire and rear brake pads. Even though the tire had more than a thousand miles left on it I was sure it wouldn't last to New York and it would lighten the load on the back of the Gold Wing. We ate across the street at a Western Sizzler. Bud got back around seven after having reached Fall River Pass in rain, sleet, and even a little snow, but he loved it and I'm sure he felt better.

Day 34 - We saw several colorful balloons take off from an open field and watched them as they sailed silently by. Later we saw the biggest feedlot for cattle I have ever seen. There must have been 100,000 head of cattle in a single, square-mile area. We saw several other feeder pens that morning as well as huge fields of corn, milo, sunflowers, and onions. The land in eastern Colorado is very flat with occasional arroyos. The land is used mainly for farming and cattle ranching. We didn't find a gas station as I had hoped in Haigler, Nebraska, so we left our planned route to get gas in Benkelman, the hometown of wagon-master Ward Bond.

Near Bazine, Kansas an old man in a car coming in the opposite direction crossed over the centerline in the road and headed directly toward me. I hit the brakes thinking he was asleep. He kept coming for another few hundred feet before finally making a left turn directly in front of me. When we got to Dan Johnson's house that afternoon I related the incident to him. He laughed and said they call that maneuver a "farmer's turn." He said that many of the older people still do it around there and you have to be constantly on the lookout for it.

We arrived at Dan's at 4:30 and were treated to an outdoor cookout with really great, fresh-killed steaks followed by ice cream and brownie cake. Dan and Elaine had planned to put some of us together in double beds, but they didn't realize our size, or that we don't do that sort of thing, especially at a point on the trip when we are already at each other's throats. John slept on the living room couch and Bud slept on a cot in the children's room. I got a really good bed in an obviously feminine room with Victorian decor and a Victorian bed. I figured I got priority because of my age. Being very tired I turned in at 9:30 while the younger folks stayed up and visited.

Day 35 - A strong, warm breeze blew through my room all night. Not being accustomed to sleeping with a breeze blowing over me I woke up a few times and dreamed a lot, but generally I slept pretty well. For breakfast Elaine served hot cornbread with honey, butter, and syrup along with melon pieces and milk -- a delicious breakfast. A few of the group also went out for coffee, which Dan and Elaine never use. We left their place at 7:45 and headed south across some sparsely populated farmland. After having run close on gas the previous day, Ed insisted that we top off our gas every 80 miles or so rather than the usual 150 miles. He was sure I would run him out of gas in the sparsely populated areas of central Kansas. A big buck deer darted across the road between Bud and Jake, and later we saw the biggest road-kill of the trip, a full-grown horse.

175

Although Kansas is generally known for being flat and boring, our route was hilly and interesting. We saw a lot of milo growing which is used mainly to fatten the cattle. We had hamburgers at Braums, a fast-food place that also sells ice cream and pastries like Friendly's. John's bike fell over in soft tar in the parking lot as we ate. The fall broke a piece off of his windshield and bent the end of his clutch handle. By then he was already looking for a dealer to get a new front tire since the sport tire he had mounted in Anchorage was almost down to the wear bars. We stopped at a rest area near the Mississippi River and chatted with a few other riders before proceeding to our motel in Joplin, Missouri.

Day 36 - Ed woke the group at six when I overslept. We had a quick breakfast at Denny's and were on the road at our usual time. We enjoyed a few good bike roads through the Ozarks in Missouri and Arkansas, and later in Tennessee. I hit a bird with the top of my windshield that I was sure would hit me in the face. We saw rice paddies, cotton fields, and a lot of milo. It was an excellent day with light traffic and good roads.

After I had made several bold passes around some slow-moving trucks and cars, I sped up for several miles as the others waited for a better opportunity to pass. Usually when this happens I would put a few miles between us to give them the sport and diversion of catching up. This time, after about five miles of going as fast as I could, I ducked into a small side road. About a minute later Bud went by doing better than 70, followed a short distance behind by Jake and then John. When I got back out on the highway I rode as fast as I could but was unable to catch them until they stopped to check the map after about 25 miles. They weren't amused. A short while after that trick I missed a turn, costing us about 20 minutes. I took heat for both incidents. We also lost some time finding our motel in Lexington, TN, which added to the growing frustrations.

Day 37 - From Jelico, Tennessee I had chosen a rarely used steep and rough pass near the Cumberland Gap. It was raining fairly hard at the time and there was some road construction along the way with soft dirt and deep gravel. A few sections of the road had literally broken away and fallen off the edge. I thought it was great fun and I was pretty proud of myself for having included it, but everyone didn't share my feelings. By the time we reached our motel that evening, wet and weary, a few of the guys had enough of my route sheet and probably of me!

Adding to their frustrations, I had called ahead and reserved the Econolodge in Bristol, which was closer to our planned route than the Super 8; but because we had stayed at so many Super 8s on the trip, most of them thought our reservations were at the Super 8. John broke away in mid-afternoon as he often did and headed for the motel. Bud slowed down and waited for Ed, who was running a few miles behind -- as Ed often did. I led Jake directly to the motel. When I pulled into the Econolodge, Jake said that Bud told him we were staying at the Super 8. That explains why John wasn't waiting for us as he usually was. I asked the clerk to please call the Super 8 and have them send any lost motorcyclists over to the Econolodge. I finally rounded up everyone, but I took the brunt of more choice words after we reassembled. We had dinner at the Omelet Shoppe next door around 8 o'clock.

Day 38 - It was heavily overcast and drizzling lightly when we returned to the Omelet Shoppe for breakfast. Jake got sick from something he had eaten there that morning or the previous night and he had all he could do to keep it down. Up to that point Jake had been bearing up to the tensions very well, but I wondered if his indigestion was caused by the stress. John was the first to abort the tour. He never revealed exactly what it was that bothered him most, but he just packed his gear, suited up, and said he had more important things to attend to at home. He left without breakfast. I couldn't convince him how great a ride I had laid out for that day, and that the first 170 miles of my Virginia route was not only great stuff but also one of my favorite rides in the country. John said he had already been on and ridden every road in Virginia. I knew that his front tire was wearing pretty thin, as was his patience, and I figured he couldn't afford much extra mileage on either. He also had a badly worn rear swinging-arm bushing on his new Suzuki that he wasn't saying much about.

Ed was the next to split. At least he waited until after breakfast. I learned that Ed had been secreting a sore butt for weeks that his ruptured air-cushion seat cover didn't help and he simply had enough of the rough, twisty, country roads I had chosen. He headed for our overnight stop in Berkeley Springs via the interstate highways.

177

Most of our morning ride was on rural roads in the Piedmont area of western Virginia near the West Virginia state line. The weather remained overcast all morning and it drizzled a few times. A roadblock on our way to Goshen Pass causing us to ride a long detour, putting us out on Interstate 81 near Lexington. The next 200 miles included some of the Blue Ridge Parkway and the Skyline Drive. Jake had trouble with the engine cutting out again in Front Royal. It sounded like we were shooting up the town, as the backfires were extremely loud. Consequently we bypassed my planned backcountry roads and took four-lane highways from there into Berkeley Springs.

We spent our last night of the trip at the home of Jake's Uncle Ed where we slept in a very rustic and interestingly furnished barn that had been converted into guest quarters. We had a beer before dinner and we ate at a newly opened Italian restaurant owned by friends of Uncle Ed. At dinner Uncle Ed asked what each of us would remember most about the trip. I answered first, "I had an amnesia attack a few years back that still affects my memory, and if I'm lucky I won't remember anything!" I said it as a joke, but at that point of the trip there was some truth to it.

Day 39 - Jake and Ed decided to take interstate highways home as Bud and I continued on my planned route, although we also split in Gettysburg so I could visit for a few hours with Donna and my grandchildren in Hanover. I tried to catch up with Bud later but that was futile. My route sheet took us through Pennsylvania Dutch country and the towns of Bird-in-Hand and Intercourse. The area was a little crowded with tourists, but it was quaint and picturesque with Amish buggies and fancy decor. My route also took us across the Delaware River at Washington's Crossing near Trenton, followed by several remote country roads through northern New Jersey and southern New York State. I had lunch alone at the Burger King in Sparta and was home by 5:30.

ALASKA 5 – THE CANOL ROAD

The primary objective of my fifth tour to Alaska was to explore several long, lonely dirt roads in the northwest that I had never been on, especially the Canol Road in the Yukon Territory. In spite of the Alaska Highway being fully paved for its entire length for the 50th anniversary celebration in 1992, I still rode more than 2,000 miles of dirt roads during the trip. I was interested mostly in traveling over remote byways with spectacular scenery and exciting rides that the RVs, campers and other tourists had not yet discovered. The Dempster Highway and the Prudhoe Bay Haul Road had already lost their luster to me because they no longer met those criteria.

My tour began with a few of my favorite southern rides through the Amish country in Pennsylvania, the Appalachians of West Virginia, and the Piedmont area of Virginia. I rode past many small tobacco and dairy farms in Tennessee and I revisited the scenic Ozark Mountains of Arkansas. I turned north soon after entering Oklahoma and traveled through many hundreds of miles of the grasslands of Kansas, Nebraska, and the Dakotas. I continued north through the flatlands of Saskatchewan and the rolling hills of Alberta all the way to Great Slave Lake in the Northwest Territories, where I finally turned west and headed for the Canol Road. I kept the following journal:

Day 1 - My investment in a radar detector paid off in the first hour of the first day when I was thinking more about my upcoming adventure than I was about my driving and I sailed out of Harriman State Park into a 20 MPH speed zone in Sloatsburg far above any allowed tolerance. As the detector let out a single loud squawk on the K band used by the NY State Police, I went for both brakes. A shiny new cruiser sat tucked in behind some bushes less than a thousand feet up the road. This close call served as a warning that I had better pay more attention to my driving and especially to my speed.

I passed many quaint Amish buggies in the lush farmland around Lancaster and later I searched along the banks of the Susquehanna River looking for a good photo-op, which I never found. I had good weather on my first day and I spent the first night at Donna's in Hanover, where Asia and Robyn were getting ready to leave on their own vacation trip to Alaska. I would see them again in 2 weeks.

Day 2 - One of the highlights of the day was Catoctin Mountain Park in Maryland near the presidential retreat at Camp David. The roads are twisty and the traffic was very light. Later I rode respectfully slow through Sharpsburg, site of the Battle of Antietam Creek where more than ten thousand young men lost their lives in a single horrible day of the Civil War. I explored a few twisty and scarcely traveled roads in West Virginia and western Virginia that I had never been on before. When I realized I had planned far too many miles of twisty roads into a single day I got onto US 19 around five o'clock and rode directly into Tazewell, VA, my planned overnight stop.

Day 3 - I had planned even more miles of byways into my third day so I got up early and left at first light. It was hazy and barely daylight as I felt my way out of Tazewell along the Trail of the Lonesome Pine. A few of the roads I had chosen were difficult to find because my maps were not too clear for the tri-state area around Cumberland Gap. TN Rte. 63 out of Sneedsville was one of the day's highlights as was KY Rte. 74 out of Middleboro. Both of these rural roads were twisty and narrow, through some beautiful countryside.

I had packed my tank bag with snacks and emergency rations before I left and I used them for lunch that day because I was tight on time. I learned that I could reach into my bag and snack while I was riding. It worked out so well that I didn't stop for lunch during the entire trip. I encountered a few brief showers that morning although the temperature rose to around ninety later in the day and it got hot and humid. I stopped at a small roadside stand in mid-afternoon and had a huge soft ice cream cone for only 53 cents. I checked in that night at a small motel in northwestern Tennessee.

Day 4 - It was drizzling and overcast when I left after a "Hardee" breakfast. I wore my rain suit all day. It poured around one o'clock and continued to rain fairly hard through the Ozarks. I rode scenic Route 16 most of the way across Arkansas and enjoyed the sweeping turns of one 175-mile section where I rarely saw another vehicle the entire time. By the time I descended into Fayetteville late that day the sky had cleared and the temperature was back up to ninety.

Day 5 - It was clear and already 70 degrees when I left at 6:15, but by 11 o'clock it was 90 and very humid. I had to panic brake a few times in northeastern Oklahoma as I went into a few

180

of the turns far too fast. I wasn't paying enough attention and the road wasn't marked that well for the curves. By that time I was also getting a little groggy. I was sore between my shoulders, in my lower back, my rear-end, my throttle hand and I was beginning to burn from the sun. I was also fighting a lot of strong crosswinds from the south that kept throwing me around. All in all it was a pretty tough 600-mile day. My radar detector sounded off several times in Kansas and I had to watch for that too. On the open prairie I could detect radar more than a mile away, which gave me plenty of time to correct. I stayed in Norton, Kansas where I found a nice room for only $18.

Day 6 - It was a cool 52 degrees and cloudy when I left without breakfast. I stopped about an hour later in McCook, NE where I spotted a McDonald's. It began to rain around Ogalala and rained intermittently for the rest of the day. I rode through a mostly grasslands with seemingly endless green rolling hills in sparsely-populated cattle country. I almost ran out of gas twice before reaching my motel in Hettinger, ND. Once was when I counted on the next town being only seven miles away but I got detoured for 25 miles just before reaching it. I entered the Mountain Time Zone that afternoon which allowed extra time at the motel to wash out a few things.

Day 7 - Anticipating a long day, I was on the road at first light. The temperature was only 42 degrees. It didn't get above 60 until around two o'clock, so I wore double-force Damarts, a jacket and my rain suit top as a windbreaker most of the day. I rode six miles of soft dirt through an Indian reservation in North Dakota. I enjoyed the grasslands of Nebraska and the Dakotas, especially with practically no traffic. After crossing the Canadian border into Saskatchewan, the terrain got flat as a tabletop and a little boring.

Day 8 - I was on the road very early again. I stopped for breakfast at eight in Vermilion, Alberta. It turned out to be an easier day than I figured. The highway bypassed North Battleford, Edmonton, and a few other cities where I thought I would lose time. I was able to maintain a 65 MPH average most of the day. Alberta scenery is much nicer than Saskatchewan with rolling hills, big valleys, and more trees, mostly spruce, balsam, and poplar. I had great weather all day. I got into Valleyview before 3 PM, which allowed time to replace the spark plugs, the oil, and oil filter. I used two 5-liter plastic containers that I got from the motel owner. I cut one into a drain pan to catch the oil and I used the other to dispose of it. Later I went downtown to eat, where I saw a local celebration going on with traditional Indian dancing. That evening a fire truck rode around town and past the motel with a musical band aboard, blaring away. A few brief showers passed through during the evening. At 3 AM a party outside my room got pretty noisy and woke me from a sound sleep.

Day 9 - I got up, packed, and had bacon and eggs at the motel restaurant, which opened at six. It was a beautiful clear, cool morning. The highway was fairly straight and smooth, with very few cars, so I was able to maintain a 65 MPH average through the sparsely-populated countryside again. I saw three deer in Peace River and later I saw a ruffed grouse with two tiny chicks where I stopped for a nature break. The mother bird was fearless and kept charging at me in a show of force to protect her babies, which were the size of ping-pong balls. It was 80 degrees at the Northwest Territories border so I peeled off a few layers of clothes, but not far from there it clouded over and got really dark. The wind changed to the north, the temperature dropped 25 degrees in 20 miles and soon it began to rain.

I stopped for photos at Alexandra Falls and Louise Falls before riding into Hay River to look for a restaurant and check on motel prices. It turned out to be somewhat of a frontier town with very high prices. I also didn't see any inviting cafes so I returned to Enterprise where I had reservations and there was a diner. It was rustic there too but clean.

I had already gotten into bed when I thought about checking on the status of the Indian-run gas station at the intersection of the Liard Trail 205 dirt miles from there. I learned they had gone out of business, making my next gas 350 miles away in Fort Liard. Even filling my two spare containers, I would have to average about 46 MPG, which was too risky through muddy construction that I anticipated. A trucker having dinner at the cafe said I could leave the McKenzie about 65 miles from there and find gas at Dory Point, just 14 miles off my route. I could easily make the 300 miles from there to Fort Liard with the two extra gallons I carried.

Day 10 - I was up at 4:45 ready and anxious to take on the first long, lonely dirt road. It was a chilly 43 degrees, very cloudy, and it looked like rain. I wore my full rain suit. Rain during the night made the 30 miles of construction very slippery. I was able to get through before the construction crews arrived, which was in my favor. Some of the work areas had deep ruts, some had standing water, and others were just plain slick, and I had to skid both feet on the ground to keep from losing it. I saw only one vehicle in the first 65 miles, a provincial work truck.

When I didn't spot a place to eat at Dory Point, I ate breakfast from my tank bag. Back on the McKenzie Highway I saw a vehicle about every hour and a half. It was actually in pretty good shape for a dirt road. I merely had to be careful to stay in the tire tracks because there was a lot of loose gravel everywhere else. Much of the McKenzie was relatively straight. I stopped for photos at Whittaker Falls and thought it was pretty wild. I transferred my spare gas into the tank about 110 miles out and realized I was getting better than 46 MPG at that point, which was unusual. It sprinkled a few times on the McKenzie Highway and began to rain harder as I turned onto the Liard Trail. The surface got messy with puddles of water in the thousands of little potholes and occasionally I hit some patches of mud. I refueled at Fort Liard and quickly pressed on, thinking that the road surface could deteriorate even more. I saw a few deer on the McKenzie and later I saw two red foxes and four bison on the Liard Trail.

The rain stopped near the British Columbia border and it got warmer. As soon as the gravel dried up it got very dusty. The 60-degree temperature felt good after 40s and 50s most of the day with rain. I was pretty tired by the time I reached the long narrow, single-lane bridge across the Fort Nelson River, onto the Alaska Highway. I had ridden 470 miles of dirt that day and some of it was pretty messy. The roads certainly didn't offer the type of riding or the scenery I had come for. They were all relatively straight and level and there was very little spectacular scenery along the way, except an occasional waterfall. It was just hundreds of miles of loose gravel with dust and sometimes mud. I ate Chinese that evening in Fort Nelson and tried to clean up some of my things from all the dust.

Day 11 - It was overcast with a lot of low hanging fog in the mountains when I started up the Alaska Highway. The fog was especially thick around Steamboat where the best scenery usually begins. I saw four caribou near Summit Lake and a large Dalls Sheep just west of there. I met some early morning rain between Steamboat and Summit, although the sun was out by the time I reached Muncho Lake. A huge forest fire was burning just west of there and smoke covered more than a thousand square miles of wilderness. I hit one huge pothole that threw me more than a foot off the seat. I thought for a moment I had lost it. The Alaska Highway was not as crowded as I thought it would be on its 50th anniversary year.

While waiting for a pilot car at some road construction 55 miles before Watson Lake, I learned from a motorist that the South Canol Road was closed a week earlier due to a landslide. If it were still closed I would have to skip it and detour north out of Watson Lake on the Campbell Highway to reach the North Canol Road and miss half of what I came for. My plan called for riding both sections the following day. I stopped at the maintenance camp in Watson Lake to inquire about the latest status. They called ahead and learned that it had been reopened.

I reached Teslin at 4:30 after going through another major construction area 80 miles west of Watson Lake where I was delayed for about 30 minutes. I decided to bypass my reserved motel in Teslin and try Mukluk Annie's Salmon Bake for lodging since I planned to eat there anyway. It also meant riding eight miles less in the morning to reach the Canol Road. I got a nice cabin for $35 and later a grilled-salmon dinner for only $12. They have a good salad bar where I pigged out before learning it was also all the salmon you could eat that night. I ate so much salmon I felt like a bear going into hibernation.

After dinner I walked down to the lakeshore where I met some cyclists making camp. Three guys and a girl were on two 1000cc Moto Guzzis and a BMW R1000GS, all with European plates. The oldest of the three guys was removing the rear wheel from the Guzzi that was attached to a stripped-down sidecar used for luggage. As I watched him change the tire I noticed a travel sticker on his tank that read, "Cape Horn, Chile." I asked if they had just come from there and the answer was yes. They had been on the road for more than two months. My own upcoming adventure on the Canol Road suddenly lost a little of its luster.

Day 12 - The name Canol Road was derived from Canadian Oil. The Canol project was undertaken in 1942 following discovery of oil at Norman Wells in the Northwest Territories. When the US Army Corps of Engineers was nearing completion of the 1520-mile Alcan Highway with more than

184

20,000 men, they were directed by the War Department to divert some of that manpower to building a 513-mile pipeline system from Norman Wells to Whitehorse in the Yukon Territory. The oil was badly needed to fuel Alaska and protect it from a possible Japanese invasion. The project included a four-inch oil pipeline with several pumping stations along its length, a refinery in Whitehorse, airfields, and other support facilities. The project was abandoned four years later, after only about a million barrels of oil had been pumped through the line.

The entire Yukon section of the Canol Road has been reopened to summer traffic and is maintained to minimum standards, which means that there would be very little vehicular traffic and no RVs traveling on it. The 138-mile southern end from Johnson's Crossing on the Alaska Highway to Ross River on the Campbell Highway has been designated the South Canol Road. The North Canol Road is a 144-mile continuation from Ross River to the NWT border. An additional 230 miles of the original pipeline road from the NWT border to Norman Wells is known as the Canol Heritage Trail. That final section is unsuitable for most motor vehicles. It is used primarily as a hiking trail, although occasionally an adventurous dirt-biker will ride it, but some of the river crossings are deep and hazardous and washouts are common. The trail passes through prime grizzly bear and caribou habitat and it reportedly features some beautiful scenery.

I assumed this day would be the toughest and probably the riskiest day of my 14,000-mile tour, with more than 450 miles of narrow dirt roads. The fact that the entire Canol Road is maintained to minimum standards also meant I had to be prepared for anything. I expected to eat both breakfast and lunch from my tank bag. I considered shortening the day but that would mean making camp somewhere along the North Canol Road, an idea I wasn't too enthusiastic about.

Johnson's Crossing was 25 miles from Mukluk Annie's. It was 46 degrees and overcast when I turned up the narrow, twisty South Canol Road at 5:30 AM, having begun the day at five. It didn't appear to be much more than a single lane. I cautiously guided the big Gold Wing through several tight turns and sharp up-and-down hills before climbing quickly to 4,000 feet. It began to rain less than a half hour after I got on the road and the surface immediately got very slick. Occasionally it would rain heavy, which gave me some concern about landslides and washouts. The road had just been reopened after having been closed for a week due to a slide. I noticed one spot where a washout had been repaired but it looked temporary at best and I wouldn't be surprised if it washed out again later that day.

I saw no one during the first 100 miles. I saw a beautiful lynx dart across the road only twenty feet in front of me near Quiet Lake. He stood more than 30 inches tall to his back. A short time later I saw a huge bull moose and then a chocolate-colored fox with silver hair on his neck, called a cross fox. I was also treated to the rare sight of a female moose with twins that were barely a week old. I have always been somewhat wary of female moose with young but she gave me no problem.

I was elated and quite excited during most of my ride on the South Canol Road. Although it was much shorter than my 1977 ride on the 480-mile Cassiar Highway, it was just as exciting and interesting. It was exactly what I had come for. I passed beautiful lakes and streams with the snow-covered Pelly Mountains and Big Salmon Range in the background. The narrow, twisty road rose to more than 500 feet above the Lapie River and it seemed as though there was nothing holding the road from falling away into the valley below. I walked near the edge at one spot and saw a large fracture in the dirt, so I tiptoed back to the bike. Just before reaching the Campbell Highway, I crossed a one-lane Bailey bridge, which spanned the rocky gorge of the Lapie River Canyon. I had spent more than four hours on the South Canol Road and saw no one the entire time.

It was 10:30 when I refilled my tank and filled two extra one-gallon containers in Ross River prior to boarding a small cable ferry. The ferry operator asked how far I was going and if I expected to return that day. I answered that I was headed for the NWT border and I did hope to be back that day. He smiled as he looked at his watch and he described to me where he lived. He said when I get back I can walk across the footbridge and find him at home. He was quite sure I wouldn't make it back before he left work at five. Two European youths waiting at the ferry crossing for a lift asked if I would tell their friends at the first Macmillan River bridge that they would be there as soon as they could find a car or truck going that far, about 120 miles. Their wait would be long if traffic on the North Canol were no heavier than the South Canol.

The river crossing took only a few minutes on the small cable ferry and I was on my way. The North Canol Road was straighter than its southern counterpart but I realized soon after leaving the ferry that I would never be back by five in spite of stepping pretty lively. I found the first ten miles to be damp and quite slick. Later I rode mostly on loose gravel. Most of the turns were unmarked and some were deceiving. A few times I went into a turn much too fast, and I would skitter precariously on the shoulder as I tried to maintain control. The thought of ending the trip right there would flash through my mind, which made me ease up a little on the throttle. The surface was pretty rough in places with potholes and sometimes baseball-size stones strewn around. I came around one turn and had to panic brake for a big caribou. He turned and faced me down less than ten feet away. I thought at first he was going to charge but I sat there and blipped the throttle a few times and he turned and ran.

Another time I rounded a bend and hit the brakes for a strange animal in the road that stood more than 3 feet tall to his back. It was completely black with a long slim tail like a panther. It had long thin legs with padded feet and when it took a few easy strides into the bush I thought it seemed to run like a dog. I didn't get a good look at its head, but what I did see of it was short, more like a cat. I've researched several books since returning from my trip but I've never found a picture of an animal quite like that one, although I think it was a huge cat.

About a hundred miles from Ross River, near where I transferred my extra gas into the tank, I came across the first of several groups of abandoned World War II vehicles, including many trucks and an old road grader. I saw buildings that were used as living quarters by construction workers and I saw the remains of a maintenance depot for repairing heavy equipment. Later I saw some sections of four-inch pipe lying loose.

I stopped to talk with a few people on foot to see if they were the friends that I was supposed to relate the message to. They spoke only French but I was able to conclude that they weren't the right guys. They looked exhausted from walking and they were both wearing head nets for protection from the insects that were very thick in the area. Whenever I stopped, even for only a minute or so, the bare areas of my skin would be covered with swarms of mosquitoes, flies, and other small insects. Just before reaching the first of several Macmillan River bridges I was approached by two young guys, one carrying a rifle. I learned after a few anxious moments that they were the ones I was supposed to give the message to. I stopped and talked for a minute but the insects were thick, I was on short time, and I was a little anxious about their strange behavior. I took off as soon as I could and pressed on for the NWT border.

The final fifty miles had the nicest scenery. Thick underbrush gave way to green, hilly tundra. Spectacular snow-covered mountains surrounded me. I saw an airstrip and a few accesses to mining areas for barite, zinc, lead, and silver. I saw only a few maintenance trucks on the road. They were usually traveling at a high rate of speed since they were more familiar with the road than I was. I hoped that I wouldn't meet one of them on a turn while I was fighting for control on the loose gravel. I saw no other travelers on the Canol Road all day.

About 8 miles from the NWT border I came upon a stream where the bridge had been washed out. The water was about a foot deep. I could see vehicle tracks entering and leaving the water and many large boulders in the swift-running stream. I studied the situation and searched for a clear path between the boulders. As I contemplated my next move a crusty-looking old guy in a four-wheel-drive pickup drove through the stream. I watched his wheels splash and bounce as he came across and decided it was a risky proposition at best for the Gold Wing. I was concerned that I could break the water pump or the oil filter, which both hang quite low and unprotected in front of the engine. I could also stall it in the middle and have quite a job pushing it out with many rocks in the way. I decided to turn around there and return to Ross River.

When the old guy -- actually younger than I am -- stopped to look at the Gold Wing, he shook his head, smiled, and said, "You're a tougher man than I, Gunga Din." I learned from our brief conversation that he is retired and lives alone up there all summer in a small cabin. He said the road is actually passable for another 28 miles. The Tsichu River, inside the Northwest Territories is the first major obstacle on the Canol Heritage Trail. A bridge is out there too and the water is much deeper and swifter, which would present a formidable barrier to most vehicles. It was 2:30 PM when I turned the bike around. It took four hours to get to that point and I was sure it would take at least three-and-a-half hours to get back, which meant I would definitely be using the footbridge to locate the ferry operator.

I got back to the river just as a maintenance truck was also arriving. I asked him if he had made arrangements with the ferry operator to get across. He said that no one is getting across on that ferry tonight. He went on to explain that its fan had gone through the radiator about mid-afternoon and he was called to work on it. I asked how long he thought it would take to fix and he said it depended on how long it took to get a radiator, a fan, and a water pump for an obsolete diesel. If they have all of the parts in Whitehorse it should be only a day or two. If he has trouble finding the parts, there is no telling how long it would take. My heart dropped as I visualized spending a week or more in Ross River with my bike on the wrong side of the river.

We walked across the single-span suspension footbridge together. It was 300 to 400 feet long and swayed slightly in spite of its heavy stay cables. The three-foot-wide walkway tilted to the left at one end of the bridge and tilted to the right at the other end. I carried most of my gear across because I didn't expect to get back to the bike that night. I walked directly to the home of the ferry operator while the mechanic went to call his boss. When I spoke with the operator, to my surprise he smiled and said, "Come on, I'll get you across." I told him about the mechanic being there so we went to find him first.

The operator said it happened while he was taking a car across. He spent hours working on the engine in the middle of the river with the anxious passenger aboard. It's a lucky thing that the ferry was attached to a cable or he would have been swept down the river in the swift current. He said he jury-rigged it so he could get me across. I was the only one stranded on the wrong side of the river. After starting the engine, the crossing took only a few minutes, after which he immediately shut the engine down. As soon as the mechanic and I loaded our vehicles aboard, the operator restarted the diesel and took us across. I'm sure the engine didn't overheat in that short period of time.

I had reservations at Sooley's Bed and Breakfast, which is a cafe with a small building in the rear that has four rooms and a common bath. After a quick shower I tried to clean up some of my things before turning in. My face shield was badly scratched, the zipper on my tank bag had stopped working altogether, and dust was in everything. Most of my clothes were filled with dust but it was too late to wash anything because it wouldn't have time to dry. I was exhausted from a long day and it was after ten when I finally got things squared away enough to climb into bed.

Day 13 - It was 46 degrees and partly cloudy when I got up at 5:30. When I learned that breakfast wouldn't be served until seven I went for a walk along the river. I also couldn't buy gas until eight, so I killed some more time at breakfast chatting with Sooley, the proprietor. I asked him if he knew anything about motorcycles traveling the Canol Heritage Trail. He said he heard that three came through the previous year, two Europeans and one from Vancouver, all on dual-sport machines. He said it was during a dry spell when the rivers were shallow. I thought it sounded like a great candidate for a future adventure. After breakfast I looked for the gas station attendant and finally found him having coffee at another small cafe.

I got on the road at 8:20, the latest start of my tour. I spotted another lynx along the Campbell Highway. I visited Dome Mountain before checking into my bed and breakfast. The "Dome" offers magnificent panoramic views of the confluence of the Yukon and Klondike Rivers, Bonanza Creek, the Ogilvie Mountains, and the Top-of-the-World Road.

I stayed at the same bed and breakfast where our group stayed the previous year, a beautiful and spotless home run by a friendly guy named Jon and his pretty Filipino wife. I ate Chinese at a downtown restaurant that evening. I didn't sleep too well, possibly because my anxiety was running high. I dreamed about the bike that night. I kept trying to start it but it wouldn't start. Then it was my camera that wouldn't work. As I kept trying to take a picture, it exploded in my face, starting little fires all around. I wondered what all the bad dreams meant. Maybe it was the Chinese food.

Day 14 - Jon's breakfast was great as usual. The strawberry-rhubarb tarts, sausage croissants, muffins, and assorted Danish pastries were all excellent. I chatted with him while eating and learned a little about Clinton Creek where he was once a supervisor at the now-abandoned asbestos mine. I decided to visit Clinton Creek that day. It was about 30 miles off the Top-of-the-World Road.

I got to the Yukon River ferry at seven and there was already a line of more than 30 large RVs waiting to cross, most of them in a convoy from Oregon. Only two large units can fit on the ferry at one time, so it could be several hours before everyone got across. I went to the head of the line to see if I could squeeze in where a car or RV couldn't. I was waved on immediately, just as they were about to raise the boarding ramp. The Top-of-the-World Road was beautiful that morning. The sky was clear and the early morning sun glistened on the mist that settled in the valleys.

I located the road to Clinton Creek easily. There were many tent campers along the first 20 miles, but I saw no one after the steep descent to the Forty-Mile River. The road is not maintained beyond there because drivers are probably wary about crossing the bridge. The planking is heavily rotted although the main structure appears sturdy. After crossing it, I learned that the road I thought might lead to the town had a bridge totally gone and the water was deep so I didn't go through it. Instead I followed a road to the asbestos mine and explored the mine area. I saw a lot of abandoned equipment lying around and I saw a small airstrip that was used extensively during the 1991 forest fire. I followed another road that led me down to the confluence of the Yukon and Forty-Mile Rivers.

When I got back to the Top-of-the-World Road, I was met by a horde of RVs from the convoy. I passed several before reaching the US customs station where the guy said he had already checked 69 RVs through that morning. I turned north on the Taylor Highway for a side trip to Eagle, Alaska. I was happy to break away from the convoy, at least for a little while. The road to Eagle was in pretty good shape considering that it clings to the sides of the hills and canyons and is prone to slides. There was a lot of loose gravel on the narrow road, which threw up a lot of dust, but I enjoyed the ride. Eagle is a typical Alaska town, very rustic and unorganized with lots of junk lying around. The river front area looked neater than the rest of the town. I gassed up before heading for Tok. On the way back up the Eagle Road I met a huge tour bus coming the other way. Luckily I had advance warning from a leading car with flags and banners flying, and a big sign saying that a bus was following.

The tail end of the convoy was just going by when I reached the Taylor Highway. I passed no less than 30 RVs on the extremely dusty and badly-worn gravel road. Several of the drivers showed resentment to my bold passes by blowing their horns. It was just about the worst hundred miles of dirt I ever rode. One of my rain deflectors snapped off of my windshield from the constant vibration. The zipper on my tank bag had stopped working the day before and everything inside was a mess from the dust, not to mention how much I got into my lungs. I cussed the RVs, I cussed the road, and I cussed the State of Alaska for the terrible condition of the road. I went by three Gold Wings from Ontario very fast, and I'm sure they thought I wasn't wired right. I got to Tok about 4:30 and checked into the same Quonset-hut lodge where our group refused to stay the previous year due to its run-down condition.

After checking in I had to admit that it was in pretty bad shape. My room was on the sunny side, which made it very hot. I opened the window but the screen was ripped out. I couldn't leave it open because it would let the mosquitoes in. The community toilet smelled strong of mildew and urine. I didn't hear anyone else in the building and my room was about halfway down a long, almost-dark hallway. My only consolation aside from the price was that although the sheets were tissue thin from wear, they were clean. If I camped out that night I wouldn't have it nearly that comfortable. There was no dead-bolt or safety chain on the door so I piled my heaviest bags against it before I took a Sominex and got into bed, an old steel Army cot.

I was asleep for about 3 hours when a jiggling in my door lock woke me. I yelled, "Who's there?" The jiggling sound continued. I said it a louder, "Who's there? What do you want?" The jiggling seemed to quicken and then all of a sudden the door began to open in spite of my heavy bags behind it. I wasn't sure if I was having a bad dream or if this thing was really happening. I presumed he had a weapon and I got pretty shook up. I thought my best defense at that point was noise, as much as I could make. I yelled at the top of my lungs, "Hey, what are you doing in my room?" The guy mumbled in a heavy foreign accent something like, "I'm looking for rope." Thoughts of what he planned to do with the rope raced through my mind. I yelled even louder, "Get out of my room!" He finally left and I got up and locked the door again. This time I moved my entire bed against it. My heart was beating so hard it took me a long time to get back to sleep, but I finally drifted off.

Day 15 - I got up at 4:15 and got ready to leave. I ate a little in the room before carrying my gear out. I was relieved to find that the bike was still there. As I was pulling out I noticed a state police barracks diagonally across the highway so I stopped to report the incident. There was only an office worker on duty. I filled out a form and signed it. The girl asked if I was returning that way, and if so would I please stop by on my return trip. She said a state trooper would investigate the case and he may have questions. I told her I would be back in three days.

I left Tok a little after five. I saw a large female moose on the Glenn Highway about an hour later. It got very overcast and began to rain so I suited up. It rained harder when I was about 50 miles from Valdez and it poured the rest of the way in. The ride to Valdez was spectacular in spite of the rain and fog. I climbed over Thompson Pass and through Keystone Canyon, and saw several big glaciers near the road at the highest pass. I stopped there and also at Bridal Veil Falls and Horsetail Falls. While getting gas in Valdez I asked the attendant if it had been raining long. He said it had been raining steady for four days. By the time I got back out to the Glenn Highway it was clear again. It was probably raining only along the coast.

I enjoyed the ride from Glennallen to Palmer, although it rained most of the way. I got into Palmer early and proceeded to wash a lot of my clothes, including my jeans and jacket and I hung them around the room to dry. I was finally able to make temporary repairs to the tank bag zipper and I cleaned the inside of the bag. I stayed at the same motel that we used the previous year with the group. I also walked to the same hotel where I ordered the same really good dinner. On the way back, I got caught in the rain the same way we did last year and I began to think about déjà vu.

Day 16 - I rode into Anchorage after a hearty breakfast at the hotel. I stopped to buy a few T-shirts and then I called Rey. He expected me on the 16th because that's what I had told Asia two weeks earlier in Hanover. I had merely glanced at my route sheet and saw 16, which was actually my 16th day and not the 16th of July. It was only the 12th of July when I arrived. I was lucky they hadn't planned something else for the day. We had a really nice visit. Rey cooked chicken soup and barbecue ribs for lunch, after which Asia and Robyn gave the bike a much-needed wash.

We enjoyed a long walk in Kincaid Park, where we saw a couple of eagles perched in a tree. Becky and the kids ran ahead and exercised the dog while Rey and I followed at a more leisurely pace. Rey's dinner consisted of a special Chinese dish, giant shrimp, and smoked haddock. His mom was there all day. I left around 7:30 and had a little trouble with a wet spark plug on my return to Palmer. I had to take the cap off the plug and clean the mud out of the drain hole in the well to let the water out. I had the same problem several times in the past year but this was the first time I took a few minutes to fix it.

Day 17 - I stopped at the state police barracks in Tok to check with the troopers about my problem of a few days earlier. A different girl took a few minutes to find the complaint and then she said, "Oh yes, here it is. That case was solved. The woman who rented you the room apparently misplaced the registration. At midnight her husband, not realizing that the room was rented, rented it again. They think that what the guy you thought was breaking in was probably trying to say that he was looking for his room, not his rope."

I reached White River Lodge on the Alaska Highway about 4:30, intending to rent a cabin that turned out to be pretty run down. One of the cabins had a pullout couch for a bed and a long outside walk to a bathroom at the lodge. The other cabin was next to a noisy diesel-power generator that provided power for the entire site. Both cabins were dirty with bare wood floors, no furniture except the bed, and no locks on the doors. The doors opened out so they couldn't even be blocked. I decided to rent a room inside the lodge instead. It cost about twice as much but it was cleaner and the bed was more comfortable.

Day 18 - It was 45 degrees and cloudy at 4:15. The restaurant was open 24 hours, so I had a full breakfast before leaving at 5:30. I saw the third lynx of my trip around Kluane National Park. It was only 43 degrees and raining at Bear Creek Summit. I gassed up at Haines Junction before turning south for Haines. The Haines Road was very scenic but it was so cold, rainy, and foggy that I didn't get much pleasure from it. It was only 41 degrees at the summit, which was completely treeless with snow patches along the road for about 20 miles. I met a guy at the ferry dock from San Jose, California riding a Gold Wing. He complained a lot about the poor condition of the Alaska Highway, especially between Lake Kluane and the Alaska border, and he swore he would never ride it again. He came by ferry from Seattle to Haines and was returning the same way, stopping a day or two at each port-of-call. I wondered how he might like some of the roads I had traveled during the previous week.

I enjoyed the brief ferry ride to Skagway but I didn't care for staging a full two hours before sailing. The scenery along the Skagway channel is nice but I am sure it would have been a lot nicer on a clear, sunny day. The wind was so strong it was difficult to stand or walk on the deck. During the one-hour ferry ride I saw a luxury cruise ship coming from Skagway and another tied up at the dock there. A girl from the National Park Service spoke to the passengers in the forward lounge about the history of Skagway with some entertaining anecdotes. I had a barbecue rib dinner in Skagway and walked around town in spite of a steady drizzle. My motel was first class, as were the prices.

Day 19 - I left Skagway without breakfast at 5:30. It was a cool 48 degrees. The scenery along the Klondike Highway was beautiful, especially up through the canyon and over White Pass into the Yukon Territory. About five miles north of Tagish I saw another female moose with twins. I estimated these to be about 4 months old. It was a clear day on the Alaska Highway with the temperature in the 50's. I got a pretty good break through the construction with only a 15-minute wait for the pilot car. I used the time to go over the bike. Later I saw a 22-wheel truck overturned near a rest area. I figured someone must have pulled out in front of the guy. He was standing there with fresh lacerations on his face, waiting for someone to come and right his rig.

There was a brief shower at the Cassiar Junction where I gassed up. Only 18 miles of dirt remains on the Cassiar between the Alaska Highway and Dease Lake where I stayed. I washed out a few things and replaced a paper-thin front brake pad with a used one I was carrying. I replenished my food supply at the local grocery store, including enough for breakfast. When I asked at the gas station about the condition of the road to Telegraph Creek he laughed and said, "That's a road?" He said it was narrow, rough, and dangerous with sheer drops of several hundred feet and he would never go up there.

Day 20 - I was up at four, the earliest of any day of the trip. Breakfast in my room consisted of heated baked beans, a can of cold sardines, and a cup of hot tea. It was barely first light when I got on the road to Telegraph Creek. The first fifty miles was twisty and narrow. It looked a lot like hard-packed topsoil. It rained during the night, which made the chocolate-colored surface slippery in spots. I imagined what it might be like in a heavy rain. I heard it gets muddy and extremely slippery with deep ruts and I could see why. I met a brief shower about 25 miles out of Dease Lake and the surface immediately got slick as water began to accumulate in the tire tracks. I saw a large bull moose about 30 miles from my start.

About halfway to Telegraph Creek I could see the snowy peak of Mount Edziza in the southwest. From there the road began a sharp descent with 20 percent grades and switchback curves for about ten miles. It descended into a small canyon and through some strange lava beds, after which it climbed sharply to a narrow ridge of the same lava-type terrain. There were 400-foot drops to the Tahltan River on one side of the ridge and to the Stikine River on the other side. The road descended steeply through another series of switchback curves to a bridge across the Tahltan River and into a small Indian village. I saw a few old smokehouses and a sign advertising fresh-smoked salmon. From the village, another steep grade scaled the edge of the Stikine River canyon. The narrow, gravel road with no side rails afforded spectacular views of the river valley far below.

Another Indian village is located near the top of a 3-mile climb. A sign there identifies it as the former home of the Tahltan bear dog, a small animal almost extinct that would bark persistently, holding the bear at bay until the hunter arrived. Telegraph Creek, ten miles farther, was yet another Tahltan Indian community. Travel services were available like gas, food, and lodging, and I saw a small general store and a public school. The town was an important center during gold-rush days. Since then it has been a communications terminal, the head of navigation on the Stikine River, and a commercial salmon fishing area. Guide services are available for hunting, fishing and river trips. A 12-mile road continues west to Glenora, the site of an attempted, although abandoned, railroad route from southern British Columbia to the Yukon Territory.

After taking a few photos in Telegraph Creek I headed back to Dease Lake and the Cassiar Highway. Only 110 miles of dirt remain on the Cassiar south of Dease Lake. Most of it was treated with calcium chloride to keep the dust down. From the original 480 miles of spectacular dirt that I rode in 1977, a total of 130 miles remains, half of which may be paved by year-end. Many RVs and campers now use the Cassiar as an alternate route to Alaska. I saw a black bear and a brown bear a few miles apart and several eagles. I ran into a few rain showers before reaching Meziadin Junction where I found the gas station closed due to a recent tragic fire in which someone died. I reached Stewart on the fumes, 254 miles from my previous fill-up. I had a very nice ride to Stewart on a newly paved road through a picturesque canyon with glaciers, white-water streams and snow-covered mountain peaks.

I got to Stewart about 3:30 and decided to go into Hyder to do some exploring before checking into my motel. Hyder, Alaska is a small town with a single, short main street and no customs check between there and Stewart, which is in Canada. The only access to Hyder is by that single road from Stewart, which led me quickly through and out the north end of town and along a glacier-fed river. I followed the road for about ten miles and was about to turn around when I saw a sign: "All vehicles beyond this point must have chains." That made it look a bit more interesting so I kept going. I climbed gradually for three or four more miles to where I was again about to turn around; but I noticed another sign, which said the Salmon Glacier was straight ahead so I continued.

The road soon began a very steep climb high into the mountains. From that vantage point I could see a spectacular S-shaped river of ice winding down through the canyon below me. As I continued to climb I realized the road actually went far above the glacier. At one point I stood looking down at the confluence of two glaciers, one coming from the north and the other from the northwest. It was a mind-boggling sight. There were huge piles of snow along one side of the road and a 300-foot drop to the glacier on the other side. The dirt road I had been following was carved out of the side of the mountain. I learned later that it continues to the Premier Mine, just a few miles beyond where I finally turned around.

During the summer, the water from melting snow builds up high in the canyon behind the toe of the glacier, and once a year the level of the water rises above the level of the glacier. This huge ice dam eventually breaks; and the water, along with tons of ice, logs, and other debris, comes cascading down through the canyon, flooding the entire valley below. It must be an awesome and terrifying sight. Local people say that when it goes it sounds like thunder and actually makes the earth tremble. I spent more than an hour exploring above the glacier before heading back to secure my room, for which I had a six o'clock courtesy hold. At $74.50 Canadian it was the highest price I paid for a room on the trip. I removed, cleaned, and lubricated the speedometer cable that evening because it had been groaning for about a week. I also did other minor bike service.

Day 21 - It was clear and 48 degrees at 5:15. It was to be my first full day on improved roads in almost two weeks. Upon reaching normal civilization, I stopped at a do-it-yourself car wash to clean away the erosive calcium chloride that had accumulated from the Cassiar Highway. I saw two large deer near Burns Lake and two black bears between Prince George and Tete Juane Cache (pronounced "Tee John Cash"). The temperature rose to 80 degrees and I felt warm for the first time in two weeks. I had beautiful scenery all day. My motel at Tete Juane Cache was on the banks of the Fraser River, with the Canadian Rockies in the background. I took one of the most beautiful photos of the trip from right outside my room. While checking out my course for the next day I realized I had made several errors on my route sheet with miles vs. kilometers, so I revised it to include a few side trips.

Day 22 - It was an outstanding day of scenery, in spite of cloudy skies and passing showers. The day began crystal clear and 48 degrees but soon after I turned south from Jasper onto the Icefields Parkway it clouded over and began to drizzle. I saw several mountain sheep in Jasper Park. It was quite cold and rainy around Columbia Icefields, which is one of the highest points on the scenic highway. It cleared up some in the lower areas of Banff Park, near Lake Louise. I came upon Lake Moraine while exploring on a side trip. It is one of the most beautiful spots I have ever been, although I couldn't even find a reference to it in the Alberta brochures.

I took off my rain suit at Lake Moraine, but as soon as I got to the Trans-Canada Highway the temperature dropped 20 degrees. By the time I got to the Kananaskis Trail it was raining and only about 50 degrees. The first 68 miles along the Kananaskis was paved and included excellent scenery. It started to rain hard as I turned off onto a forestry trunk road that was all dirt. It rained for the next 67 miles into Coleman and the road got real slick in a few places. The only areas where it wasn't slippery the surface was rough with a lot of loose gravel. I saw a beautiful young elk along there.

On one of the muddiest sections I spotted several competition dirt bikes parked in a field alongside the road. There were about a dozen pickup campers and some makeshift rain shelters with guys sitting underneath, drinking beer. I saw a sign: "OVER THE BARS X-COUNTRY CLUB." They might have been on a weekend dirt-bike outing when the heavy rain and cold temperatures might have turned them off to riding. I wondered what they thought when they saw a Gold Wing splashing by through the mud. I blew my horn in a mocking gesture as I turned up the throttle a little and waved.

My reservations were in Blairmore, an old coal-mining town, where the mine was closed. It was still cold and raining when I arrived. My room was in an old-fashioned hotel near the center of town. I was concerned about parking in that area and I thought about looking for something else, but I had guaranteed reservations there. It turned out to be a really nice place with good food and friendly people. I asked what time they served breakfast and the answer was, "Our normal time for breakfast is seven, but what time would you like to have breakfast? We will have someone there to prepare it for you."

Day 23 - It rained most of the night and it was still overcast in the morning. An older gent was up and waiting for me when I got to the restaurant about 5:45. He prepared a hearty breakfast of sausage and eggs, and we talked for quite a while. I finally broke it off and left for Spokane.

I saw a young elk as I approached Kootenai Pass. I entered Washington at a small customs station at Nelway and rode through a very dense forest of huge evergreens. Later I took a wrong turn and found myself on a remote forestry road in some mountains. The rough gravel went on for almost 30 miles and came out in Chewela. South of there I saw two young deer feeding in a guys garden.

Ralph Spencer was waiting at the Motel 6 when I arrived in Spokane at 2:30. He had driven his Mazda Miata from Sun City, Arizona. After my shower we went together to find Roy Bodnar, another friend, and we visited with him for a while. Ralph and I had dinner at the Holiday Inn, after which I serviced the bike. The cap on the radiator expansion tank had come loose and the tank was empty, which could explain why the fan had been coming on more than usual. I filled it, added the last of my spare engine oil to the engine, and added water to the battery. I noticed that mud had taken its toll on my left-front fork seal, as the oil was running down the left fork leg. I also saw a trace of oil on the right-rear shock.

Day 24 - A strong thunderstorm passed through during the night with lots of thunder and bright lightning. It went on for almost an hour. In spite of having only 450 miles on my route sheet for the day, I felt anxious about the day and I had a feeling that I needed extra time; so I was up and on the road by 5:45. Ralph and I didn't even have breakfast together although we talked while I packed. It was a comfortable 60 degrees when I left but it got considerably cooler an hour later in Idaho.

I had a nice ride along Coeur D'Alene Lake where I saw two deer and a young elk. One deer gave me a close call when he crossed my path. I had another beautiful ride along the St. Joe River where there was 16 miles of construction along the dirt road. I made a wrong turn onto a logging road, thinking it was the road that led over St. Joe Pass into Montana. I climbed the steep grade for about 10 miles through switchback curves until I reached the top of the mountain where the road ended. I had to retrace my route back down the mountain. The error cost me about 45 minutes, but I got several nice pictures.

It was almost lunchtime when I stopped for a late breakfast in St. Regis, Montana. I was stopped by construction 40 miles east of there that cost me another 45 minutes. In Missoula I learned that I had made a 60-mile error on my route sheet. These three problems and the time change from Pacific to Mountain Time brought me into Lewistown around 7:45 PM, which was four hours later than I had planned. I had been on the road for 13 hours. It seemed odd that I would anticipate this time crunch when I got up that morning.

It was 56 degrees and raining when I arrived at the motel. The temperature crossing the Continental Divide at Rogers Pass was in the forties. I noticed during my nightly check of the bike that the rear tire was wearing quite thin and I doubted it would make the last 2700 miles to home.

Day 25 - I had breakfast in a small cafe and left in my rain suit. As soon as I got through the Judith Mountains it began to clear up. By ten o'clock it was sunny but still cool. I bucked a strong head wind most of the day. The speedometer cable that had caused problems earlier on the trip finally snapped around midmorning. Consequently I had to plan my fuel a little differently and use the tachometer to figure my speed. I spent the entire day on Route 200 through the gently rolling grasslands of Montana and North Dakota. There was very little traffic. I saw cattle and a few sheep grazing and I saw lots of barley and wheat growing. I saw a car only about every 20 or 30 minutes. I reached my motel in Washburn, ND about two hours early because of another route sheet error. I used the time to wash out a few things and to look around the town.

Day 26 - The terrain in eastern North Dakota and western Minnesota was generally flat. I saw mostly barley, alfalfa, and sugar beets growing, as well as some corn and beans. I continued on Route 200 most of the day. I encountered a few showers in northern Minnesota and crossed the Mississippi where I could almost step across. Around midday I realized that the front fork was losing quite a bit of oil and it was getting onto my right trouser leg. I even got some on my glasses. I stopped to let air out of the front suspension to relieve the pressure and I wrapped a rag around it to contain the leaking oil. I was preoccupied with working on the fork when I forgot about my saddlebag cover sitting loose. As I started to pull away it flew off and went skittering along the road, scratching it up pretty bad. With the speedometer cable broken, my front suspension losing oil, my rear tire getting close to the cords, and my saddlebag cover getting scraped up, I began to wonder if the good luck that had been with me for so long had finally run it's course.

I saw a lot of marshlands in eastern Minnesota near where I crossed the St. Croix River into Wisconsin. It started to rain lightly and continued to come down for the rest of the day. Wisconsin seemed a lot greener than most places I had been for several days. The forests were thicker too. I found riding without the speedometer to be tricky. Four separate police cars put their radar on me while I was using the tachometer for a speedometer. For my gas stops I kept track of the mileposts, especially after I went on reserve. I got a nice room in Hayward, Wisconsin that was almost the last room in town, since they were having logrolling competition that weekend. I noticed a bald spot on the rear tire and figured it would last another full day at

201

best. I called the Honda Riders Club and got the name of a shop on my route that might have the tire.

Day 27 - The motel was supposed to have a continental breakfast at six, but I waited until 6:10 and saw no one around so I left to find breakfast on the road. The temperature was in the thirties and there was quite a bit of frost around. Good weather was with me all day. I bought a tire in Escanaba, Michigan, which was the only Dunlop K491 they had in my size. It was a "blem," which I assumed meant that it had a cosmetic defect. I tied it onto the back seat for later.

I saw four deer that morning, all young. One was a tiny fawn. I followed the Circle Route along the north and east shores of Lake Michigan. The beaches on the north shore are almost always empty when I go by. Towns on the east shore are mostly picturesque vacation areas. One town had flowers planted along both sides of the streets all the way through town. I encountered a lot more traffic than I had seen in several weeks. I stayed at a Days Inn on the shores of Lake Cadillac. I mounted the new tire close to an air machine at a nearby gas station, which took me an hour and a half. I also swapped a rear brake pad with a used one I found in the bottom of the saddlebag. The muddy roads certainly took their toll on brake pads.

Day 28 - I had breakfast at a small cafe and was on the road by 6:30. It started to rain a half hour later and drizzled for about two hours. I passed through mainly small towns and rural farm country in southern Michigan and Ohio. I got to the AMA Headquarters in Westerville at 2 PM, where I attended the Life Members Dinner that evening.

Day 29 - I rode home via the interstate highways. My total mileage for the trip was just over 14,000 miles, 2,000 of which were ridden on dirt roads. My longest day was 610 miles, while my daily average was 480 miles for the days that I rode.

VISITING MAYAN RUINS

It was overcast when I left Buchanan on Wednesday, February 17th, a change from two days of intermittent snow. I was leaving ten days earlier than it would normally be necessary for my annual ride to Bike Week in Daytona Beach because I planned to tour the Yucatan Peninsula in southern Mexico "on my way" to Florida. The temperature was below freezing and the Palisades Parkway was slippery in spots. It cleared up and got warmer in Delaware but it was still quite windy. I stopped for the night at the Gold Rock exit in North Carolina where there was a Motel 6 and a Shoney's. I had chosen mostly interstate highways to get to Texas and from there back to Florida after the eight days I planned to spend in Mexico.

Just before leaving on the trip I noticed that the left fork leg was slightly wet with oil, which apparently began leaking during the Crotona Midnight Run the previous weekend. The leak got progressively worse and by the end of the first day I had oil on everything. I lowered the air pressure in the forks and wrapped rags around the leg in two places to keep it from blowing up onto the tank bag, from running down onto the front brake, and from blowing onto my clothes. I realized I would have to stop somewhere and get it fixed before reaching the rough Mexican roads. Other than the oil leak, the Gold Wing was in fairly good shape in spite of its more than 100,000 miles.

Day 2 - It was 38 degrees and cloudy when I left the motel. Although it cleared up around lunchtime it didn't get much warmer. When the fork leak continued to get worse I called it a day in Tallahassee so I could locate a dealer to replace the seal. I called the dealer listed in the phone book, hoping to get it done that evening, but he said he didn't stock fork seals for Gold Wings. I called the Honda Riders Club for the location of other dealers on my route and then tried one they told me about in Pensacola, but he also didn't stock seals. I finally connected with the dealer in Fort Walton Beach who had the seals and was eager to do the work. I made an appointment for the following morning at 9 AM.

DAY 3 - I slept well for the first six hours but couldn't get back to sleep after 3 AM. I got up at five and left at six, figuring that the ride to Fort Walton Beach would take about 3 hours. My estimate of the driving time was OK but my memory of the time change to Central Time wasn't, so I got there at eight instead of nine. Luckily they started a little early and finished the job by ten. I returned to the interstate and stayed with it for the rest of the day. I also didn't remember about the shortage of places to eat around the Lake Charles exit. I ended up eating at Popeye's again, the same place I had eaten the previous year. I covered 650 miles in spite of the detour into Fort Walton Beach Honda and the two-hour stopover for repairs.

Day 4 - It drizzled a little during the night and I encountered some fog and light drizzle near Houston, where the weather became hazy and warm. The sun came out after lunchtime and it was nice enough except for a strong head wind that cut my gas mileage considerably. I came up behind an older 1100 cc Gold Wing traveling in the same direction. I was doing about 10 miles over the speed limit and was about to pass him when I noticed it was a cop on a motorcycle. I followed him for several miles until he turned off.

It was 82 degrees when I reached Brownsville a little after three. I exchanged some traveler's checks for pesos at an exchange house, since it was already too late to catch a bank open. I got only 120 dollars worth because I didn't want to carry more cash than that. I really wasn't too enthused about the exchange rate either. I remembered from an earlier trip to Mexico that prices were very low and I was able to use my Visa for lodging. I checked over the bike at the motel and added a little oil that I was carrying. I rearranged my bags, studied my maps, and went out to buy some food supplies to use whenever I couldn't find a decent place to eat. I declined the property insurance for the bike because the cost for eight days was more than I pay for an entire year of bike insurance in the US.

Day 5 - I was up at 5:20 and out by six for a quick breakfast at McDonald's. The Mexican immigration procedure took about 45 minutes. I had to go to four different counters to complete everything. They gave me the necessary sticker for the bike this time in addition to a tourist card. A local uniformed sentry in Matamoros stopped me before I even got out of town. He acted real official and wanted to know where I was going. He proceeded to give me directions that I hadn't asked for and then he put out his hand for money. I reached in my pocket and handed him a shiny new 500-peso coin. He looked at it in obvious disgust and said "Agh, that's a penny!" In hindsight, I think it was worth only about sixteen cents. I didn't have anything smaller than a 10,000-peso note (about $3.20) so I showed him that, thinking it would be better not to insult him further and possibly get into a longer delay. He smiled in obvious approval and snatched it out of my hand. I would certainly run out of cash quick that way.

The streets in Matamoros had a thin layer of dirt on the surface that made it quite slippery in the early morning dew. Outside of town I ran into a thick fog, which I felt my way through for about two hours. The temperature rose to over 90 degrees that afternoon. At my second gas stop I was quite sure I had been shortchanged but I had already dropped a handful of coins into my pocket and I didn't feel sure enough then to challenge the guy. I figured it was 10,000 pesos and I decided to check my change closer after that.

I got lost in Tampico while looking for the ferry that I had seen on my maps, not realizing they had built a bridge since the map was printed. One thing I learned about Mexican maps was that they are frequently out-of-date or just plain wrong. I was riding on a nice, smooth road through a park when a police car coming the other way signaled for me to stop. He could see I was American and he assumed I was lost. That far into Mexico no one speaks a word of English, so I exchanged a few words with him in Spanish. He figured he had better lead me to the bridge, which he did, and I thanked him very much. He drove very fast through town and it was a chore to keep up. Again I wasn't sure if it was done for money and I didn't offer any.

All of the roads were very rough and every little town I passed through had at least two speed bumps that they call topes. Some towns had five or six topes and some of them were huge. I must have bounced over hundreds during my eight days in Mexico. Many vendors sell their wares at these topes because vehicles have to come to almost a complete stop before going over them. Motorists become a target for high-pressure sales, which reminded me of the unsolicited windshield washers in New York City. I didn't recognize most of the food sold there except the cold pineapple juice and cold coconut milk. I was wary of the cold juices because of the ice. You can't be sure where the water for the ice came from. I saw bananas and coconuts growing wild along the highways and I also saw them cultivated on farms around Tuxpan, Poza Rica, and Vera Cruz. I saw orange groves, pineapple fields, corn, vanilla, and date palms. I saw huge bunches of dates hanging from some of the trees.

The roads were especially rough around Tuxpan and Poza Rica. One of my favorite signs of the trip was "Tramo Peligroso." I soon learned that it warned of a very dangerous situation ahead. I knew that the word peligroso meant dangerous but my dictionary didn't have a translation for tramo. The word reminded me of trauma and it didn't take long to learn that whatever it was, the circumstances of not heeding the sign could be traumatic. A few times after seeing the sign I would round a turn and the road would be completely washed out. A few times the macadam ended abruptly and I would face huge holes. Once I hit a hole so hard that a plastic cover flew off the inside of my fairing, both mirrors turned down, and the instrument panel came loose.

The front and rear suspension bottomed quite often. I made emergency repairs to the fairing with silicone seal that evening. I found that my bottoming problem was due at least in part to the mechanic in Florida not putting air back into the front suspension. After I pumped it up it worked a lot better. In one place between Tuxpan and Poza Rica, I followed a truck through a very rough section of road; and as the truck was negotiating a series of deep holes I saw his front axle cock as much as 30 degrees one way, while his rear axle was cocked 30 degrees the other way. I scraped the bottom of the bike three times through there. I was often down to 30 MPH and less for long distances.

I reached Poza Rica at 5:30 and spotted an old hotel with a garage. I stopped because it looked comfortable enough and the 63,000 pesos were reasonable -- around $20.00 -- although they didn't take Visa. I asked the woman where I might find a place to get something light to eat and she pointed to a house across the street. I knocked at the front door and the woman who answered it offered to prepare a meal with eggs, onions, tomatoes, and peppers. It sounded fine but I asked her to go easy on the peppers, which I assumed were of the hot variety. Her teenage son had a makeshift stand in front of the house where he sold refresca (cold sodas). I bought one with the meal and ate at a small homemade table and chair in the dark near the edge of the busy road. I enjoyed the meal in spite of the meager trappings.

I rinsed out a few pieces of clothing in my room in spite of having washed most of my clothes in Brownsville. The temperature rose into the 90's that day and I had sweat profusely into everything. The clothes I washed the previous night were still damp, but I decided to ride with them in the morning. I noticed the gas prices were up considerably since my earlier trip to Mexico; and the hotels weren't taking Visa, so my cash was depleting faster than I had expected. I was extremely dehydrated and I drank quite a bit from the gallon of fresh water I was carrying. Aside from the money, I also needed to locate more drinking water. I watched a Spanish speaking show on TV before turning in. I couldn't follow the dialog because they spoke too fast. The room had a noisy air conditioner, the bed was very hard and lumpy, and the noise from the street continued all night, so I didn't get much sleep.

Day 6 - I had breakfast in my room from my provisions. It was foggy again when I started, which stayed with me until after ten. It was actually a blessing because it kept the temperature down. I saw more bananas, coconuts, pineapples, and oranges, and I began to see a lot of sugarcane. I was surprised to learn how many people still live in adobe huts with thatched roofs and dirt floors. It seemed like a contradiction that the women and children from these hovels all look so clean and well dressed. The young girls are often dressed for school in very clean-and-pretty party dresses, while the boys wore sparkling white shirts and black pants.

I saw many men walking with large machetes in one hand and a water jug in the other. I assumed they were on their way to work in the sugarcane fields. The old cane trucks I saw were all loaded to capacity with stalks. They would churn their way slowly out of the fields onto the road and then struggle under the huge load of sugarcane as they headed slowly toward the processing plants, dropping many stalks along the way. Road signs warned motorists of slow-moving cane trucks.

The temperature climbed to over 100 degrees. I was tempted again to stop and buy some cold juice but I drank from my water jug instead. A few times I stopped to buy bottled soda. I ate lunch from my bag. For lunch I had hard salami, which kept fairly good in the heat, although it got shiny-wet from its own oil oozing out. I also carried a supply of granola bars and a large plastic bottle of lightly-salted peanuts. For breakfast I carried canned sardines, instant oatmeal, raisins and tea. I also carried soup and canned tuna for an occasional dinner.

The heat and terrible roads combined to make it my toughest day. The seat takes a greater toll on my butt in the extreme heat, and it also gets very hot behind the fairing when the temperature rises above 100. There was a lot of smoke around from farmers burning off their sugarcane fields after the productive part of the stalks are harvested.

I rode for miles along empty beaches on the beautiful Gulf of Mexico coast. The prettiest area I saw was around Lake Catemaco, where it was hilly and picturesque. The apartments and vacation condominiums in Vera Cruz are built close to the beach, as the highway passes between the row of buildings and the sea wall. The first two gas stations I stopped at in Vera Cruz were closed for some reason and I had to search for one that was open before venturing into the countryside again.

That evening I spotted a new motel along the highway near Minatitlan. I checked in after learning that a room with a double bed was only 45,000 pesos ($14.50). I thought it was odd that I didn't get a key to the room. I put my things away and locked the door when I left to make a long distance phone call. I went in search of a small shop like a Western Union office displaying a "Larga Distancia" sign. Since I was running short on cash and wouldn't pass a bank until the next day, I first asked the price -- 27,500 pesos ($9.00) for three minutes. To talk for ten minutes would have cost over thirty dollars. I had quite a time communicating with the young girl there as she seemed frightened by my poor Spanish and she was having trouble understanding what I was trying to say. I guess it didn't help that I was giving her a hard time about the price.

When I got back to the motel the clerk unlocked the door for me. Just outside was a garage bay for the bike with a large curtain to conceal it from outside view. I thought that was pretty neat from a security point of view. I took a shower and looked for a place to plug my razor. There was none, so I used the TV outlet. I realized from looking around the room that there were other things that made the room quite unique. A toilet paper roll was mounted on the wall next to the bed. There were drink prices posted on the mirror, and prices for several other things that I couldn't translate. There was a small turntable device in the front wall that was apparently used to deliver drinks and collect money without opening the door. There were no windows in the room. As soon as I turned on the TV the whole thing became shockingly clear. It was a sex hotel with porno flicks on every working channel of the closed-circuit TV.

Day 7 - I left before first light in a thick fog and heavy mist. Trucks were using their windshield wipers as well as their headlights. Although the roads were wet they were much smoother than they had been for the past two days. I got to Villa Hermosa a little before nine and went directly to the bank. I waited quite a while in a teller's line and then had to wait in another line to get approval for exchanging money. I asked for pesos with $160 worth of travelers' checks and an additional 200 dollars against my Visa card. Asking for an amount in dollars against the Visa instead of pesos seemed to confuse the girl. When she finally got management approval for the Visa transaction she sent me to the teller, who began to peel off a huge stack of 100,000 peso notes, possibly 200, which would have been over $700 worth. I finally got her to understand that it was far too much and how much I really wanted, but it was almost two hours before I got out of there. Reversing the original Visa transaction was a big problem for them. At one point they told me to come back in three days, but I persevered. When I got home I waited for my Visa statement to make sure the earlier transaction got reversed. To my surprise neither transaction appeared on my statement so they were out $200. I hope no one got fired over the mess.

The road to Palenque was in pretty good shape. It was the first of eight Mayan archaeological sites I visited on the Yucatan Peninsula. Palenque is located in the State of Chiapas at the foot of a chain of low hills in the midst of a rain forest. It is a classic Mayan site, unique in its beauty and technical perfection. The most interesting of the many buildings I visited was the Temple of the Inscriptions, which was built sometime around AD 700. I climbed four tiers of stairs to the top of the sacrificial temple and saw the ancient hieroglyphic inscriptions from which the temple got its name. Mayan priests are said to have cut out the hearts of their sacrificial victims at the base of the temple, after which they would run up the stairs carrying the still-beating heart to sacrifice it to their angry god. It is believed that thousands of victims were sacrificed in this manner. I also visited many of the other buildings including the palace, the ball court, the House of the Jaguar, and the Temple of the Sun. I took a short walk into the jungle where I saw the remains of several other buildings yet to be uncovered and restored.

I met a young couple from California who were there on a bus tour from Can Cun. They gave me the name and address of a hotel in Merida where they thought I might like to stay. They asked how I was ever going to get across those temporary pipe bridges with a motorcycle. I didn't have any idea what they were referring to. But after spending a few hours at Palenque, I headed for Francisco Escarcega where I planned to spend the night; and that afternoon I came upon the largest Tramo Peligroso sign of my trip. It was before the first of three ominous-looking temporary pipe bridges I had to cross. The bridge was made up of several long, eight-inch-diameter steel pipes, laid across the span. Several pipes were used for each wheel track. When heavy trucks or busses crossed very slowly, the pipes would bend under their weight. I chose two pipes that were butted fairly close together to ride between and I kept both feet down for security. It was tricky and I wondered what it would be like in the rain when the pipes are covered with slick mud. I looked down between the pipes and saw water running several feet below the bridge.

I found a big old hotel in Francisco Escarcega that was typical of the classic Mexican hotels I remember seeing in old western movies. My room was large and stark. There were two hard double beds in the room and a huge old-fashioned ceiling fan overhead. The fan originally had five speeds, but only one of the speeds still worked -- high. There was no seat on the toilet and no curtain for the shower, which allowed water to spatter all over the bathroom. The mirror had fallen off the wall and was leaning against it. There was no hot water, although the cold water wasn't that cold, so I took a shower anyway.

I rinsed out my jeans, shirt, socks, and shorts before heading out to look for a place to eat. I had eaten breakfast and lunch from my supplies and I was ready to try the Mexican food. I found a bus terminal in town with a restaurant that displayed an easy-to-read menu. Most Mexican menus were a little too complicated for my level of Spanish. I had bifstek ranchero, which I figured would be ranch steak, but it turned out to be like a thin beef stew. Of course it could have been the fault of my pronunciation when I ordered. It was spicy-hot and served with rice and refried beans. They also served flat, tasteless stuff they call tortillas instead of bread. I enjoyed the meal except for the tortillas and the hot spices. It was so hot that I had to keep sipping soda to relieve the burning. It was expensive by Mexican standards, about $7; but then it was in a bus terminal where you might expect higher prices. Speaking of expensive I paid the equivalent of $1.30 for a small soda at Palenque. All of the prices in the gift shops at Palenque were also quite high.

I checked the oil in the bike and added a little. It was hot in my room so I used the high-speed ceiling fan to get relief. I was awakened around 11 PM by a bus right outside my room with a defective muffler. The bus driver started the engine and proceeded to warm it up for 20 minutes right outside my open window. The strong exhaust smell permeated the room.

Day 8 - I had breakfast in my room and left before six. It was warm and muggy as I headed for the Mayan ruins at Edzna. I found what I thought to be the right road, which turned east about where my map said it should, but it was a narrow, rough road that led through a small town past a large sugarcane processing plant. There were about forty workers milling around outside the plant, apparently getting ready to work in the fields. Almost everyone carried a huge machete in one hand and a jug of water in the other. They didn't look very friendly. I felt uneasy when many eyes turned my way as I bounced slowly over the topes. I was hoping it was the right road because I would feel even more uneasy returning that way. Sure enough I got about a half mile out of town and the road petered out to a narrow, dirt wheel-track road. I met an old man walking alongside the cane field and asked if I could get through that way. He answered "Si," so I kept going, but the road was actually only a shortcut through the fields for the cane trucks. I finally made it through and located the road to Edzna after about four miles of churning through a lot of soft dirt.

I got to Edzna about 8 AM. No one else was there except the caretaker who took my money as I signed the guest register. I had the place all to myself. The potential danger involved in wandering around alone crossed my mind but it really didn't bother me much at the time.

Edzna is situated in a wide valley in the State of Campeche in the midst of a dense scrub forest. Although the Edzna site covers more than two square miles, it has not been fully excavated, as was the case with most of the Mayan sites I visited. It is laid out like a large plaza with buildings around the perimeter and a small sacrificial altar at the center. The grass that covers the plaza is kept very neat. The most interesting and tallest of the structures there was the huge Five-Story Building. The base of this pyramid-shaped structure is about 200 feet on each side. It is believed that the priests occupied the first four floors. The temple, which makes up the fifth floor, stands 16 feet high and has a 20-foot-high roof comb perched on top, the purpose of which a mystery to me. I assumed the roof comb was either a decoration or it could have been used for defense. The building including the comb is more than a hundred feet high. I climbed to the temple level and later visited the Great Acropolis, the House of the Moon, and a few of the other buildings.

Just before turning onto the secondary road that leads to the Sayil and Labna sites I went through a huge arch that separates the Mexican states of Campeche and Yucatan. An access road that appeared relatively new leads to both sites. The road twists through a dense scrub field where thick vegetation grows over the road from both sides, making it extremely narrow for busses. It was still early for bus tours and I noticed only a few other visitors. The highlight of the Sayil site is the Palace, a large three-story building with terraces around the outside of each floor. The Palace has magnificent architecture with a pair of heavy columns adorning each of four entrances. The building features clustered columns around two other doorways and a decorative frieze that extends for the length of the building. The frieze contains masks of their gods, serpents, jaguars, and other motifs in mosaic. I visited the Mirador, a large, very weathered temple with a decorative roof comb. Many of the buildings at Sayil are badly weathered and crumbled. I saw live iguanas darting in and out of cavities in a few of the buildings.

Four miles farther east on the same road I located the Labna site, where the main attraction is the beautiful Arch of Labna. The inside opening of the corbel-shaped arch is about 16 feet high and 12 feet deep. It is adorned with very decorative mosaic, beautifully set into the front and rear of the structure and on the frieze. Decorations include many intricate mosaic patterns. The arch is flanked on both sides by rooms with entrances facing northwest. Two stone reliefs of Mayan thatched huts project out from the roof like dormers above the room entrances.   There was also a palace at Labna and a large weathered Mirador temple with a tremendous roof comb.   The buildings were grouped in a somewhat haphazard fashion around a large, well kept plaza.

The Campeche-Merida road bisects the Kabah site.   The most well preserved buildings at Kabah are on the east side of the road where I pulled in.   Little is known of the history of this site, which lies about 12 miles south of the huge Uxmal site.   It is believed that the Kabah site may have been linked with Uxmal by an ancient ceremonial road.   I explored the main palace known as the Teocalli, the Palace of the Masks, and the Temple of the Columns.   The buildings at Kabah are huge and the architecture is very beautiful, but many are badly weathered and partially crumbled.   I bypassed the huge arch on the west side of the road so I could spend more time at Uxmal.

Uxmal is one of the finest and most complete Mayan archaeological sites in all of Mexico.   Located in the same scrub-covered plain as the other sites I visited that day, it was certainly the highlight of my entire Mayan tour.   The classic architecture and technical perfection of the buildings at Uxmal were amazing. The tallest and most spectacular of these structures is the 125-foot-high Pyramid of the Magician that derives its name from a fictional legend claiming that a dwarf with the help of his mother, a witch, built the temple in a single night.   I climbed to the top of this exceptionally steep temple, which is as tall as a 12-story building.   There was a heavy chain stretching from the ground all the way to the top for the safety of climbers.   The steps are so steep that many climbers, including myself, use their hands on the steps like mountain climbing, as an alternative to holding onto the chain.   The sacrificial temple at the top is decorated with several masks of the Mayan rain god Chac, a common feature of many of the sites I visited, as is the figure of a priest's head protruding from the jaws of a huge snake.

I used the chain occasionally on my way down because my feet didn't fit on the narrow steps and I didn't feel secure climbing down on my heels alone, facing outward.   Many people climbed down backwards as I did, facing the temple and using their hands to steady them.   I didn't count the steps but I think there were about 140.   Some of the unique features of the pyramid are its oval base and a large stone cistern at the foot of

213

the temple. The stone surface around the temple slopes toward the cistern to direct rainwater into it.

The largest of the excavated and restored buildings at Uxmal is the Governor's Palace. The architecture and beautiful workmanship of this structure may be the finest example of pre-Columbian architecture in the Western Hemisphere. About a dozen entrances providing access to as many as twenty-four inner chambers, each of which has a corbel-arch ceiling. A ten-foot-high mosaic frieze across the entire front of the building is richly decorated with Chac masks, serpents, thatched huts, and many other forms and geometric patterns. A large, sculptured head with a feather headdress adorns the center of the frieze above the main entrance. It is estimated that more than 20,000 stones, weighing an average of 100 pounds each were used in the construction of this huge mosaic frieze. The precision evident in the stonework of the entire structure is magnificent. On the terrace in front of the palace stands another sacrificial altar with a double-headed jaguar in the center. The huge altar appears to have been cut from a single block of limestone.

Another exceptionally beautiful group of buildings at Uxmal is the Nunnery Quadrangle located directly behind the Pyramid of the Magician. The four buildings in the quadrangle surround a 30,000-square-foot courtyard, access to which is through a large corbel-arch entrance to the building on the south side. The largest and oldest of the buildings is the Temple of Venus on the north side. Each of the four buildings has a tall frieze facing the courtyard, and each frieze is adorned with Chac masks, snakes, serpents, jaguars, monkeys, thatched huts, and many geometric forms.

Many other buildings at Uxmal were badly weathered and have not yet been restored. Some have not even been uncovered from the heavy underbrush that still surrounds the site. A few of the partially restored buildings that I saw included the ball court, the Great Pyramid, the Pyramid of the Old Woman, and the Temple of the Phallus, which derived its name from a row of sculptured phalli on the frieze, some of which serve as rainwater spouts.

It may be many decades before excavation is completed at Uxmal. At least five tour busses were in while I was there and I would guess that several hundred people were visiting at the time. Uxmal was my favorite of the eight sites I visited. The temperature was in the 90's all the while I was there climbing, exploring, taking pictures, and trying to learn as much as I could in the few hours I had allotted myself. I could have spent the entire day at Uxmal. I saw several live iguanas while I was there, one of which was more than five feet long.

I passed the Dolores Alba Hotel in Merida twice before stopping to recheck my notes with the address I was given. I finally pulled up in front of the place and stared at the number. I was certain there must be a mistake. It was a high brick wall with big old double doors that made it look like a parking garage. A guy on the sidewalk asked if I wanted to go in. After hesitating for a moment I replied "Si." He banged his fist on the big door, which then opened slowly like it was motor-driven. I rode up across the narrow sidewalk and through the doors. The next thing I knew I was sitting on colorful flagstones in a pretty little courtyard directly in front of the hotel reception desk.

I felt a little awkward because I had never sat on my motorcycle in front of a reception desk before. I immediately turned off the engine and smiled at the female desk clerk. It was an old, attractive three-story hotel. Each floor had balconies with iron railings that surrounded and overlooked the attractive open-air courtyard, where several small cars were parked between the trees and plants. After a quick shower I found the pool that was in another part of the hotel, and I took a quick dip. There was a refrigerator just outside my room with complimentary water in sealed bottles. My ground floor room was very reasonable -- only 55,000 pesos ($17.75). It was not without fault though, as the shower drain was clogged, causing water to run all over the floor, and the bed was actually a block of concrete with a very thin mattress on top. I did have at least one pleasant surprise when I learned that all five speeds of the huge ceiling fan worked.

I got directions from the desk clerk for the "Larga Distancia" telephone office. I left on foot when I learned it was less than a half-mile away. Walking on the sidewalk was not easy because it was very narrow and filled with people. Whenever I passed someone I would have to turn a little sideways to avoid bumping into him. If I met a couple holding hands I would step into the street. It took about ten minutes to walk to the telephone office. I first asked the girl in Spanish what time in the evening the rates were reduced. She answered

215

in Spanish that she doesn't speak Spanish! I asked in English if she spoke English and she looked even more frightened and blurted out a loud "No!" She motioned for me to wait as she went through a connecting door into the shoemaker's shop. A small, smiling Italian shoemaker came in carrying a tacking hammer in one hand and a ladies shoe in the other. He said in fairly good English, "Can I help?" I asked him first -- just to make sure, "She doesn't speak Spanish?" He smiled and said, "No, she is Mayan." He said that the long distance prices are always the same. I made my call and was shocked to learn that my five minutes with Lilli cost 75,000 pesos ($24). I paid her and returned to the hotel. –

Before I left for the telephone office I had taken my secret wallet, a thin travelers' check folder, out of a hidden inside pocket of my traveling jeans and I stuck it in my back pocket along with my regular wallet -- which was a big mistake. I reached for it when I got back to the hotel to put it in a more secure place in my luggage, but it was gone. It had $300 worth of pesos inside, plus $110 in US cash. I had visions of delaying my trip to get another Visa advance. It could have really messed up my trip because aside from the delays, I would have kicked myself over and over again for my dumb mistake. My first thought was to go back to the telephone office and see if I had dropped it there. I didn't have much hope but I headed back anyway. I kept wondering how I would ever communicate with the girl if the shoemaker had closed for the day and gone home.

When I got there I was relieved to find that he was still in his shop. I rushed in and said with both my palms facing upward and dismay in my voice, "I have lost all of my money!" The woman standing with him turned to me and said in a contentious tone, "What? What? What are you saying?" I assumed that was his wife! I explained to him that I must have dropped my wallet in the telephone office. He asked how much money I had in it and I told him. With a smile he reached under the counter and asked if that was my wallet. I could hardly believe my eyes. I immediately reached in and took out a 100,000-peso note and handed it to him with profound gratitude. He smiled and said he would give it to his wife. All the way to the hotel I kept thinking about all the bad things I had heard about Mexico. Even during my call home, Lilli said she heard about bandits who held up a tour-bus that very same day at one of the Mayan sites in the Yucatan and robbed everyone. She was afraid that I might have been among the victims. I learned later that it was along the entrance road to the Labna site where the underbrush grows right out to and over the narrow, twisty road, and the busses have to wind very slowly through. I got back to the hotel and counted my remaining money and thought I there was another 100,000 peso bill missing. Either the girl or the shoemaker got it, but I forgave them and hoped that it would bring them much happiness for having returned my wallet.

I walked to the center of town to get something to eat, about seven blocks from the hotel. I learned after arriving at the park that it was the last night of their annual Carnival. The main festivities were taking place right there in front of the church. It was very crowded. I ate something from a street vendor that looked, smelled, and tasted pretty good. I sat at a small table next to the vendor's stand in the park and watched the festivities as I ate. There was loud music and dancing girls in colorful costumes. Later I met a Cuban guy from Miami who recognized me as an American and asked if I needed any help understanding what was going on. He proceeded to explain the significance of the last day of Carnival, which has something to do with the killing of the devil and they are now celebrating his demise.

I asked the guy how he made his long distance phone calls to Miami and I learned that I could have bought a special credit card that works in a few special telephones in the town square. The card can be purchased for the amount you wish to spend on the call. It is inserted into the telephone and there is a timer to tell you how much time you have left. The final cost is only a fraction of the Larga Distancia prices.

Day 9 - I had tea and some raisins in my room and decided to wait for breakfast at the hotel. After packing and loading the bike I went out for a short walk in the early morning quiet. About a block and a half from the hotel I saw a large patch of blood on the sidewalk, about three inches wide by two feet long. Someone must have been either stabbed or hit over the head on the sidewalk during the night.

I had a large dish of fruit for breakfast including banana, muskmelon, grapefruit, and watermelon, with a main course of scrambled eggs and ham. After breakfast I asked at the desk for directions to Chichen Itza -- another mistake! The senora sent me west instead of east and I was 45 minutes just finding my way out of town.

Chichen Itza is one of the largest and best restored archaeological sites in Mexico. It is probably the best-known Mayan site in all of Mexico and Central America, which may be partly due to its proximity to the resort area at Can Cun. Many tour busses visit Chichen Itza every day with vacationers. It was founded around AD 450 and was a sacred center of the Mayans for more than 700 years. One of the most popular and favorite attractions is the Pyramid of Kukulkan, a very impressive square pyramid with stairs on all four sides. This pyramid is often used as an icon for Mexico. It stands 80 feet high, which is about 45 feet shorter than the Temple of the Magician at Uxmal, and it's not nearly as steep; however it offers magnificent views of the entire area from the atop the temple. I climbed the 91 steps to the top and rested there for quite a while and took in the sights.

Not far from the pyramid is the Temple of the Warriors, a huge building adorned with large serpent columns, jaguar heads, snakes and a well-preserved Chac-mool, which lies on its back in a semi-reclining position. The stone Chac-mool is holding a bowl on its stomach for sacrificial offerings, usually the victim's heart. There are several Chac-mool figures around the site and there is even a Tomb of the Chac-mool. It is believed that he was a temple guardian of some sort. Adjacent to the Temple of the Warrior is the Group of the Thousand Columns, which is believed to have been a market mall or a place of assembly. No one is sure what its purpose was and I'm not exactly sure how many columns are still standing in the group, but it's certainly far less than a thousand.

The Great Ball Court at Chichen Itza is in excellent condition. The Mayans took their games very seriously. The object of the game was to get a hard rubber ball through the stone hoop that is situated high on the wall. The hoop is mounted vertically as opposed to present-day horizontal hoops used in basketball, and it is much higher. The ball could be hit with the elbows, hips, and knees, and was never supposed to touch the ground. It is believed that the entire losing team was often sacrificed to the gods, so they played with great fervor and enthusiasm. Along the bottom of the court wall are projected reliefs of losing players being led off to the sacrificial altar, possibly the one at the Temple of the Jaguar, which is on the opposite side of the plaza that makes up the Great Ball Court. An altar in the form of a large jaguar is located there. Many of the sites I visited had ball courts in various stages of restoration.

Other gory reminders of the barbaric ways of the Mayans can be seen at the Well of Sacrifice (or Sacred Cenote) and at the Platform of the Skulls. It is believed that in times of natural calamities, especially droughts, living humans as well as precious objects were cast into the well to appease the gods. Many skulls and precious objects have been recovered from the well in recent times.

The Platform of the Skulls is about eight feet high and 60 feet square. Four rows of skull reliefs are sculpted around the face of the platform. Sacrificial skulls as well as all of the skulls from battles with their enemies are believed to have been piled onto this platform. The most current "gifts to the gods" are believed to have been displayed on the ends of long stakes, which made up a palisade fence around the edge of the platform. Another smaller platform nearby, called the House of the Eagles, was believed to have been used for celebrations, possibly by warriors before and after their battles, or by dancing girls during their festivals.

A week earlier, I had stopped for lunch in Alabama on my way to Mexico and spoke with a guy who had visited many of the Mayan sites. He told me that one of the most impressive sites was Coba. Most people I spoke with never heard of Coba. My map showed a road going from Chemax to the Coba site, but I had trouble finding the road after finding Chemax. I learned later that the road I was looking for is used only by cows, or possibly that was a figure of speech describing the road, i.e. a cow path.

I continued for more than 50 miles past Chemax looking for the road and asking people in the villages for directions. In one village I stopped to ask a boy about 14 years old, who appeared to be on his way to school. I asked in Spanish and to my surprise he replied in English, "You need to go to the second town and there will be a road on the right for Coba." I told him that his English was very good. He smiled broadly and said, "Thank you. I hope you have a nice trip." His face was beaming as I left. It was probably the first time he had an opportunity to use the English he had learned and he could hardly wait to tell his teacher about it. Later I stopped to ask a guy for directions who was walking along a lonely stretch of highway. He was an Indian carrying a huge machete in one hand and a rifle slung over his shoulder held by the other. He looked scary to say the least. He didn't respond at all to my question and kept walking.

I located Coba in a dense scrub forest in the State of Quintana Roo. It is one of the largest Mayan sites ever discovered, but it's far from being fully uncovered. Coba is believed to have been occupied for well over a thousand years beginning sometime between AD 300 and 600. It was rediscovered near the end of the 19th century. Since then 6,000 buildings have been identified, although only a small percentage have been excavated. Access to all of the buildings is by way of long jungle paths.

A large pyramid called the Church stands near the entrance. I climbed to the top of the Church and looked over many square miles of jungle. About a mile to the northeast I could see the huge, 138-foot-high Castle of Nohoch Mul, which stands alone, protruding far above the jungle foliage. I followed the paths all the way to the weathered castle and saw many smaller buildings along the way. It was just a long walk in the heat from my point of view, and somewhat anticlimactic after seeing Palenque, Uxmal and Chichen Itza.

From there it was at least a three-hour ride back to Merida, and I hoped to get back before dark. I sped along searching for an entrance to a new four-lane-divided highway I had heard about from Chichen Itza to Merida. I spotted a sign pointing to an access road that I thought said Autopista. After turning off, I picked up speed on the access road. Suddenly I sped by a large commuter airplane discharging passengers and I leaned hard onto what I thought was the main highway lanes. I immediately recognized the telltale markings of a runway and did a big sweeping U-turn. A guy came running toward me, swinging both arms wildly. I said to him in Spanish that the sign said Autopista! He screamed back at me, "Aeropista, Aeropista, no Autopista!" It was an airstrip. I sheepishly expressed my apologies and got out of there as quickly as I could.

After arriving back at the hotel I realized I had given a gas station attendant a 100,000-peso bill instead of 10,000. I had handed him what I thought was the exact change with a combination of bills and coins. Of course he wouldn't say anything and I didn't notice it until later when I found the hundred missing. I had concluded long before this that my biggest problem of the trip was with those lousy pesos. There is no consistency about where on the bill they put the markings, and they are currently in the process of changing the currency to where 100,000 pesos will become 100 "new pesos," etc. Some are marked the old way and some the new way. It was very confusing.

I took a shower and a quick dip in the pool when I got back. I must have walked more than five miles at Chichen Itza and I lost track of the total number of stairs I had climbed. I had dinner at a small restaurant in town where my table was out on a busy sidewalk. I recognized pollo frito on the menu, so I ordered that and ate my fried chicken while watching the people. It seemed as though everyone in the city was on the sidewalk. Their living quarters are probably too hot in the evening, so they all take to the streets. Later I searched the gift shops for a few things to take home.

Day 10 - I was up and ready to leave before six, but the night desk clerk didn't have change for my $50. I had arranged to pay in US dollars because I wasn't sure how my pesos would hold out on my trip back to Texas, after having accidentally lost or given away at least three 100,000 peso notes. I waited 45 minutes for the senora to come and open the safe. The morning traffic had become heavy, although most of the traffic lights were in my favor, so I still got out of town in good shape.

It was quite windy but the temperature still rose into the low 90's by afternoon. I stopped a few times to drink from the water I had stocked up on at the hotel, and once I stopped for a Pepsi at a roadside stand. I got shortchanged again at a gas station and argued successfully with the guy to get the 10,000 pesos he had shorted me. I usually tried to have the exact change so I wouldn't have to argue about it.

After 500 miles I checked into the same sex hotel, mainly because I had slept well on the new bed and the price was right. The clerk tried to tell me something when I checked in that I just wasn't translating. I asked him if it was a problem and he said no, so I just forgot about it. I went out for dinner and ordered the "comida corrida" or meal-of-the-day. It was a mixture of several things including fish. It was good but not very filling, so later I heated a cup of soup in my room.

Day 11 - I got up early after a good sleep and was loading the bike when my phone rang. It was the night desk clerk. I recognized the Spanish for "forty-five" and I told him that I already paid the forty-five last night (45,000 pesos), but that didn't satisfy him. We weren't doing too well on the telephone, so I said wait a moment and I walked up to the office where three guys were waiting. I finally understood what he was saying: that my original forty-five was for only five hours, and I stayed all night. He wanted another 45,000 pesos for the rest of the night. Apparently I had gotten away with it the first time before they had a chance to hit me up for more money. That's apparently what the desk clerk was trying to tell me when I checked in the night before.

I still wasn't sure how my pesos would hold out before reaching the border, so I argued with them about the extra forty-five. After seven days in Mexico I was getting much better at Spanish than when I came in. I knew only a few hundred words when I started, but picked up another dozen or so each day while I was there. I was pretty proud of myself when I managed to come up with the right words to present an argument, which was: I am one person, not two; I was there only for sleeping, not for sex; I have only enough money to get to the border; it was Saturday and tomorrow is Sunday and no banks are open; if I give my money to you, I won't eat for two days. I offered to pay by Visa, but they couldn't take Visa. At one point, they wanted me to leave something like my clothes in lieu of money. I argued that my clothes wouldn't fit anyone there anyway. It took about fifteen minutes to soften them up, and when I thought my timing was right, I pulled out 20,000 pesos and offered that. They looked at each other and mumbled a few words before the guy reached for it. It was just breaking daylight when I got on the road. I was pretty happy to get away for a total of about $21.00, which was still a bargain. I rationalized that it was compensation for some of the money I had lost from being hustled and shortchanged during my week in Mexico.

I figured this was going to be my toughest day of riding. On the way south I rode only 350 miles of this particular section in one day, and it was my toughest day then. On the return trip I planned to cover more than 500 miles, which would put me into Tampico that night. By the time I reached the really rough roads north of Lake Catemaco it was raining. They must have had a

222

heavy downpour just before I got there because the water was rushing across the road in a deluge of mud, rocks and water. I saw a pickup truck that had lost control and hit another pickup. The busses really fly as they continually dodge potholes and breaks in the road, which makes it treacherous to pass because they are more intent in looking for holes than they are in their rearview mirror. A few times I had close calls passing a bus or truck when the guy would dodge a hole while I was passing, reminiscent of my earlier days on the Alaska Highway. Anyone who thinks the Alaska Highway is rough today ought to come to Mexico.

It rained lightly all the way from Lake Catemaco to Tampico. I finally took a chance that morning with the cold pineapple juice sold at the topes. It was delicious and I was thankful I didn't have any bad aftereffects. I stopped for lunch at a roadside restaurant along the gulf about halfway between Vera Cruz and Poza Rica. I ordered roast beef with a strange enchilada, which tasted pretty good. I told the woman to go easy on the spices and she obliged. A few miles before reaching the Tampico Bridge, I went through one of several toll stations. The smallest bill I had was a 50,000-peso note. Toll attendants usually folded up the change before sticking it into my hand. This time, with my newfound wisdom, I paused to unfold the bills and count the change. Sure enough, it was 5,000 short! I turned and said loudly, "Hey, cinco mas," meaning five more. He just handed over the other five with a nervous smile.

I rolled over the Tampico Bridge at 5:30 PM. I was really tired and anxious to get into a good bed. I saw a large sign for the Bahia Motel and asked a young guy on the street how to get there. He said it was very far away and it would take more than an hour to get there. He pointed uptown and said there is a very nice hotel called the Monte Carlo, only five minutes away. When I got there I realized it was the classiest hotel in town. I stopped the bike in front of the place and two uniformed attendants opened the double doors for me. I trudged in with my muddy rain suit and boots and stood dripping at the first-class reception desk. Yes they had a room and the price was fifty-five. I thought he meant pesos so I put 55,000 on the counter. He said no that was 55 dollars. I said wait a minute, I think I have more on the bike. In pesos it cost 165,000. It's a good thing I had argued with the guy in Minatitlan that morning or I would have

223

run short, even in US dollars. I also tipped the bellhop to carry my bags, giving him all of my heavy coins. I put my bike in the garage overnight, instead of in a parking lot. I had a light supper from two different street vendors as I strolled around town, which was packed and noisy with overcrowded sidewalks and music blaring from loudspeakers. It seemed like the entire population of Tampico was on the sidewalks.

Day 12 - I had a king-sized bed that was about eight feet wide with four pillows. It was the strangest bed I ever saw. It was shorter than a regular king-sized bed and a lot wider. I think four people would have fit comfortably in it. It reminded me of "Bob and Carol and Ted and Alice." It was cool in the room and I slept well for about 6 hours. When I couldn't get back to sleep, I got up at 4:45, had breakfast in my room, and left before first light. The only problem was that as soon as I got out of town I was at the mercy of holes and unmarked topes in the dark. The roads had no white lines on the edges, or even in the center.

About five miles out of Tampico I made a wrong turn that led me through a small town. As I felt my way out the north end of town I ran out of macadam and onto rough, muddy dirt. I stopped to ask if this was the right road for Matamoros and they nodded and motioned for me to keep going. Although it was raining lightly when I left the hotel, I didn't put on my rain suit because I thought the main weather front had already passed. Wrong! I got hit around midmorning with a torrential downpour and got thoroughly soaked. It rained all the way into Matamoros where the roads were slick. I was a wet, muddy mess when I passed through customs. I stopped for the day at one o'clock in Brownsville so I could clean up and dry my clothes. I called home and also called a friend in Florida who had invited me to stop by. Since I was running a day ahead of schedule I decided to take him up on his offer if I could cover 1350 miles in two days. It should be a snap in good weather, but tough in the rain.

Day 13 - I got up at 4:15, had my tea, oatmeal, and raisins before loading the bike. I spotted a Whataburger and stopped for a breakfast sandwich and orange juice. It was still dark, drizzling, and 62 degrees when I left Brownsville in my full rain suit. It drizzled for the first five hours. Just as I entered the outskirts of Houston the skies opened up. Cars were sliding all over the place. One girl spun out and hit two other cars only a few hundred feet in front of me on a wide, busy expressway.

Sometimes I could see for only about 200 feet. Another accident held up traffic for about 15 minutes on the Houston beltway. Later a guy in a pickup truck spun out directly in front of me. First I was following his taillights and a moment later I was looking at his headlights.

Besides the pouring rain, there was a fierce crosswind. I got into some heavy truck traffic and got thrown around quite a bit. The random wind currents around the trucks were so strong that my tires kept breaking loose sideways and the bike was doing a ballet as the tires would break traction one way and then the other. The deep furrows in the road and the rumble knobs between the lanes didn't help.

After I got out on I-10 I tried three times to pass a truck, but every time I got even with his front bumper, I was struck by a heavy blast of wind from his front end that would hit the bike so hard the front wheel would break traction. I was finally able to get by when we went behind some trees, which temporarily blocked the strong crosswind. It poured steady for four hours before easing up in the Iberville Parish of Louisiana where the long bridge crosses the Henderson Swamp. I decided to call it a day in West Baton Rouge, after 650 miles. I didn't get wet except for my gloves and a little on my seat where a seam must have a pinhole leak, but it was a tough day.

Day 14 - Expecting another long day of rain, I got up at 2:55, after 6½ hours sleep. I packed, ate, and left at 4:15 in the dark. It rained for about 2 hours and was overcast for another five. It finally cleared up around Tallahassee and got warmer. I stopped in Ocala to secure a room for the following night, and I had supper on the road before pulling into Ken Arnold's driveway at 6 PM. That evening we went to his weekly Retreads meeting where I met some of his friends.

Day 15 - I was up at 6:15, and had breakfast at Ken's home. I serviced the bike there and replaced the right-front brake pads while he went to a doctor's appointment. We left around 11 AM for Daytona Beach over some of his favorite back roads. Florida 19 was the highlight of the ride. It passes lakes, hills, orange groves, and some really nice country.

We visited most of the afternoon at the enduro sign-up area, where I spoke with several old friends and made a few new ones. When it clouded over and threatened rain I headed for my motel in Ocala. It poured that night, which promised to make the enduro pretty messy the following day.

Day 16 - I went directly to the enduro start area near Bunnell. The entrance road was very muddy. There were a few cars and a pickup truck stuck in the deep ruts. I got around them and made it all the way in, but I don't think many people on two wheels, or four for that matter, got in after me. I heard that they opened a different access road to get the rest of the competitors in. The enduro start had to be delayed an hour, and very few spectators showed up, most of whom had gotten discouraged by the weather and the condition of the entrance road. I left around noon and went to check out the bike shows and to buy a few T-shirts before checking into a motel in Jacksonville.

Days 17 & 18 - I rode 325 miles to Surfside Beach, S.C. to visit with Bill Claus and his wife Dolores. I spent the afternoon there and stayed the night. I left at 6:30 AM and had a long and uneventful ride home on the interstate highways. I covered the final 725 miles in just less than 12 hours.

ALASKA 6 - THE THREE MUSKETEERS

My 1996 tour was intended mainly to accompany Bud, who had been befallen by bike troubles when the RAMS rode to Alaska together in 1991. Jake also found the opportunity to go again, so the three of us took the trip together. I tried to plan a ride that would be interesting and challenging to all, although much of it retraced my earlier Canol Road tour. I planned the ride to be fairly aggressive since we were seasoned dirt riders, and because Jake and I both had chores to attend to at home.

I left home on the Fourth of July, heading north through the Catskills toward Jake's house in Slingerlands over a series of scenic country roads. It rained most of the way, which I hoped wouldn't set a precedent for the trip. Bud arrived about the same time from his home in Stow, MA. Arlene treated the three of us to steaks and lobster for dinner that evening.

Day 1 - It was chilly when we left Jake's. We crossed the Mohawk River at Canajoharie where we saw locks along the old Erie Canal, now called the New York State River Thruway. We enjoyed a scenic ride through the Adirondacks and saw what appeared to be another small set of locks in Lowville near where we stopped for a second breakfast.

We crossing the St. Lawrence River via the Thousand Islands Bridge and got a scenic view of some of the many small islands for which the area was named. We covered 500 miles and reached North Bay, Ontario before nightfall. Our reservations weren't in the best part of town, raising some concern about the security of the bikes, especially Jake's BMW R1100RT, the most valuable of the three; so we located a secluded spot behind the building before checking in.

Day 2 - Soon after we got up, Jake realized that his bike key was missing. He searched all of his pockets, his bedding, and his luggage. When I went outside to load up I found it lying in clear view on the pavement beside his bike. Enough said for security. We had coffee in the room and rode 100 miles before breakfast. The temperature was 52 degrees when we left and it stayed cool and cloudy for several hours. The sun broke through around midmorning, although the overcast soon returned and we had a few sprinkles before lunch.

Lakes and rolling hills on both sides provided the nicest scenery of the day. By afternoon the road was much straighter with balsams, cedars, and poplars along the highway. Daisies, buttercups, and many other wild flowers flourished in the broad clearing between the highway and the forest. We located our reserved motel about five miles east of Geraldton, Ontario.

Day 3 - The room had no rollaway so I slept on a plastic inflatable mattress that I carried for such emergencies. It didn't provide a very restful night for me. My clothes and my skin would stick to the plastic whenever I turned and the mattress gradually lost all of its air, putting me on the floor by morning.

We started in the rain at 5:50 with the temperature at 55 degrees. The rain continued for about an hour before we saw gradual clearing. We stopped at a small cafe near Nipigon Bay for breakfast. The scenery was nice all day. I recognized some of the area north of International Falls from my 1981 trip, with its bare rocky ground, trees that seemed to be stunted, and black rock on the surface that looked a lot like lava or exposed magma. We rode through a few showers with raindrops as big as grapes before reaching the eastern edge of the prairie near Winnipeg, where we stopped for the night.

Day 4 - It rained quite heavy during the night but stopped just before we checked out of the motel. We rode through several light showers that morning and saw a lot of wheat and other grain in the fields, which was followed by about a hundred miles of mostly poplar trees, and then balsams for another hundred miles as we headed due north. The roads became gently winding, two-lane macadam with a coarse surface. Bud and I had to transfer gas from our spare cans into the tank before reaching The Pas, as distances between gas stations got much longer. We found a bank in The Pas where we exchanged travelers' checks for Canadian currency.

About 10 miles from Flin Flon we began to see rock on the surface everywhere. It seemed as though the earth's underbelly was coming right out through the surface, with very few trees or other vegetation able to grow. Flin Flon is a city of approximately 7,000 people built entirely on this rock surface. The water supply as well as the sewer system is built on top of the ground because it would be impractical to bury pipes into the solid rock. Flin Flon is a mining town where mainly copper and zinc, but also precious metals such as gold are extracted from the ground. Copper and zinc deposits were discovered there in 1914, the year the town was founded, although the mines were not developed until 1929. The huge smoke stack from the m can be seen for miles. Most of the population appears to Scottish or Irish. We visited a museum where Josiah Flintabatey Floniton, a mythical character who is said to have founded the town is featured. We rode around town to take in the sights before heading for our motel.

Day 5 - Having eaten too much too late I didn't sleep too well. We left at first light knowing it would be a long, tough day with a lot of dirt roads. After entering Saskatchewan we had a spectacular view of the sunrise directly behind the huge smokestack in Flin Flon. The Saskatchewan border is at the west end the town. The temperature dropped to 46 degrees during our first two hours on the scarcely traveled and very rough road.

We stopped in the middle of the road around eight o'clock for a nature break. Bud said, "What are we doing about breakfast?" I reached into the trunk of the Gold Wing for a can of sardines. Bud's first remark was, "You've got to be kidding." Breakfast in the middle of the dirt road consisted of canned sardines and granola bars; and although Bud refused to partake of the sardines, he was carrying a few sticks of his own beef jerky. Many flies, gnats, and huge mosquitoes swarmed around as we ate.

We rode about 65 miles of rough dirt roads to reach Rte. 2, where I planned to get gas. We found no gas near the intersection so we went north into the town of La Ronge. We encountered considerable construction in the next 100 miles, with much loose dirt and coarse gravel. We met logging trucks traveling in both directions on the dirt road. Upon entering Alberta the roads improved. We saw wheat and canola growing and cattle grazing in the fields. It rained for the last 20 miles of the day. Our reservations were at a beautiful, modern inn at Athabasca. It was by far the longest and toughest day of our trip. We covered more than 700 miles in 13 hours, of which about 175 miles was on loose dirt and gravel.

Day 6 - I slept well on a much better rollaway cot. I was awake by 4:30 and got the others up then. We were on the road in only an hour in a steady rain. It had rained most of the night and continued for about an hour into our day, after which we got intermittent showers for the rest of the morning. The temperatures stayed in the low fifties. We had breakfast at an IGA grocery store where we found a small restaurant inside.

We passed through Dawson Creek at "Mile Zero" of the Alaska Highway around noon. There was construction and heavy traffic for the first 40 miles, which cleared up after Fort St. John. The sun came out and stayed with us for part of the afternoon as we climbed through the scenic Pink Mountain area. There was dust in many spots where loose gravel was used to fill potholes and huge frost breaks in the pavement. Otherwise the road was in fairly good shape. A truck followed us for several miles at 75 MPH and finally passed us doing 80 or better. We stopped for the night at Fort Nelson.

Day 7 - I woke up at 2:50 and couldn't get back to sleep so I got up at 4:15 and made some coffee. We were on the road an hour later. It was 55 degrees and mostly cloudy, dropping into the mid 40s in the mountains. I saw bears, Dalls sheep, and caribou as we passed through some of the most scenic areas between Steamboat and Muncho Lake. We rode on about 20 miles of loose gravel and 10 miles of messy construction before calling it a day at Mukluk Annie's Salmon Bake in Teslin where we rented a cabin and enjoyed a good salmon dinner.

Day 8 - I woke up early again, around 3:30, and got the others up at 4:15. By the time we turned onto the South Canol Road the temperature had dropped to just above freezing. The guys were beginning to tire of my breakfast fare of sardines and granola; although traveling mostly on long, lonely dirt roads you don't find cafes that easily, and I wasn't about to wait for the restaurant at Mukluk Annie's to open.

The South Canol Road was the highlight of our tour as it was on my previous tour. We stopped several times for photos. It was actually the first time we stopped for any photos, which was another thing that didn't please Bud and Jake too much. The first thirty or forty miles of the Canol Road were a little dusty, but it got progressively better and the good weather held. We spent about four hours enjoying the spectacular scenery and riding the scarcely traveled, 138-mile, winding dirt road. I saw a female moose with young, but not as many animals as I saw on my previous Canol Road adventure. We went into Ross River for gas before heading for Dawson City, which was a long and tedious ride on the Klondike Highway consisting of many miles of gravel with construction along the way. Although it was very scenic, I didn't appreciate it as much as the first time I saw it in 1977. I had traveled that stretch of road several times. We stopped for lunch at a small cafe in Carmacks.

As we neared Dawson City we stopped at the Dome for a spectacular view of the city and the confluence of the Yukon and Klondike Rivers. On the 21st of June it is possible to see the Midnight Sun from the Dome. We arrived at the Dawson City Bed & Breakfast about 5:30. It was the third time I had stayed there. I was recognized immediately and I felt like I was returning to a regular vacation place. After cleaning up, we walked into town and had dinner at Klondike Kate's.

Day 9 - Our gracious host Jon had breakfast ready at six as I had requested. The food was excellent as usual. We were out of there by 6:45 and we got to the Yukon River ferry about a minute before it shoved off. No one else was waiting so we were the only three vehicles aboard for the 10-minute crossing. There was also no one waiting on the west bank when we landed. The Top-of-the-World Road was beautiful that morning. We could see the Richardson Range very clearly far to the north. There was very little dust on the road and no traffic.

We cleared US customs quickly and headed for Tetlin Junction. The Taylor Highway was also, as usual, rough, dusty, and in terrible condition with at least 25 miles of construction. We spread out to avoid fouling each other's air cleaners. I rushed ahead so I could stop at the abandoned 1898 gold dredge for a photo of it with Bud and Jake rounding the bend in the background. When I got there I quickly put the bike on the side stand, ran to an ideal spot, and readied my camera. I waited a minute, then two, then several, and no one came. My first thought was about a downhill, off-camber turn about six miles back, which had a lot of loose, marble-sized gravel all over the road. I thought about Bud's stiff right leg resting up on the highway peg and about him favoring the hand brake. It was not a good spot for using the hand brake. I turned the bike around and headed back, expecting the worst.

But I found them after going back only two miles. Jake's plastic covers were already removed and laying all over the ground, as they looked for the reason why his BMW engine had suddenly quit. My initial glib comment was, "The saga continues," referring to our earlier Alaska trip that I called "Saga of the Ailing BMWs." I said I had been thinking about an appropriate name for this tour and this could be it: "Alaska 6 -

The Saga Continues." After standing back and watching them work for a few minutes, checking the connections and fuses under the seat, behind the headlight, and under the tank, I asked Jake if he had an operator's manual for the bike.

I opened the book to the troubleshooting page and began to read aloud: "Bike will not start: 1. No gas in tank. 2. Ignition switch in off position. 3. Kickstand down." Enlightenment came over Jake's face at that point and he immediately looked under the bike where the broken kickstand interlock switch was dangling at the end of a wire. It took only a few minutes to bypass the switch, button up the covers, and we were on our way. The final 25 miles into Tetlin Junction were extremely rough with heavy washboard and thick, loose gravel.

We stopped for lunch in Tok before heading east on the Glenn Highway, which was very rough, with frost heaves and many breaks in the blacktop, several of which were temporarily filled with loose gravel. I had reserved a cabin in Glennallen, but after seeing the shabby condition of the cabins and finding no place nearby to eat, we decided to press on for Palmer, 126 miles farther west. We had run through a few brief, light showers between Tok and Glennallen, so when a light shower began just 20 miles from Palmer we thought it was just another brief shower and we continued to ride, but the rain suddenly came down quite hard and we got soaked.

We stopped briefly at the Matanuska Glacier before heading for the same motel we stayed at on our previous trip with the RAMS. Finding no vacancies we continued on for a few miles and found another motel. The rates were reasonable but there was no rollaway, so I used my defective inflatable mattress again. That evening while going over my bike I noticed that I had lost the front bumper on one of the rough roads we traveled that day.

Day 10 - We located a Wal-Mart in Anchorage where Bud purchased some oil, a funnel, and paper towels. He did his oil change in Rey and Becky's driveway. Rey was at work when we arrived but he got time off and came home for a few hours for lunch. He prepared baked halibut and Alaskan sea crab for our lunch, along with corn on the cob, salad, and other assorted dishes. I took Robyn for a short ride on the bike and later tried to no avail to fix his computer, which appeared to be missing a few key files. Jake went in search of the BMW dealer, where he had previously ordered a tire. The dealer was too busy to work on it that day but they made an appointment for the following morning. We got back to Palmer about 6:15 and had a late dinner at the hotel in town.

Day 11 - Bud and I headed for Denali Park as Jake went to get his tire mounted. The temperature was only in the mid 40s and it got considerably colder as we approached the entrance to Denali, where it also began to rain. After a short tour of the Visitors Center we returned to the bikes and headed out in the rain. It rained intermittently for the rest of the day. We got to Tok about 4:45, a half hour before we were scheduled to meet Jake coming from Anchorage. He arrived an hour later than he planned after having been delayed looking for a lost saddlebag along an extremely rough section of the Glenn Highway between Tok and Glennallen. The bag literally snapped off the side of his new BMW in one of the deep dips in the road. He never heard it go and couldn't find it.

As we were on our way to dinner we spotted a salty-looking guy with a BMW K1100 getting gas. We walked over to talk with him and learned that he was on a tour from his home in Brazil. He had gone first to Tierra del Fuego at the southern tip of South America and then to Prudhoe Bay, the northernmost point accessible by road in North America. As Jake was talking with him I was looking at the huge pile of gear he had tied onto the bike. I noticed Jake's saddlebag perched on the very top of the pile. The guy had found it lying alongside the road. Jake offered to treat him to dinner for finding the bag.

We learned at dinner that his name was Mario Francisco del Castro Filho. He was an entrepreneur in his home country, a dealer in boats. He was a very interesting guy. He told us about a motorcycle accident he had a few years earlier, after which he was in a coma for three days. Before the accident he was able to speak fluent French and English; but as a result of the accident he got total amnesia and completely forgot both languages. Although he was relearning English on this trip, he struggled with it. He was headed for the Summer Olympic Games in Atlanta where he was entered in the competition with the Brazilian rowing team. He said he had been sleeping on the ground in his bag, and he was traveling a lot at night because of the heavy RV traffic and road construction during the day. After dinner we all took photos of each other and exchanged decals.

233

Day 12 - We were up early for our ride to the Haines Ferry. I was anxious to get an early start due to the possibility of long delays in some of the construction areas. I wanted to make sure we didn't miss the ferry, for which we had no reservations. The temperature was 51 degrees when we left Tok but it soon got down into the mid 40s. We enjoyed a scenic ride through the Beaver Creek area with practically no traffic. We arrived at the construction in the Yukon just before a heavy rainsquall. The mud wasn't very deep but the surface was wet and slippery, with a lot of washboard and many puddles.

I had a close call when I ventured too close to the edge of the road to avoid some of the severe washboard. My rear tire suddenly broke loose on the slant edge and the bike began a long broad slide at 65 MPH. Luckily it corrected itself because there was a steep drop off the edge and it could have been a really bad scene. Most of the construction was between the Alaska border and Burwash Landing. It was overcast around Lake Kluane, which is usually one of the better spots for photos, and for which I had allowed extra time.

The electric power was out at Haines Junction and we had to wait for one of the gas stations to start up their auxiliary power. It rained during our ride down the Haines Peninsula. Patches of snow lay in several places on the treeless, tundra-like summit. It was very cold and raining most of the way with fog. We arrived at the ferry building in Haines at 3:30, five hours before we had to queue up for boarding. The ferry was scheduled for a 10 PM departure. We had more than enough time to eat, explore a little around the area, and get back.

We had a high-priced meal at a local restaurant and filled up with some of the highest-priced gas we got anywhere on the trip. We browsed through a few souvenir shops and rode around town to see the sights. The ferry loading operation with the large RVs went extremely slow and it appeared as though the crew had never done it before. Several of the huge motor homes got hung up as they eased their way down the steep loading ramp onto the main ferry deck. The difficulty may have been due to it being dead-low tide. All of the vehicles were loaded through the side of the ship. Our short ferry ride up the Skagway Channel occurred well after dark, so we missed seeing any scenery from the deck of the ship. We finally got to bed in Skagway at 1:20 AM.

Day 13 - After not much more than a nap, we headed up through the scenic canyon toward White Pass and Canadian customs. We stopped several times for photos on our way up and over the pass before proceeding to Jake's Corner on the Alaska Highway where we had a full breakfast. The original crusty owner for which the place was named had sold out several years earlier but his collection of old trucks, snow-removal equipment, and other machinery still adorned the complex like a museum. Some of the equipment dated back to the mid 40s when the Alaska Highway was built.

We rode mostly on good roads in good weather from there to the Cassiar Highway junction. There were a few areas of light construction on the Alaska Highway and again on the Cassiar, where we experienced about 15 miles of dusty gravel. The rest of the roads were in great shape. We had lunch from some of the smoked salmon that Rey had prepared for our return trip. Our overnight reservations were at the North Country General Store Bed and Breakfast at Dease Lake. We had a suite of rooms in this unique inn where they stretch the "bed and breakfast" definition. A community kitchen in the hallway is stocked with only cereal, coffee, and filtered water, which is considered the breakfast. We enjoyed a full, roast-beef dinner that evening at the Other Place Restaurant.

Day 14 - We were up at 4:15 for what I figured would be a long and potentially difficult day on the Telegraph Creek Road. I made coffee in the hallway and we had granola cereal for breakfast, after which we were on the road by 5:40. If the road had not been quite so dry and dusty we would have gone all the way to Telegraph Creek; but it was extremely dusty that day and we had to spread out to avoid fouling each other's carburetor air filters. I saw a large gray fox dart across the road at one point, but no other animals. We went as far as the confluence of the Stikine and Tahltan Rivers in the Tahltan Indian Reserve. The views from the narrow razorback ridge, far above the two white-water rivers, were spectacular.

We aborted our trip to Telegraph Creek right there and returned to Dease Lake where we stopped at the bed and breakfast one last time to use the toilet facilities before heading down the Cassiar Highway. It started to rain around 10:30 and continued for most of the time we were on the dirt sections, which helped to keep the dust down. Some places got messy and we got splashed with muddy water several times by oncoming trucks. We saw a guy and a girl on a BMW Paris/Dakar dual-sport bike. They seemed to be having serious problems in the slippery mud. We assumed they finally gave up and turned back because we saw them later near Stewart.

We got a room in Stewart before heading into the mountains north of Hyder where we hoped to see the Salmon Glacier as I did on the previous trip. We ran into rain and heavy fog as we picked our way up the twisty, rough access road that leads to the glacier. The road was full of deep, muddy potholes, which were hard to see in the fog. We went 22 miles into the mountains along these treacherous roads without ever seeing the spectacular glacier that was one of the highlights of my previous tour. The fog was too thick to see anything, so we finally headed back to the motel in Stewart where we had a late dinner.

Day 15 - We turned in at 8:45 PM, although I didn't get to sleep until around one o'clock. I got the guys up a little after five. We packed the bikes and left in a steady rain. We ate some smoked salmon in the room with coffee but we still stopped for a full breakfast at Meziadan Junction. The rain continued for more than four hours. After that it became overcast for the rest of the day with occasional showers. It was heavily overcast for our long climb into the Canadian Rockies.

Our overnight reservations were at Tete Juane Cache on the banks of the Fraser River where I stayed on my previous trip. The restaurant where we ate dinner had become a Korean barbecue. We shared a large table with several people who were also guests at the motel. The Korean chef named Kim was said to be famous in his home country for several of the dishes that he served. His menu included barbecue beef, bean sprouts, fiddlehead fern, (whatever that is), hot radishes, and hot cabbages. We enjoyed the meal. It was a long tiresome day for me without enough sleep.

Day 16 - It was raining and 48 degrees when we rode into Jasper for breakfast at a fancy restaurant there. A group of Swiss people from a tour bus came out of the restaurant about the same time we did. We talked with a few of them as we prepared to leave. One guy kept smiling and saying to me in poor English, "You're goving?" I answered twice, "Yes, we're going." He kept saying it like I didn't hear him the first time and each time I answered the same way. I thought he might be a

236

little simple, or maybe hard of hearing, but finally his wife, who spoke English clearly, enunciated, "He asked if this is your Gold Wing." Meanwhile he was smiling and nodding. As we were pulling out he said "Goot fahrt!" which Jake told me later was German for "Have a good trip."

We made our way down the Icefields Parkway through Jasper and Banff Parks in the rain, which became mixed with snow and sleet as we climbed over Parker Ridge. The temperature at Columbia Icefields, where we stopped for a few photos, was only 36 degrees. We finally ran out of the rain near Lake Louise but it was still heavily overcast. After turning east, we rode through some road construction on Trans-Canada One and saw several Rocky Mountain sheep along the Kananaskis Trail. The Forestry Trunk Road that runs parallel with the Continental Divide was dusty with a lot of marble-sized gravel on the surface, but it was a ride that we all enjoyed.

Day 17 - It was 53 degrees and partly cloudy when we left Blairmore at 5:30. It dropped into the mid forties near the crest of Crowsnest Pass. We saw several BC provincial cops with speeders pulled over, so we took it easy along Route 3. We had a nice half-hour ferry ride across Kootenay Lake after riding a great 50-mile twisty road along the east side of the lake. We got to Spokane, Washington at 3:30, where we were supposed to meet Ralph Spencer. He had planned to accompany us for a day or so but he never showed. It was 82 degrees in Spokane, which felt particularly hot in long johns.

Day 18 - It was a beautiful, clear, crisp morning leaving Spokane. We negotiated several scenic and twisty secondary roads through some rolling wheat fields in eastern Washington, and across the state line into Idaho. We learned while having breakfast in St. Maries that heavy damage from early spring flooding had not yet been cleared; and that some of the roads we planned to take along the St. Joe River leading over the Continental Divide into St. Regis, Montana were still being repaired. The flood had taken out several roads in the area. We used the interstate highway as a detour and later we experienced several construction delays in Montana. We got to our motel in Lewistown around six. I washed the radiator core because the engine was running hot during the day from all of the mud in it.

Day 19 - We had breakfast in Jordan. It was cool and clear all morning as we rode through some barren areas of eastern Montana. We had lunch at a taco stand in Watford City. It was becoming increasingly cloudy in the afternoon, and we rode through a few showers late in the day. We rode another 350 miles with several construction delays before reaching our reserved motel in Carrington, ND.

Day 20 - We experienced several rain showers during the day, a few of which were heavy. We crossed the Mississippi River where it is only about 10 feet wide and later checked into a doublewide trailer at the Woodland Motel in Augusta, WI before looking for Phil Bourdon's house. My tire had arrived at Phil's, so I proceeded to change it in his barn. We enjoyed a dinner that Connie prepared, and afterward we visited with our hosts for a few hours before returning to our doublewide.

Day 21 - Phil led us over several remote farm roads for more than 240 miles to the Michigan state line where he turned back. We rode along the Upper Peninsula of Michigan to the Macinaw Bridge and then followed the Circle Route on the east shore of Lake Michigan for a while. Many of the towns had flowers planted along the roads. We located our Super 8 in Cadillac but when we learned there was no rollaway cot, we got a room at another motel nearby.

Day 22 - We were on the road at first light for the day we planned to visit the AMA in Westerville, Ohio and the motorcycle museum there. We spent a few hours browsing through the museum and we stopped to see a few of the people we know there. After leaving AMA Headquarters we headed into the farmland and saw a lot of Amish buggies around Mount Eaton. A few times there would be as many as three and four buggies in a group holding up traffic in the hilly terrain. Cars would crest the blind hills and have to panic brake for buggies that were traveling very slowly the dips. We ran into a heavy shower just before reaching our motel in Massillon.

Day 23 - We traveled several scenic secondary roads on our final day, including a few dirt roads in the mountains of central Pennsylvania. The main regret of our trip was the shortage of photo opportunities. Since I had planned a daily average of more than 520 miles of secondary roads, some of them dirt, it allowed very little time for anything other than hard riding. I think we had a good ride.

GOOSE BAY ON A LIGHTWEIGHT

The thought processes involved in deciding to take a 3300-mile trip on a 225cc dirt bike get a bit complicated. It involves a lot of "been there, done that," and wanting to do something different while staying within the general definition of adventure touring. Having been to Alaska six times on big bikes I once said that if I ever go again it would probably be on a 200cc motorcycle just to be different. But then I may never get the desire to go to Alaska again and I may never own a 200cc motorcycle. Besides, it would probably take me at least two weeks just to get there on that size bike.

A few years ago I heard about a new road opening in northeastern Canada that connects northern Quebec with Goose Bay, Labrador, so I wrote for more information. Along with a lot of other printed material about Newfoundland and Labrador I received a three-page brochure on the Trans-Labrador Highway. It described the final 180 miles of road into Goose Bay as "pit-run gravel." Another 40-mile section south of Labrador City was described as "under construction and rough." It sounded interesting. I was fairly sure there would be no RVs or campers on the road to cope with and it's my kind of ride. I decided it was the place I should go next and maybe I should do it on a small machine like I once thought about for Alaska.

After I began thinking more seriously about it, I couldn't find the right bike for the trip. I considered taking the Gold Wing but figured the 180 miles of "pit-run gravel" meant a lot of stuff the Gold Wing just doesn't handle very well in. It could even take a lot of the fun out of it if the gravel was deep and loose. The thought of taking my old 1974 500cc Triumph TR5 crossed my mind. After all, it held together for six days in the Berkshires only two years earlier, riding with a group of Europeans and some legendary New England dirt riders. That idea stuck for a while. I hauled the Triumph out, cleaned up the carburetor, and got it running again.

I mentioned the idea to a few friends and learned that several thought it was a great idea. Jake Herzog was the first to express a serious interest. He said he would restore one of his own old 500cc Triumphs and join me. The next to express a strong interest was Emil Cocce of New Jersey. He said he liked the idea, but said emphatically that he would use his more up-to-date, 350cc-dual-sport Suzuki. Others also expressed a desire to go including Frank DeGray on a restored 650cc Triumph.

Emil's sudden and tragic death while touring in Virginia began to thin our ranks. The Triumph idea eventually dissolved when the old machinery just wouldn't cooperate on a few shakedown rides. A month before the trip was scheduled, I jumped at the chance to buy a used 225cc Yamaha Serow. Jake in quick succession jumped at this opportunity to switch to his 650cc Kawasaki KLR. One by one the others dropped out until there was only Jake and myself heading for the Canadian border on one hot day in July. Frank was still a maybe for the next day in Maine. Following is a daily journal of the tour:

Day 1 - I left Buchanan for Jake's house on July 17, 1997, having ridden the Yamaha for a total of less than a hundred miles. I soon learned that it was necessary to shift down on many of the hills. The little engine sang soprano as it whirred loudly in the lower gears over Storm King Mountain behind West Point. Coming down the north side it let out a high-pitched whine as my speed edged up over 65 MPH. I swore I could hear it saying, "Hold on old man, we're going to Labrador." I stopped briefly at Jim Moroney's shop in Newburgh before heading into the Catskills. I got a few chuckles and a few expressions of skepticism about the little bike, but I think no one doubted my resolve -- my sanity maybe but not my resolve. Jim Moroney made the comment as I left, "He won't make Albany on that thing." A short time later I passed through Phoenicia where I saw people preparing to "tube the Esopus," a local water sport in the Catskills.

I decided early into the trip to try and maintain my constant speeds below 65 MPH. I figured that RPMs above that speed might be approaching redline on the tiny machine and I didn't want to blow it up. The speedometer indicated a red line from 55 MPH up, but I figured that was because the national speed limit was 55 when it was manufactured. Of the people I spoke with about it, no one knew very much about the RPM redline for a Serow.

I arrived at Jake's house in Slingerlands at 4:30 PM, about a half hour earlier than planned. I wanted to miss any late afternoon thundershowers and I wasn't sure of the average travel time I could make with my new steed, or should I say my pony, especially in the hilly areas of the Catskills. I traveled on a few wet roads but I saw no rain that day. It was a beautiful day at Jake's with a warm breeze and low humidity. Arlene prepared a great lobster picnic that we ate outdoors by their pond. I turned in at 9:30 while Jake finished his packing.

Day 2 - We were up before first light, had coffee and croissants at Jake's, and we were on the road by six, after Arlene took a few photos of our intrepid start. We rode superhighways around Albany to avoid the early morning traffic and soon we were on some of Jake's favorite dirt roads northeast of Troy. We emerged from the farmland to have breakfast at an old country diner in Whitehall, leaving there a little after eight. We traveled a few more rough back roads along the state line, as we gradually made our way east into picturesque Vermont.

We stopped at one farm and waited as the farmer led his herd of milking cows across the road. Around 9:30 we came through a second farmyard where Jake slowed to let a cow cross. I slowed down behind him and turned to look at the cow as she sauntered through a gate. When I turned back to see where I was going I saw to my horror that Jake had suddenly stopped for the farmer's wife, who was leading another cow across about a hundred feet up the road. There he was just sitting there and here I was closing fast at about 20 MPH. I went for both brakes, but my time quickly ran out. The next thing I knew I had rear-ended him square in the middle. The little Yamaha stood right up on the front wheel as the rear wheel raised a few inches off the ground, depositing me soundly onto the pavement and also knocking Jake off of his bike. I was sure the trip had ended right there as I envisioned the fork and front wheel pushed back to the engine. As I picked myself up, Jake proceeded to pick up both bikes. It was soon evident that the damage was minor and the greatest loss was to my camera, which was attached to my belt when I landed on it. We both sustained multiple bruises and I got a few minor abrasions. We got the usual "Are you all right?" from the farmer's wife before we got back on and continued on our way a little worse for wear.

A short time later Jake motioned for me to lead. Although it was where my route sheet took over, I thought he probably felt safer with that arrangement. My planned route took us over several rough back roads in Vermont, New Hampshire, and Maine. By the time we got to Stratton we were both thankful that we were on modern dual-sport motorcycles with good suspension rather than the vintage Triumphs. I felt really beat up. We also realized that if we had taken the big touring machines we probably would have incurred major cosmetic damage in the mishap and possibly even disabled one or both of the machines.

The temperature was in the high 80s when we rolled into Stratton, our first-night stopover. We had covered 380 miles and celebrated with a few beers and a first-class dinner. Frank DeGray had said he would join us there, and we looked for him all evening, but he never showed. We figured he must have changed his mind at the last minute. Our room was very hot with no air conditioning, so we slept with the door wide open and the box fan set on high in the doorway. The room finally cooled down around 3 AM, but neither of us slept very much that night due to the heat.

Day 3 - We were up at 4:45 and I walked over to a 24-hour convenience store for coffee and donuts for the two of us. The temperature was in the mid 60s, it was hazy, and there was a light fog in some areas as we left Stratton. It never got above the 70s all day. We traveled a few wet roads while approaching Quebec City. I put on my rain suit, which became my standard for the rest of the trip; if not for the rain, then for the cold. Jake wore his high-tech, dual-sport outfit. We stopped at a bank in Quebec City to exchange currency.

We had a 15-minute ferry ride at Tadoussac that took us across a scenic fjord. I was glad to be eastbound after seeing a mile-long queue waiting for the westbound ferry. They probably had up to a two-hour wait, whereas our wait plus the crossing was only about a half hour. We got to Baie Comeau around 4:30, having traveled 435 miles that day. Baie Comeau is divided into two sectors and we chose a motel in the west sector before learning that our morning route north was out of the east sector, five miles farther up the road.

Even though we rode more miles that day, it was less tiring than the previous day because the roads were smoother and the pain from our bruises had a chance to subside. My gas mileage dropped quite a bit, probably because of the higher speeds and stronger headwinds. I could hold the speed fairly constant between 55 and 60 MPH, although sometimes I would be able to maintain as much as 65 on level ground. Occasionally I would hit 70 or better downhill, and when we climbed several

11% grades, my speed would usually drop below 40. I added oil to the bike at Baie Comeau. I watched the oil carefully during the trip because the engine held only a liter of oil. Being down only a pint meant that almost half of the oil is gone.

Day 4 - I slept like a rock for seven hours, after which we were on the road by 5:15. The electric power in town had failed around five so we left without breakfast, or even coffee, because of the power outage. The day started out with bright sunshine and temperatures in the mid 40s. The first 30 or 40 miles of Route 389 consisted of twisty blacktop through a hilly, scenic countryside with lakes and rock outcroppings along the way. We saw vacation homes around a few of the lakes we passed. About an hour after we started, the temperature dropped to around 40, it got overcast, and began to drizzle.

Having bucked a strong headwind most of the way from Baie Comeau, the Serow ran completely out of gas two miles short of Manic 5. We stopped to transfer gas from the two-and-a-half-gallon plastic can that I carried on the back.

It's 130 miles from the west sector of Baie Comeau to Manic 5, a hydroelectric power facility with a huge dam and power station. After refueling both bikes there we rode another 105 miles of gravel road to Gagnon. A light rain that was more like a heavy mist kept the dust down. The road was wide and relatively straight with a fairly smooth surface. Many of the shoulders were soft and there were some soft ridges and loose stones up to baseball-size in the center, although it was fairly easy to stay in the tire tracks and hold a reasonable speed. We topped off the gas at a small station 62 miles north of Manic 5 in expectation of the 165-mile stretch with no gas at all.

Gagnon is a ghost town right out of the "Twilight Zone." Except for the divided pavement, concrete curbs with indentations for driveways, steel storm-drains, and evidence that there were once streetlight stanchions, we saw no other signs that a building of any sort ever existed there. No foundations or any type of construction materials were visible anywhere. The town of Gagnon was completely disassembled, picked up, and carried away. In effect, it was a ghost town without buildings. Today it exists in name only, as a reference on the map. There are 55 miles of good blacktop road from there to another place on the map called Fire Lake. The improved blacktop road appears completely out of place as it crosses a high plateau seemingly from nowhere to nowhere. We saw only two other vehicles in the entire 55 miles. It was raining and quite chilly, with the temperature in the low forties. The landscape consisted mainly of thin northern balsams. There was a pale-green, lichen-like moss covering the rocks and much of the ground.

The forty miles of dirt from Fire Lake to Mount Wright had some of the worst road surface we found anywhere on the trip. It would have been passable by a big road motorcycle but there were millions of huge potholes and a lot of washboard surface with many soft spots. It was a challenge to ride with any kind of bike. The narrow, low maintenance dirt road, which the brochure refers to as "under construction" meanders all over the countryside, crossing the active railroad tracks several times. The railroad connects Labrador with the seacoast town of Sept-Iles, Quebec. I thought the road surface was more in need of maintenance than it was under construction, because we didn't see construction equipment anywhere. A heavier rain settled in and it got quite cold.

The poorly maintained road ended near a huge iron mine in a place called Mount Wright. Twenty-five miles of fairly good road then took us past the access road to the town of Fermont, Quebec, and eventually into Labrador City, a town with nice accommodations and some nice people who spoke English. We stayed at the Two Seasons Inn where the food was good but expensive. Most of the entrees were priced in the mid $20 range. I noticed that Chateau Briand for two was $52. I ordered the salmon steak, one of the lower-priced entrees, while Jake opted for Big Jim (somebody's) sirloin. There were other restaurants nearby but we were cold and tired so we chose to stay put in the warmth of the inn. There was a wedding reception in progress when we arrived. Our room on the first floor cost $72 (Canadian) after my Senior Citizen discount, which was the same price we paid in Baie Comeau with no discount.

Day 5 - When we left Labrador City at 5:30 AM the temperature was one degree Celsius (34 degrees) with no rain. It didn't take long for the rain to return and the temperature to drop to around the freezing mark. I wore every bit of clothing I brought, including my spare jeans and all of my spare T-shirts. Luckily I brought double-force Damart underwear. My fingers felt very cold through my 60-year-old lightweight Harley mittens that happened to be in the bottom of my saddlebag. To justify our pain we reminded ourselves more than once that this is what we came for. By the time we got 50 miles out we were "cold to the bone" and Jake was wet underneath his outer clothes in several places.

The 150 miles of gravel road to Churchill Falls was in fair shape. There was some washboard surface with a few soft ridges in the center, but for the most part it was a standard Canadian gravel road with a little less maintenance than some. Light rain kept the dust down. The scenery was fairly good although the road was generally straight and level. Neither of us would go out of our way to come back and ride this piece of road again, since there are certainly many more interesting dirt roads closer to home. We made the average time listed in the brochure, which was 3 hours.

Churchill Falls is a small, neat village owned and operated by the hydroelectric power company, which I think is in turn owned by the government. The hydroelectric plant offers tours of the facility when booked in advance. All standard services are available including banking, shopping and a post office. We lingered over a late breakfast at the inn before tackling the main object of our tour, the final section of the Trans-Labrador Highway into Happy Valley/Goose Bay.

While at Labrador City we had heard several comments about how bad the final 180 miles into Goose Bay was. Very few people we spoke with there had anything good to say about it. Some mentioned being stuck for hours while construction crews had the road torn up and blocked. Others told us about up to five accidents in a week along the road, where cars or pickups slid off the sometimes-slick surface into the ditches. Everyone we spoke with in Labrador City seemed to be negative about it. In contrast, the people we spoke with at Churchill Falls had very little negative to say about the road. The conversation there centered mostly on the average time to drive it, which was 6 to 8 hours. Some made it in 5.

The road started out narrow and fairly straight with just two tire tracks. Vehicles meeting from opposite directions had to slow down and make room for each other. One of the first things I noticed about the road was the lack of "pit-run gravel" that the brochure had alluded to. I would characterize the road more as a narrow, minimum-maintenance dirt road. It got more interesting about 50 miles out near the Metchin River, where the road was twisty and scenic. Rain threatening to wash away some of the road surface and we were concerned that if the rain continued to come down like it was, we may have difficulty returning that way. We even discussed the possibility of taking a ferry out of Goose Bay if the road got completely washed out and they closed it to all traffic.

The road is actually a great ride for an adventurous dual-sport rider. Of course it's a long way to come just to ride 180 miles of challenging dirt. It's what we came for though, and we enjoyed it in spite of the rain and cold. The rain caused many muddy ruts and a few washouts along the edges and sometimes a mild washout across the road. These obstacles are not a big deal for a dual-sport bike but they could give most road-bike riders a case of "white knuckles." It would take an experienced rider with a large road bike much longer to get through than the time we made it in, and I'm sure that certain weather conditions could render it impassable. I suppose in a couple of years the road will be greatly improved and maybe even paved.

My greatest concern was with my failing eyesight. Being practically blind in one eye and having low vision in the other, when my face shield and glasses become covered with rain, it doesn't afford a very good view of the obstacles. Several times I hit ruts and deep puddles that I didn't see. My concern then would be regaining control after hitting whatever it was. We made the trip from Churchill Falls to Goose Bay in six hours, which included a stop to refill the tank from the spare can, oiling the chain at least once, and stopping for a few photos. I was dry inside my rain suit, but Jake was wet to the skin in a few places. His high-tech riding gear wasn't designed for riding all day in steady rain on a dual-sport bike.

We had heard much about the construction on the eastern end of the highway, which began about 70 miles from Goose Bay. The entire final 70 miles is considered to be under construction, although there were only two or three pockets of actual work activity. We came upon one spot where a bulldozer had the road torn up pretty bad but when the operator saw us coming he back-bladed a section for us to ride across, which might have been difficult for a large touring machine. Because of the extremely light traffic, the construction crews use no flag people to stop or direct traffic. We had to find our own way through and hoped that we didn't get dead-ended by taking the wrong path.

We checked into the Labrador Inn, our most expensive lodging of the trip. Being tired, cold, and wet we ate at the inn and skipped the sightseeing. We went by the old US Air Force Base at Goose Bay before locating our inn in the Happy Valley area. The air base was used by the Northeast Air Command for defense and early warning in the 1950s, and later by U2 reconnaissance aircraft. We assumed there was a coastal village nearby, but at that point we weren't interested in anything other than warming up, taking a shower, getting a meal and some rest. We toasted Emil Cocce at dinner and figured he was probably looking down on us and smiling. I walked out to the convenience store after dinner for breakfast snacks since we planned to leave before the restaurant opened.

Day 6 - The temperature was in the low 60's when we left the motel at 5:30. We were both fully suited even though it wasn't raining. It was a good bet that it would be raining again soon anyway. It did start to rain near the first construction activity about 30 miles out, where a large piece of machinery was cutting a swath through the trees with a huge cutting wheel. The machine threw chunks of bark and branches all over the place. I caught a piece of something on the end of my toe that was quite painful. Around 50 miles out a huge backhoe was digging on one side of the road and depositing its bucket loads on the other side. We had to time our passing to be between swings of the huge bucket.

About 20 miles past the construction I thought I saw a deep washout across the road in front of me as we were traveling about 40 MPH. My clouded, rain-covered face shield blurred my already poor vision. I thought I didn't want to hit the ditch at that speed, so I went for the rear brake. Unfortunately I hit it a little too hard, throwing the bike into a slight broad-slide. Consequently it was crossed up when it struck the minor washout and I did a really ugly departure from the bike, landing on my head. Jake said when the bike landed it hit first on one side and then did a complete somersault, landing on the other side. It's amazing how much that little machine can take, not to mention my 72-year-old body. I bounced along the ground and heard my helmet hit the dirt road three times before I finally came to rest. As Jake was picking me up, he said I was lucky I landed on my head; otherwise, I might have really gotten hurt!

The only damage that resulted from the spill was that the brake pedal got bent, which Jake straightened while I regained my composure. I sustained a slight concussion and we had to stop a few times to rest when I got dizzy and nauseated each time we took off. Only a few miles up the road I picked up a nail in the rear tire, which went flat very quickly. The flat gave my head the little extra time it needed to clear. The tube had at least one large hole in the sidewall in addition to the expected hole on the face, so we used Jake's spare tube rather than trying to patch it. I stuffed his 450x17 tube into the narrow 18-inch tire and we used two of his CO_2 cartridges to put about 15 pounds of air into it. That was enough to get us the remaining 95 miles into Churchill Falls where I got more air.

The 180 miles from Goose Bay to Churchill Falls took us about seven hours. The rain was lighter than on our eastbound trip and the surface was in better shape. The ride would have been a blast had I not dampened the joy by crashing and having a flat, but that spiced up the experience and gave us something to talk about.

We had lunch at Churchill Falls and made the 150 miles into Labrador City in three hours. I had a headache most of the way and my ears were ringing pretty loud. I also had some pain in my neck where I had ruptured a disk a few years earlier in a serious road accident with the Gold Wing. I stopped using the face shield before we reached Labrador City and decided to brave the cold and rain on my bare face rather than risk another bad scene. Riding the rough terrain was much easier once I was able to see where I was going.

Day 7 - The temperature was 40 degrees and it was raining when we left Labrador City, although the sky looked promising for a change. I had breakfast in the room, having picked up a few cereal bars and some orange juice at the local food store the night before. Jake carried his breakfast and ate en route about an hour later. It was very cold for the first 100 miles, especially on my bare face. We were not carrying enough clothes for that type of weather.

Near the end of the rough 40-mile section, which again crisscrossed the railroad several times, we saw an 18-wheel semi that had apparently went into a turn far too fast and overturned in the ditch. The engine was cold so we assumed it had been there for quite a while. It would certainly take a heavy-duty hook to set it upright and get it out of there. It appeared from the tracks and skid marks around it that another truck had already tried in vain to move it. We stopped briefly to look it over and Jake took a few photos.

We ate a full breakfast at the small truck-stop 62 miles north of Manic 5. Being in Quebec where many people spoke only French, they enlisted the translating assistance of the only English-speaking woman in the place to wait on us. The breakfast took a long time because we had to wait for her to cook the bacon that came directly from the refrigerator.

As we were getting gas at Manic 5, Jake mentioned that it was still quite early and he suggested we catch an earlier ferry to the Gaspe Peninsula. Our original plan was to leave Godbout at 8 o'clock the following morning and tour the Gaspe. I remembered seeing a 2 PM ferry listed on the schedule that left from Baie Comeau rather than Godbout. We figured there was still time to catch it if we hustled, so we rode the next 125 miles of mostly twisty macadam in 2 hours. The little Yamaha sang a high-pitched tune all the way. It actually ran better than it did a week earlier when I left home. Any carbon buildup must certainly have been cleared out by then. We rushed to the ferry landing in Baie Comeau to find only a few maintenance workers painting lines in the queuing area. I rechecked my ferry schedule there, and saw that the 2 PM ferry from Baie Comeau ran only on Mondays and Fridays. It was Tuesday.

We peeled off a few layers of clothes there and decided to skip our planned tour of the Gaspe Peninsula and head back the way we came. We could reconnect with our planned route near Solon, Maine the following day. We each had several chores waiting for us at home and we had already done what we came to do, which was to ride the Trans-Labrador Highway to Goose Bay. After a late lunch in Baie Comeau we rode another 140 miles, stopping for the night at Tadoussac. We rode a total of almost 500 miles that day, 150 miles of which was dirt. In my wildest dreams I would never have believed that I could accomplish that on a 225cc dirt bike just one day after landing on my head. It took its toll though, because I was beat and had a real sore butt as well as a headache.

Day 8 - The temperature was in the low 40s when we boarded the ferry across the fjord. We had to wait about 20 minutes before it shoved off. It was only 5:30 AM and the ferry probably ran hourly when traffic was light. We saw a water spout from a whale near the mouth of the fjord in the St. Lawrence River as we stood near the rail of the ferry. We stopped for breakfast at a McDonald's in Baie St. Paul and used the superhighways to bypass the expected morning congestion in Quebec City. We had lunch at an old restaurant in Jackman, Maine and stopped for the night in Gorham, NH.

Day 9 - The temperature was in the forties when we left Gorham. Our final day included an excellent gravel road over Jefferson Notch near Randolph, NH, a really nice series of twisty, scenic roads through New Hampshire and Vermont, and an enjoyable ride on another gravel road over Lincoln Gap. We both remarked what a beautiful ride it was through the picturesque villages and the scenic New England countryside. The weather was perfect. It made me wonder as I have many times in the past why we travel thousands of miles in search of the very same thing, when we have it right here in our back yard.

We split around lunchtime in Salem, NY. Jake headed southwest for Slingerlands while I rode straight south for Buchanan, hoping to beat the weather that looked threatening in my direction. I did run into rain near Poughkeepsie and rode the last 50 miles in a heavy downpour.

ALASKA 7 - ROBYN'S GRADUATION

My primary objective for riding to Alaska for a seventh time was to see my grandson Robyn graduate from high school. I would also get to see my granddaughter Asia, who had taken a brief hiatus from her college studies to accept a government job working for the Air National Guard there. I figured the main thing I would get from the ride itself would be seeing some outstanding scenery in the mountains during the spring season when everything is still white with snow and the roads are free of traffic. There should be practically no RV traffic to contend with in mid May, making it a safer and much more enjoyable trip than during the tourist season. I left on May 19th, almost two weeks earlier than I had ever left for Alaska before and a full eleven days before Robyn's graduation. The eleven days included at least two extra days in case I ran into snow. My original plan included nine fairly short days of riding in each direction, which I figured should be more than enough.

I would turn 76 in June and my physical condition was pretty good for my age. When I mentioned the trip to my cardiologist he just smiled and said, "Go for it." Of course he's an eternal optimist, which is why I chose him. I think my ophthalmologist may have had a few concerns because I have blind spots and a few other problems involving both eyes; but I recently passed my motor vehicle eye test and I've learned to live and ride with my eye problems. Aside from that, I have several stiff and aching joints, especially in the morning, but I can live with those too, as long as I can manage to get my shoes on and tied, and get my rain suit and boots on when I need them.

Initially I planned my route via Spokane, WA to avoid possible snow in the northern Rockies, but when I researched the British Columbia area on the Internet I learned that the Cassiar Highway between Hazelton, BC and Watson Lake in the Yukon Territory was in poor condition. Deep mud was reported along some of the dirt sections and there was considerable one-way, single-lane traffic due to washouts. If I had all the time in the world to get there, and if I was packing a tent and sleeping bag, I would risk it, because it's more scenic that way. But I didn't have all the time in the world and I was traveling as light as possible. Typical spring weather, including some rain and sleet was also reported in the area between Spokane and Hazelton.

The Alaska Highway route through the northern Canadian Rockies on the other hand didn't seem half-bad for spring travel. The road surface was reported clear with reports of some frost heaves, many breaks in the pavement, and a few minor, isolated landslides. It's always been that way, even during some of my better trips, so I revised my route to enter Canada via Saskatchewan and head straight for the Alaska Highway at Dawson Creek, BC. Twenty-two miles of construction were reported on the Alaska Highway in the western part of the Yukon Territory, but I would have to cope with that section on either route I chose.

Choosing which motorcycle to ride was the next decision I had to make. Originally I thought because of the weather, my old 1986 Honda Gold Wing was probably the best machine for the job in spite of its 95,000+ miles; however I had concerns about the original stator, which had failed on each of my other two 1200 cc Gold Wings in their first 100,000 miles. A second potential problem was the rear-wheel spline, which had failed once on this machine already and the new spline had run dry of grease on an earlier trip to Alaska, so it was well worn and probably not totally reliable. Either problem had the potential of delaying my trip for several days if not weeks; consequently, I chose my new BMW for the trip.

In spite of my having named an earlier trip to Alaska "Saga of the Ailing BMWs," where all three BMWs had mechanical or electrical problems en route, I felt fairly confident that my 2001 R1150GS would not follow that lead, especially after having broke it in with 11,000 trouble-free miles since Labor Day. The only concerns I had with the BMW related to its being a sport motorcycle, as opposed to a touring bike. It was not equipped with a long-distance-touring saddle, full wind protection or touring tires. In January I installed a tall aftermarket half-fairing, although the lower part of the fairing system would not be available until later in the summer. After acquiring and testing a pair of tank panniers to hang across the tank in front of my knees, I concluded that these bags provided all the additional wind protection I needed. Knowing that my rear tire would last only about 8,500 miles on the coarse Canadian road surfaces, I calculated that it would get me back to Phil Bourdon's farm in Wisconsin, where I could make the change on my return trip; so I shipped the new tire to Phil's house just before leaving. I put an extra six pounds of air into each tire to extend the tire mileage and to protect the wheels from potholes and traumatic breaks in the pavement that I knew were inevitable. I was ready to leave.

Day 1 - I was about ninety percent packed and loaded when I got up that morning, so my biggest chore was to "suit-up" and get myself onto the machine. The temperature was in the mid 50s and there was some fog in the valleys as I headed west through Harriman Park. I did a lot of thinking during the first few hours and didn't sing to myself right away as I normally did on my trips. Mostly I was thinking about how far I had to go. I finally began singing as I climbed into the Poconos, with lines from "It's a long way to Tipperary."

The first day went relatively smooth and quick. It was an uneventful ride over a familiar set of interstate highways that I had gotten to know pretty well when Donna was stationed in Ohio. I got to my motel just west of Columbus before four o'clock. I felt I could have gone another hundred miles but I stopped mainly because I had reservations. I also remembered that all of the motels I had checked earlier around Dayton were booked. It was an easy 600-mile day and when I called Jim and Barbara to tell them I was OK, I said it was "a piece of cake." I picked up some juice for my breakfast before turning in.

Day 2 - My day started with a clear blue sky and temperatures in the low 50s, which called for long johns and my rain suit bottoms to break the cool wind. I had no trouble suiting up with only a few minor aches and pains. I ate breakfast bars that I carried, along with the juice. I thought it would be an easy day with only 576 miles of interstate highways showing on my route sheet. Including an hour gained entering the Central Time Zone I figured I would be in Menomonie, Wisconsin by 3 PM at the latest.

The first of a series of route sheet errors became evident in Indianapolis. I had written I-65 rather than I-74 to go from there to Bloomington, Illinois. I suspected something was wrong when I realized that I-65 was making a big sweeping turn, so I took the first exit and got out my road atlas. My eyesight is barely good enough to read the map except in bright sunlight, but I was able to see my error and I went back to find I-74. I got to Bloomington where I ran into my second error. It was becoming obvious that the combination of my poor eyesight and not spending enough time studying the maps with a magnifying glass were beginning to eat into my travel time.

Soon after circling Bloomington and heading north, I realized yet another error. I had omitted a huge chunk of I-39 when I calculated the mileage to Portage, Wisconsin. I had written that it was 38 miles from Bloomington to Portage and it turned out to be a whopping 255 miles. All of these errors were in the area where I had made some quick changes after deciding to enter Canada via North Dakota rather than near Spokane. I simply didn't spend enough time with the revision. Extending my day by an additional 200+ miles and taking a few wrong turns brought my total mileage for the day to over 800. I thought about stopping before Menomonie, but decided to go all the way since I had reservations. I checked in at six.

About an hour and a half before reaching Menomonie I ran through a thundershower with heavy downpours, for which I managed to suit up in time. I ate dinner at a nearby Perkins, after which I picked up my juice for breakfast. I noticed that from riding a few hours with bare hands, the strong return spring on the throttle had caused all of the heavy skin on the entire palm of my right hand to break loose from the flesh like a huge blister. It meant that I would have to use my heavier gloves and I'd have to hold the throttle mainly with my fingers and thumb until the skin had a chance to reattach itself. It also meant no more riding with bare hands until I could get different return springs installed.

Day 3 - I saw light coming around the drapes when I woke up during the night. Without ever looking at my watch, I peeked out and saw a bright light at horizon level and assumed it was the sun coming up. I immediately started packing my things to get ready. Before I rolled up my rain suit, I looked out again to check on the weather. This time I saw that it was still very dark and that the light I had seen was actually a security light in the parking lot. I saw that it was also raining very hard. I continued to get ready, ate some breakfast in my room, and left at first light in my rain suit.

The traffic heading into St. Paul was heavy and it was quite windy. I assumed it was rush-hour traffic, although it was still quite early. The strong crosswinds caused me some concern because I was riding very close between cars and trucks at a fairly high rate of speed. I thought about the time I was on the

Gold Wing in west Texas when a blast of crosswind struck me so hard from the side that both tires broke traction.

It stopped raining by the time I was halfway around St. Paul but the winds got much stronger and the temperature dropped considerably. It was a challenge just to hold the bike on the road for the 240 miles from St. Paul to Fargo, ND. I stopped once to strap the tank bag tighter to the tank with a bungee cord because the crosswinds kept blowing the bag over onto my leg. I even had to tighten the strap on my helmet when it too began to get thrown around by the wind. I was being literally tossed all over the highway. I stopped in Fargo to put on my snowmobile top over both the heavy leather jacket and my rain suit because I was getting cold. The crosswind and head winds continued all the way into Minot where I stopped for the night. I noticed a sharp drop in gas mileage from the mid 40s per gallon that I got at home, down to around 28 MPG.

I got to Minot at 4 PM in spite of two construction delays, both of which used pilot cars. I stopped at the Harley shop to get a recommendation on lodging and I was advised that the Days Inn had the best deal. The price was far less than the Motel 6 of the previous night with a much larger room and a coffee maker. A check of the oil level in the bike indicated that I needed some, so I searched several places around town for Mobil 1 before locating a Target store. I walked from my motel to a nearby Perkins for dinner, and later picked up breakfast juice.

Day 4 - There was a thick layer of frost on the seat when I came out in the morning, although it was a very clear day. I wore my 3 layers of high-tech Damart underwear and my full snowmobile suit. It was a beautiful day except for the wind. It was Lilli's and my anniversary, which would have been our 54th, so I spent much of the day reminiscing those years. Crossing the Canadian border was a nonevent that took less than a minute, a huge difference from the last time I came through that same border crossing in 1981.

Saskatchewan was as flat as I had remembered from previous trips. I saw very few cattle, and the wheat fields were bare. The crosswinds were very strong, which became annoying after a while, especially the loud wind noise against the side of my helmet. Gas prices were running around 93 cents per liter. I recalled from my earlier trips that Saskatchewan gas was not the greatest, so I burned high-test gas whenever I could find it, but many places in the farmland only carry low-grade regular.

I decided to lengthen my planned day because the weather was good, except for the wind. I tacked on about 90 miles and reached Lloydminster, Alberta where I stopped for the night at an old travel-type motel.

Day 5 - I was up at 4:30, stiff and sore all over. I recalled that the fifth day of most of my trips was usually the roughest from a soreness point of view. I left at six after eating breakfast in the room, but I felt lousy. I hoped I would loosen up and feel better soon. I also felt weak, all of which I attributed to my fifth day on the road. With the temperature in the mid 40s, I opted for the snowmobile suit again.

I finally cleared the open prairie and got into some scenic, hilly terrain with trees. Less wind and a better grade of gasoline combined to improve my gas mileage a little. Of course I was traveling at much higher speeds on this trip than I usually do around home, and the tank panniers created additional wind resistance, all of which were working against my gas mileage.

I stopped at a McDonald's in Edmonton for a second breakfast, after which I felt much better and a little stronger. I decided to stretch my riding day to at least 10 hours if the good weather held, although my eyesight usually deteriorated by late afternoon. I couldn't see oncoming cars at a distance, which made passing more difficult and riskier. I don't always see traffic lights in the towns either, and the ones I did see I often couldn't distinguish whether they were red or green because of the glare from the sun. I reached Fort St. John, about 47 miles up the Alaska Highway and called it a day there after 572 miles. I was starting to get tired by then and I knew that the distances between populated areas get much longer after Fort St. John. I stopped at the first motel I saw, which turned out to have all housekeeping units. It cost a little more but the room was very comfortable.

The muscles in my throttle hand were getting sore from the strong throttle return spring, since I was using only my thumb and fingers to hold the throttle open due to the loose skin on my palm. Sometimes I rested it by crossing over and holding the throttle with my left hand, but I wouldn't have a great deal of control in that position in case I faced an emergency. Using my heaviest gloves to hold the throttle open kept some of the pressure off my palm, as the heavy glove tends to take much of the strain from the twisting action. The hand was almost healed, although still a little sensitive.

Day 6 - An incredible day: I woke up at 4 AM and when I wasn't able to get back to sleep, I got up at 4:30. I ate a small can of tuna in my room with a strawberry breakfast bar and a liter of tropical juice. The morning weather report said it was 10 deg. C. outside, which is about 50 deg. F., so I opted for three layers of Damart underwear and my leather jacket on top, and long johns with jeans and rain suit pants on the bottom. That was good for leaving Fort St. John, but by the time I got to Pink Mountain I had to slip my snowmobile jacket over the top of everything, as the temperature dropped into the 40s. I was getting a little chilly, even before reaching the high mountains.

The sky was clear blue with unlimited visibility. The scenery around Pink Mountain with its many snowcapped peaks along the horizon was beautiful. Being aware of the long "dry spell" coming up, I topped off my gas there. The surface of the easternmost section of the Alaska Highway in British Columbia was smooth and well maintained with exceptionally light traffic. Seeing a vehicle approach from the opposite direction about every 5 minutes and passing one in my direction about every half hour made it fairly easy to maintain a constant speed of 75 MPH. I saw a few animals like moose, caribou, sheep, and fox along the way that I had to be particularly careful of, because they didn't always move out of the way very quickly.

I gassed up in Fort Nelson and headed into the Rockies with very light traffic. The scenery around Steamboat Mountain, and from there past Summit Lake and Stone Mountain was spectacular. Ice still covered Summit Lake, and Stone Mountain was completely blanketed with snow. Muncho Lake where I stopped a third time for gas also had ice covering about half of the lake, while heavy snow covered the surrounding mountains.

When I reached Watson Lake I was beginning to feel cold on my knees and I was a little tired from having run through a few showers and several rough sections of road in the Yukon Territory. It was barely 2:30 and I had already covered about 585 miles of beautiful country; but I wasn't crazy about the idea of staying at Watson Lake, or of quitting that early. I hadn't eaten since 5 AM and I was beginning to get a little hungry. I pondered my alternatives as I stood taking a photo at Signpost

257

Park. I realized that if I stayed at Watson Lake I would miss eating my favorite salmon dinner at Mukluk Annie's Salmon Bake in Teslin, and I'd also miss spending the night in one of their cabins. I had come to like Mukluk Annie's as a stopover and I had been looking forward to it. By gaining the extra mileage during the past few days, my original plan of spending the night there had been put in jeopardy.

I reached into my bag for a granola bar, and after wolfing that down for my lunch, I headed out for Mukluk Annie's, 176 miles away. I ran through a few showers, some very rough roads, and an eight-mile stretch of loose gravel along the way. About 50 miles from my goal it got quite cold, possibly dropping into the 30s, and my knees felt cold. Snow accumulation was visible between the trees, and patches of snow were visible along the grassy right-of-way. I may have been at a fairly high altitude at the time. I took a photo there and pressed on. After crossing the long steel-grate bridge over Teslin Lake, I finally pulled into Mukluk Annie's at six o'clock. I had been on the road for 12 hours and had covered almost 760 miles of the Alaska Highway, for an average speed of more than 62 MPH, which included four gas stops and a half-dozen photos.

After checking in I ordered the deluxe salmon bake along with the salad bar, which included baked beans and a delicious potato salad. My salmon plate consisted of a salmon steak plus a generous fillet, which together covered my plate. I talked with the young cook as he grilled it in the center of the dining area. My cabin was very small with no shower. A toilet and small lavatory sink were situated in the corner of the same room. Hot water was available in a central facility that houses the community showers as well as additional sinks and toilets. The tiny cabin, which is adorned with wall-to-wall carpeting, is heated with an electric space heater. The heater was definitely needed that night because it got down below freezing.

Day 7 - I had a little trouble getting to sleep so I took two Tylenol PM pills. I thought it might have been caused by the waitress accidentally reversed the coffee pots. When I awoke at five I was not only sore and stiff as I usually was in the morning, but I was also groggy from the pills. It took me quite a while to get all of my clothes on. Since the temperature outside was below freezing, and since an earlier forecast I heard called for rain in the area, I chose to wear my full snowmobile suit over the top of my leather jacket, and then my rain suit over everything else. It restricted my movements considerably and it was quite a chore to get it all on with my stiff and aching joints and the miserable way I felt. An alternative would have been to leave without the rain suit, but if I were to run into rain, it's doubtful I would be willing or able to get the suit on at the roadside without a place to sit. Getting onto the tall BMW that morning was another challenge because I couldn't bend very well with all the clothes I had on.

After the first 100 miles I considered going into Whitehorse for a quick second breakfast in order to get a few cups of coffee to wake me up, but when getting into Whitehorse seemed like too much of an effort with heavy early-morning traffic, I made a U-turn and returned to the highway, gassed up, and continued on. The road surface got progressively rougher west of Whitehorse and before I reached Haines Junction I had run through several huge breaks in the road at a speed, which if I had the Gold Wing, I would have bottomed the suspension very hard and possibly damaged to the machine.

I took a 15-minute break at Haines Junction after noticing a fresh pot of coffee in the office. While there I took a chance and removed my rain suit, which took about 15 minutes while I finished my coffee. I had to peel off some of it anyway to use the toilet.

West of Haines Junction the road surface got much worse, and if I hadn't put extra air in the tires I think I would have bent the rims on at least one of the huge potholes I hit. It was particularly rough around Lake Kluane, where the road skirts the edge of the lake for several miles. That was where I encountered some rocks in the road from a minor landslide, and also the first traffic of the trip. There were about a dozen large motor homes, house trailers, and pickup campers traveling slowly because of the roughness. I assumed they had just gotten off the ferry in Haines because of the way they were bunched together. I had no trouble getting by, but I was glad I didn't have to cope with that kind of traffic all the way.

Between Burwash Landing and Beaver Creek I ran into the 22 miles of road construction I had heard about. It was dry, with loose gravel on the surface, which made the bike fishtail quite a bit and I left a long trail of dust. I met a few large motor homes along there too, which were more difficult to pass because of their huge dust trails. I would usually wait until the dust was blown away by a gust of wind before I attempted the pass. There were several pockets of work activity, but I was stopped only a few times for a few minutes each time.

After clearing US customs near Beaver Creek I also found the Alaskan roads to have several huge frost breaks. I got to Tok around 2 PM Alaska Time, having gained two hours crossing the border. If I had not been nodding off from the lack of sleep I would have continued; but I was already more than a day ahead of my schedule and I had been on the road for 10 hours, so I decided to take a motel there. I also wasn't too enthused about stopping in Glennallen. I chose the same motel in Tok where I had stayed a few times before. The room cost $67, which was the highest price I paid for any night of the trip. Gas prices were also high there, especially considering that they pay no state taxes in Alaska. It was about 20 cents higher than the average price of gas in the US. In Canada I paid as much as a dollar a liter. It was my toughest day of the trip so far, having covered 520 miles of very rough road on a few hours sleep.

Day 8 - I slept more than nine hours, which made up for the previous night. There was frost on the seat when I came outside. Coffee was ready in the lobby so I had that with the rest of my breakfast in the room. It was partly cloudy and it looked promising in the western sky. The Glenn Highway was fairly rough, with many deep dips in the pavement between Tok and Glennallen. That's where Jake's saddlebag snapped off in some dips a few years back. I gassed up in Glennallen.

Eureka Summit was crystal clear for the first time in about eight times that I remember coming through there. I had never realized how spectacular the scenery was from the highway because it was usually overcast, foggy, sleet, snow, or raining when I came across the summit. There was considerable snow alongside the road. Sheep Mountain and Gunsight Mountain were spectacular. The highway descends from there to Matanuska Glacier and the Matanuska River Gorge where the roads become extremely twisty for the first time on the trip. I noticed that the bike ran much stronger at the lower altitudes. It was much more responsive than it had been for over a week in the mountains. The whirring sound of the engine, which is not totally unlike an electric motor, sounds almost the same pitch whether I'm traveling at 65 or 85.

I encountered some construction near Sutton, but I was lucky because there was very little traffic in either direction and I didn't get stopped. Several miles of hard-packed dirt brought me quickly through the construction area. I stopped at the McDonald's in Palmer for a second breakfast. Actually it was almost lunchtime. I arrived in Anchorage and went directly to Rey and Becky's house, getting there a little after noon. It had taken only 7½ days from home, during which time I clocked about 4650 miles for an average of 620 miles per day.

Days 9 through 13 - I spent 5½ days in Anchorage. I visited with my hosts, Rey, Becky, and their four children; with my wonderful grandchildren Asia and Robyn; with Andi Meisler, who is Ralph Spencer's daughter; with Don Rosene, the local BMW dealer, who I had known from enduro days; with many of Rey's family who also live in Anchorage; and last, but far from least, with Donna, who had come up from Richmond, Virginia for the graduation. Aside from these visits, other highlights of my stay in Anchorage included the graduation, a big barbecue party that Rey and his family threw for Robyn, visiting Asia's workplace, shopping downtown with Asia and Robyn, shopping with Becky and the children and spending quality time with Rey, Becky and the children at their home. I had a really wonderful time. They all had head colds while I was there, which I managed to catch before I left.

Day 14 - I left Anchorage on June 1st in bright sunshine, but by the time I had gone only 40 miles to Palmer, I already saw more clouds than sun and it kept getting darker. Just past the Matanuska Glacier it began to rain, and before I reached Eureka Summit the rain was steady, mixed with sleet. I stopped at the summit to put on my rain suit. With all of the clothes I was wearing it took more than a half hour to get my rain suit on over the snowmobile suit. I was also wearing my heavy leather jacket under the snowmobile suit.

I should have gotten gas at the summit but I thought I could make Glennallen only about 60 miles from there. To my surprise and chagrin the bike went on reserve only about 5 miles past the summit, which meant that I would have to make 55 miles on the reserve -- doubtful if not impossible, even downhill. I thought about returning to the summit but I kept going and began looking for a gas pump, although they are very scarce in the hinterlands. Luckily I spotted a single, rusty old pump in front of a cafe about 30 miles down the mountain. I went inside to ask if they had gas and would they please turn on the electricity for the pump. The rain had stopped by then.

I saw a few patches of sunshine after Glennallen, but soon after gassing up in Tok it began to rain steady. It rained all the way into Beaver Creek in the Yukon. I decided I had gone far enough for the day so I checked into a motel there after only about 435 miles.

Day 15 - What a terrible night! Having left Anchorage with a head cold, it seemed to have gotten much worse in the past 24 hours. There was a steady flow of fluids from my nose all night. When I lay on my side it would pour out and run down my face onto the pillow. When I lay on my back it would run down my throat, and I'd have to keep swallowing so I wouldn't choke on it. I lay there for almost two hours before finally getting up to take some Tylenol PM. That knocked me out but I kept waking up whenever it felt like I was drowning from the postnasal drip. I didn't sleep much.

I woke up at five and peeked out through the drapes. I thought the weather looked promising, like maybe the rain had passed over. I felt terrible as I sat on the edge of the bed doing nothing and wondering how I was ever going to get myself starting that morning. It reminded me of Eddie Mac on the Cassiar Highway that night in the rain, when he couldn't see and he just stood there and didn't want to move. I also thought about the story Jake told about the cow that got his head caught in the fence and would lie down and die before he would fight his way out. I was determined I was going to fight my way out of there. I proceeded to choke down a tin of sardines, a liter of juice, some heart medication, some vitamins, and my Citrucel. I still sat for a long time waiting to conjure up enough strength to get my clothes on, not to mention getting my leg over the machine. It took almost two hours to get out of the room and on the road.

After finally getting started I realized it wasn't clearing up after all. It rained the entire day between Beaver Creek and Watson Lake, 570 miles of the roughest part of the Alaska Highway. Most of the dirt in the 22 miles of construction was soft from the rain and offered no better handling than the loose gravel on the way up. At least there was no dust and it was still early, so there wasn't much machinery working and I rode through most of it between 65 and 70 MPH.

The road surface was particularly rough around Haines Junction and Lake Kluane. Going across some of the huge breaks in the pavement at 75, the GS would let out a loud "Brrrrumf," as the paralevers and cantalevers soaked it up like it wasn't there. Even though I had several extra pounds of air in each tire, the sound it made was sometimes unnerving.

I stopped at Haines Junction for gas, coffee, and a brief rest. It was beginning to look like it would rain all day, so I slipped the homemade "hippo hands" that Jake had given me several years ago over the ends of the handlebars. With the temperature in the low 40s, my hands had been getting wet and cold in spite of the electric handgrip heaters. I was able to maintain my 75 MPH most of the day, thanks to the superb handling of the bike, but it got a bit hairy at times. I came across the quarter-mile-long, steel-grate Teslin Lake Bridge at about 70 in heavy rain, enjoying the sensation of the wheels weaving in and out of the rain-slick grooves. I often wondered what it would be like in the rain. Actually it didn't feel any different from dry and I concluded it was all in the mind.

As I neared the Cassiar Junction about 12 miles from Watson Lake it was raining so hard that I was having trouble seeing where I was going, especially when a car in front of me was hidden in his own misty spray thrown up from the wet road. At the speed I was traveling I got far too close behind several of these vehicles before realizing there was actually someone hidden in the cloud. Then while passing I would have to flip my face shield up to see, and I'd get rain on my glasses too, making the visibility afterward even worse. I pulled in for gas at the junction and had to carefully pick my way to the pumps around huge patches of mud and deep water puddles.

I called it a day in Watson Lake at barely 4 PM, because I was nodding off from the lack of sleep and I felt beat. I was reminded that Watson Lake is still in the high-rent district when I paid $89 for a single room; and that was with the senior discount that I insisted on. Otherwise it would have been $94. In US funds that was almost, but not quite, as much as I paid in Tok. The tank panniers had quite a bit of water inside, although I didn't carry anything in them that had a problem with the water. The bag I carried on the back seat also took on water, although my tank bag stayed fairly dry inside, as did my saddlebags and trunk. My wallet got soaked and several of my

Visa receipts were totally unreadable. There was a restaurant in the building, so I ate there and walked next door in the rain to get my liter of breakfast juice.

Day 16 - It was still raining hard and barely 40 degrees when I got up after sleeping well for about 8½ hours. There was a coffee maker in the room so I had coffee with a can of tuna and my liter of juice. My nose was stuffed, my throat was sore, and it was still raining when I got on the road about 6:30. My cold had also settled into my voice box and I could barely utter a clear sound from the laryngitis. I would try to sing a little to myself, but couldn't get any of the words out. Some of the words I was trying to voice were, "Though it be raining, have no regrets." and "What a glorious feeling, just singing in the rain." They are songs that usually cheer me up in the rain, although I didn't feel that either song was cheering me up that morning. I was wearing most of what I brought with me, including the rain suit over the snowmobile suit, with my leather jacket underneath.

I saw three bears, a moose, an elk, and several Rocky Mountain sheep. There was a bighorn sheep in the road at one point as I rounded a bend at speed and I came very close to hitting him. I almost didn't see him at all. By the time I reached Muncho Lake the sun was trying to break through, it finally stopped raining, and cumulus clouds were beginning to form. The ice was practically gone from Teslin Lake, Muncho Lake, and even Summit Lake, although it had snowed about 4 to 6 inches overnight around Summit Lake. There were still signs of it, including slush in the road near Stone Mountain.

I reminisced a lot during the day about Lilli, being her 74th birthday. The temperature rose into the 60s in British Columbia and it turned out to be a very nice afternoon. I blew by a guy on a new Harley about 100 miles east of Fort Nelson. He had been traveling about 65 MPH when I first saw him. My passing seemed to spur him on, as he began to follow me. When I pulled into a gas station at Wonowon, he also stopped and we got acquainted. He was riding a 2001 Ultra Classic, which he was breaking in on a ride to Alaska, so there was less than 5,000 miles on the bike. He was keeping up the pace I was setting, except whenever I'd cross a steel-grate bridge. Then he would slow down considerably, not liking the sensation of the wheels weaving from groove to groove. He introduced himself as Patrick Powers from Minneapolis.

I stopped at a motel in Dawson Creek and Patrick also pulled in. He asked if I minded that he tag along in the morning. I said it was fine with me if he's up when I'm ready to leave. I also told him I eat in the room and wouldn't be stopping for breakfast. I learned that he was traveling without credit cards and he was practically out of Canadian currency, so he had to negotiate for an exchange rate wherever he stopped for gas, food or lodging. The first place I stopped had two rooms, so we stayed there. At dinner that night a guy at the next table said, "How does that BMW go?" Patrick answered for me. He said, "I'll tell you how it goes -- it goes like Hell." He told me about some of the recent problems he had with "battle fatigue" from his Viet Nam experience. After spending time in a psychiatric hospital, his wife left him and took the children. It was a sad story of unrequited love, since he was still in love with his wife.

Day 17 - After turning in, I couldn't get to sleep. I thought it might have been from regular coffee accidentally switched with decaf at dinner. I'll have to stop having coffee at dinner to avoid the problem. I even took extra Tylenol PM, but only got a short nap for about two hours. I got up at four and started to get ready. There was a microwave oven in my room, so I opted for a can of Vienna sausages I was carrying. They taste much better heated than cold. I went out to wake Patrick around five and learned that he was already up and dressed and just about to walk over to a 24-hour restaurant for breakfast. Had I known there was one nearby, I probably would have gone there with him. I continued to get ready while he went to eat.

We were both ready to leave at six, but when Patrick started his Harley he said something didn't sound right because he didn't hear a certain humming sound that he usually heard when he started the bike in the morning. He thought that the fuel pump wasn't working. It took a few extra tries of the starter, and after it started it wouldn't drop back to idle, even after it got warm. He thought it was probably a function controlled by the computer. He checked his owner's manual and found that the nearest dealer was in Edmonton, about 360 miles away, although on our route. We gassed up and headed out, as the idle kept getting higher and higher. He thought it was also burning a lot more gas than usual. I told him I would try to stay with him until he was safely at the dealer's shop, even though he said he didn't want to hold me back. We stopped every 125-130 miles for gas and each time we stopped the engine idle seemed to be getting higher, until it reached about 3400 RPM. The construction between Valleyview and Whitecourt was difficult for him to negotiate with the idle that high, especially since we were stopped often by flagmen.

When we finally reached Trans-Canada 16, a limited-access highway just 30 miles from Edmonton, I was watching him in my rearview mirror on the huge cloverleaf. I thought I saw him split off onto a different highway exit. I wondered if he used this opportunity to cut me loose, or if he decided to ride the back roads instead of the superhighway on his own. I thought about my options, which were: should I go back and look for him or keep going. In order to go back I would have to go several miles to get off the limited-access highway, and then double back to the cloverleaf where I would go for some distance north in order to make a U-turn to retrace the way we came around the first time. Not knowing how I would ever find him, and thinking that if he was stopped he really needed someone with a cell phone far more than he needed me, I continued on my way rather than returning. I had been nodding off from the lack of sleep and I had many miles to go that day. I never saw or heard from him again.

East of Edmonton, it began to rain fairly hard, accompanied by strong crosswinds. I had two cups of coffee with my breakfast and a Mountain Dew later in Whitecourt, but I was still nodding off quite a bit. I had all I could do to stay awake long enough to reach Lloydminster, where I stopped at the same motel I used on the way up.

Day 18 - The weather out of Lloydminster looked pretty good when I started, although I had difficulty with the bright sun as I headed southeast directly into it. The temperature was only about 40 degrees. Approaching North Brattleford I couldn't read the signs because of the sun in my eyes and I got onto the wrong route. As soon as I realized it, which was a few miles down the road, I turned around and headed back.

After North Brattleford it got very windy as I emerged onto the open prairie. At that point I was traveling directly into the wind as well as the sun. My first tank of Saskatchewan gas ran out in only 135 miles, for an average of approximately 29 MPG. I looked for high test at a few places I passed, but most places had only 84 or 86 octane, which was mostly at coop stores. By my third gas stop I was exhausted from fighting the wind. Once after finding a small coop store about a mile off the highway, I gassed up and got a cup of coffee, hoping it would revive me. It was clouding over at the time so I decided to change from my sunglasses to regular glasses there. I put the ¾-full cup of coffee on the pump while I got out my sunglasses. A gust of wind blew the coffee cup clear off the pump and the cup went tumbling across the road faster than I could retrieve it. I had actually placed it on the leeward side of a sign on the pump. Whenever I stopped for gas, I'd have to secure my gloves under a bungee cord to keep them from taking flight.

I left the coop store totally exhausted and thinking, "Oh well, it could be worse; it could be raining with strong crosswinds instead of the head winds." Almost like magic, the strong winds changed to the side and heavy rainsqualls started. I cut my speed to 70 and a few times down to 65 when the crosswinds got up to 40 and 50 MPH. Having had the Gold Wing break traction once with both wheels at the same time in similar conditions, I was very leery of what could happen next. The BMW was about 250 pounds lighter than the Gold Wing, and my tall tank bag, high trunk, and back-seat luggage all contributed to giving it a huge silhouette and making it want to act like a kite, wind-surfing me across the prairie. I had to constantly struggle for control and I worked for every mile.

It got the most hair-raising when trucks coming the other way at the same high speed would momentarily block the wind and I would become entangled in their turbulence. I would be instinctively making the necessary corrections behind the truck when all of a sudden I would be spit out the other end; which left me to struggle with regaining control on the wet, slippery road, while the crosswinds would again hit me hard from the side. I'd laugh about it at the time, but after a few of those I tried to find a different track whenever a big truck approached. The tire tracks on my side were usually filled with water, there was a lot of loose sand along the shoulder, and the center of the lane was shiny with oil drippings; so there wasn't a clear track anywhere, and I was continually aware that the wind could knock the bike out from under me at any moment.

I also had problems with my eyesight in Saskatchewan whenever I passed long trucks. I couldn't see far enough to get a clear view for my pass and sometimes I would think I had a clear shot when I would start passing a truck moving around 70 or 75 MPH. But when I would be partway by, with my speed up to around 80, I would realize that the truck was a tandem rig with two trailers and a huge 12-wheel dolly between the trailers. Some of those rigs were more than 150 feet long. I'd usually have the throttle screwed on all the way; but when I would be ¾-of-the-way by, I would then see someone coming fast from the opposite direction. It would be far too late to change my mind and drop back, so I'd have to continue my pass. Before I could get all the way by, the oncoming car would be there, and I would have to tuck in close to the truck's cab. The other vehicle would have to take to the shoulder, usually with his horn on high. I thought about Jake and how he would have choice words for those passes. I think they should either ban that length truck from 2-lane roads or have a sign on the back informing motorists of the length of the rig; but with my eyesight, I probably wouldn't be able to read the sign anyway.

I ran into some roadwork during one torrential downpour with strong crosswinds. I sat there for several minutes as the flagman controlled the one-way traffic. I think I got more rain just sitting there than I did while riding. I had to brace myself against the crosswind to keep it from knocking me over. The flagman was dressed in a rain suit with his back to the wind. He didn't look very happy to be there. As the traffic started through, I could barely see where I was going and had to ride through soft dirt and slick mud.

Several times the wind got under my route sheet holder and ripped it clear off the top of my tank bag because the Velcro wouldn't hold it tight enough against the strong gusts. When one end of it ripped off earlier, I attached a safety strap to it, to keep from losing it.

I bought my last Saskatchewan gas about 80 miles from the US border with every bit of Canadian currency I had left in my pockets, which paid for only about 5 liters. I figured I had a little more than a gallon in the tank in addition to that, which should get me to the border, especially if I took it a little easy. Later the reserve warning light came on long before I thought it would, so I stopped at a gas station about 10 miles from the border, but the station was closed. When I finally got to my first gas in North Dakota, it took 5.6 gallons, which was more than it had ever taken.

By the time I got to the Days Inn in Minot I was more tired than I had been after any day of the trip. It was a really tough day and I still had laryngitis and other signs of my cold. I noticed that the rear tire was almost to its wear bars. With that little tread it was a small miracle that it didn't break loose during the day in the crosswinds. Maybe it was only the coarse Canadian road surfaces that kept it from slipping.

Day 19 - It was cloudy when I left Minot and it looked like it was about to start raining. I slept a little late and was on the road around seven in my rain suit. I was stopped twice by road construction. I went through a freshly bulldozed area at one spot and almost got stuck as my wheels sank several inches into the soft dirt.

About two hours after leaving the motel it got quite dark and the sky looked very threatening around Carrington. I was about to stop to put on my hand covers to keep my gloves dry, but before I could stop, a torrential downpour continued for about ten minutes. It felt like I was under a waterfall. I had to come to almost a complete stop. I couldn't see for even a few feet in front of me. Fortunately I wasn't on the interstate highway with trucks following close behind.

I rode through strong head winds and crosswinds for the first six hours of the day. After Fargo the sun came out several times while I rode on Interstate 94 and I maintained almost 80 for four to five hours. The speed limit on the interstate was 70. Traffic on the beltway around St. Paul was extremely heavy.

Soon after clearing St. Paul, it began to rain again and rained all the way to Phil's farm in Augusta, Wisconsin. After exiting from the interstate at Eau Claire, I found my way easily through some back roads and I pulled into Phil's driveway at 4:30. He was in his dooryard when I got there and the first thing he said was, "What are you doing here today?" He had apparently not received any e-mail about my progress because I had given Barbara the wrong e-mail address for him. She had been sending out progress reports to several friends every two or three days and I thought Phil knew where I was at all times. Luckily he was home, because he didn't expect me until the following day.

I secured the motel and returned to Phil's to tackle the tire change. The change went smoothly and we were finished in less than an hour. Phil and Connie took me into Augusta and treated me to supper. I told them I preferred something light, so we ate at a 1960-style drive-in, where we were waited on and ate at an outside picnic table. We got there and back in Connie's huge 1969 Cadillac. It was a very pleasant evening, as we shared a few laughs and a few stories. I also saw some, but not all of Phil's tractors. He said that of the 13 he owns, only two are "workers" while the rest are part of his collection.

Day 20 - I got up at 5:15 feeling pretty rotten. I was sore in several places in addition to a headache and a sleeping-pill hangover. When I couldn't get to sleep in the first hour of lying there, I took two Tylenol PMs. I felt like I did in Beaver Creek and I started the day by choking down my sardines, Citrucel, vitamins and medication as I struggled to get dressed in a hurry. I managed to get on the road in 45 minutes. It was very overcast and raining lightly with some fog around.

The rain stopped by the time I reached Interstate 94, about 40 miles south of Augusta. I had planned to take Interstate 80 from south of Rockford, Illinois and bypass Chicago; but when I got to the I80 split, the exit was on the opposite side from where I was riding and I blew right on by. I figured I would then continue on I90 through Chicago, thinking it wouldn't be too bad; and after all, it was 50 miles shorter that way.

I couldn't read the signs once I got into Chicago and I was in the wrong lane several times there too, so it took me an extra hour to get out of the city and finally find I80, where I ran into about 10 miles of stop-and-go traffic. Due primarily to my poor eyesight I had been on the Eisenhower Expressway, I494, I290, I94, I90, I57 and I80, all before I finally located the Indiana Toll Road. Aside from the glare of the sun, thick smog hung over Chicago and its suburbs, which added to my vision problems. My left hand got numb from pulling the clutch so many times in heavy traffic. I realized that I would have been better off to have gone north from Phil's, across the Upper Peninsula of Michigan, bypassing the Chicago area altogether.

When I got to Toledo, I spotted the Motel 6 where I planned to stay, but I saw it just as I was passing the exit – my poor eyesight again. I got off at the next exit and doubled back for about 5 miles. I got in at five, still managing to complete 600 miles in ten hours. I was really beat after a very frustrating day and I got into bed around eight o'clock.

Day 21 - I got up at 4:30 on my final day. As I sat there on the edge of the bed I thought that I couldn't take too many more of these days. I was getting really tired and feeling weaker and more achy every morning. After going through my morning ritual of getting myself started, I got on the road at first light, which was before six.

I didn't get gas the night before as I usually did, and figured I'd gas up somewhere along the Ohio Turnpike. A short while after entering the turnpike, I passed a service area where I saw a sign that said the next gas was 70 miles. I checked the gas gauge and figured that I had plenty of gas to go 70 miles so I didn't stop. When the reserve light came on long before I expected it to, I was still 35 miles from the gas station; but I thought with good "eastern gas" I could easily make 35 miles, especially if I cut my speed to 70 MPH from the 75 I had been traveling."

I entered a construction area about ten miles from the gas. The two lanes got very narrow with practically no shoulder on the road. I had a sinking feeling in the pit of my stomach that I'd hate to run out of gas in an area like this, with the huge trucks taking up practically all of the available space and traveling at highway speeds. I passed a sign saying that the service area was two miles just as the engine sputtered and quit. I pulled over to the edge of the pavement and couldn't even put the bike on the stand at first because the gravel edge sloped off. I couldn't stay in the travel lane because the traffic was too heavy and moving very fast. As I sat on the bike trying to hold it upright, the trucks and cars roared by, almost scraping my arm. What a hell of a predicament.

I managed to gouge out a hole in the hard dirt for the kickstand by scraping it back and forth against the ground. Then I climbed over the barrier and stood on the outside, hoping the trucks wouldn't sideswipe the bike. They often came within a few inches. About 10 minutes later one of the construction guys came by in a protected construction area. I hailed him to stop and told him my problem. He said he didn't have any gas on the pickup but he would go for some. Another construction pickup came by and stopped, this time in the heavy traffic lane. He pulled in ahead of the bike and parked. He said he had gas on the truck but he wasn't sure about it's quality. As we started to pour some of it into the tank, the first pickup returned with fresh gas, so we put that into the bike instead. I slipped the guy a ten and thanked him profusely for going for the gas.

After that incident I had an uneventful ride home with blue skies, fluffy white clouds, and the temperature in the 70s. I got home at 3:45. All in all it was a very memorable trip. Although tough at times it was also emotional at times, because I thought a lot about Lilli. I got home two days before my 76th birthday.

I was very proud of my grandson Robyn, who graduated cum laude in the top 10% of his high school graduating class of 300. I wished Lilli could have seen it. He'll be going to college this fall in Arizona.

Asia will probably be graduating from college in Anchorage in two years. I mentioned to her while she was chauffeuring us back from the graduation that Grandpa is just going to have to do that ride one more time. Her immediate reply was, "No you don't grandpa. That's what they make airplanes for." I hate airplanes. Besides, they can be dangerous.